The Delusional Divas

Doing Italians *oops* ... Italy

a travel memoir

This book is nonfiction. While the places and incidents are true, the "charac-ters" are only loosely based on real persons. Their names and personal information have been changed, and factual assertions have been altered and embellished in some instances for the sake of creating a literary work.

DELUSIONAL DIVAS, INC.

Somewhere on the planet

oops
Doing Italians...Italy

This book is dedicated to our parents. Thank you for everything you have done big and small. Much love.

Acknowledgments and Authors' Notes

No amount of thanks is enough to our families for their unstinting support and encouragement. In particular, to Debra's children Giselle, Maurice, and Adelaide: thank you for being her shining stars and guiding lights since your birth...and for not poisoning Stephanie when she and the book commandeered your mother's time. Many thanks to Stephanie's sister, Sharon, for reading the book and being our loudest cheerleader. To friends and book readers Dee, Kim, and Jen, thank you for your beyond enthusiastic support. The same goes to Stephanie's aunt Sheila and cousin, Michelle. Your editing efforts will never be forgotten. We would also like to thank Stephanie's sister, Ross, and editor, Marlene Adelstein, both of whom read the first version and said we were capable of so much more. It was not easy to hear, but you were right and we hope we have lived up to your vision for us. To Lazurù, a truly heartfelt thanks for our fabulous book cover and putting up with our million requests. Finally, our sincere gratitude to the "cast of characters" who appeared in our lives and on the pages of this book, even those whose performances chose to depart from the Divas' preferred script. Without your grist for our mill, there would be no book.

One final note:
This is a true story, but names have been changed to protect privacy. Additionally, our names were changed. One might ask why since we reveal ourselves as the authors. We can only say that the process of revealing so much of our lives seemed easier when thinking of ourselves as other people. Hence, Debra and Stephanie became our beloved Dena and Shelby.

On Delusion:

There are some people who live in a dream world, and there are some who face reality; and then there are those who turn one into the other.

-- Douglas H. Everett

Prologue

"Hatboxes, how divine! I haven't seen ladies travel with hatboxes since forever." Standing on line at the airline ticket counter, the woman who'd been eyeing Dena and Shelby up, down, and up again had decided to speak.

Turning slowly, Shelby smiled with satisfaction, fondly stroking the violet floral hatbox hanging from her hand. Maybe Dena's harebrained scheme of dragging hatboxes to and through Italy hadn't been sheer lunacy after all. Still, Shelby would never admit it.

Dena stood a little taller, squaring her slim shoulders with pride. Finally, someone impressed with their Divaness. Yes, it was a woman, but she would take what she could get at this point.

"So, tell me," the woman with a distinctly British accent continued, "Are there really hats in there?"

No amount of willpower could stem the crimson tide creeping across Dena's cheeks. Like a child caught with her hand in the cookie jar, the wheels of her brain whizzed, searching for the right answer. She struggled to keep her voice normal.

"Of course," she answered a little too quickly. Before continuing, she hazarded a furtive glance at her own pink version of Shelby's hatbox, making sure the top was on securely and revealed nothing.

"What else would be in here?" Dena asked. Besides every condom she and Shelby had carried across the Atlantic minus one or two.

The Englishwoman leaned in closer. A conspiratorial smile played across her face. "You could be smuggling good-looking, young Italian waiters out of the country," she whispered a little too loudly.

A high-pitched squeal of laughter erupted from Dena. She prayed the nervous tittering didn't give her away and shot a pleading look toward Shelby. The devilish twinkle in her friend's eyes gave Dena a momentary scare. She had seen that look many times before, the look that told how sorely tempted Shelby was to leave her swinging in the wind. Oddly, it was the remembrance of all those previous times that quieted Dena's fears. She knew her best friend of thirty-odd years would not only keep her secrets, but also leap in to rescue her.

And, predictably, Shelby didn't miss a beat. "Nope, no wait-ers. But we certainly won't deny that we came here looking for romance," she said, dismissing the woman's suggestion with an airy nonchalance.

"Not once, mind you, but twice. Two trips in less than six months! A spring trip, and another in the summer," Dena blurted out. As soon as the words tumbled from her lips, she wanted to kick herself. Did anyone else really need to know the depths of their delusions?

Shelby cringed at her friend's slip of the tongue, but willed her body to show no trace of embarrassment. If only the synapses in the girl's brain fired as swiftly and surely as the words from her mouth. For one delightful second, Shelby allowed herself to picture just once letting Dena burble on, making a complete fool of herself. It might be fun seeing how she extricated herself from the mess, kind of like watching a spider tangled in a web of its own making, thrashing around desperately for freedom.

Shelby sighed. It was a pleasant thought, but one that would have to wait for an occasion when Dena hadn't managed to trap Shelby in that web with her. Long years of friendship making her adept at the practice, Shelby quickly threw out a diversion.

"But in the end, we found something much more important than romance," she said with a tease, expertly baiting the hook. "Ourselves, and perhaps, an exciting new career!"

Maddeningly, the Englishwoman didn't bite, her curiosity still fixed on Dena's impetuous revelation. Ignoring Shelby's tidbit, she instead wondered aloud why two women would travel to Florence twice in less than six months.

A worthy opponent, Shelby mused. What should she answer? Quickly calculating they'd never see the woman again, so why bother taxing herself devising a lie, Shelby offered the truth. "Well, I came to see if anything was left of a long ago romance," she confessed with a bit of defiance.

"And I came to feel what it was like to have romance in my life again," Dena added.

"We completely transformed ourselves...into divas," Shelby said. A derisive little laugh accompanied her words, and she rolled her dark brown eyes self-deprecatingly before continuing. "Or what we thought was a diva...the desire of every man and the envy of every woman!"

"Yeah, we deluded ourselves into thinking that we were 'The Divas.'" Dena raised her hands with a flourish, painting quotation marks in the air. "We were sure it would get us what we want-ed."

"And that was...?" the Englishwoman prodded.

*Twin expressions on the friends' faces bespoke their won-
derment. Was the woman a hitherto undiscovered life form, one
without a brain or hormones? This time, they answered what
they considered a rather silly question simultaneously.* "Why,
men, of course!"

*The woman was all ears as the two outlined their plans. How
they'd hopped a plane and immersed themselves in the ultimate
delusion: a campaign to shock and awe, accepting nothing less
than total defeat of the enemy. Complete surrender.*

"In the end, barely a shot was fired, and both sides retreated," *Shelby finished up.*

"Yeah, we were in retreat...but never in defeat."

"Heavens no! We had new worlds to conquer."

"Yes, an exciting new career to start."

*The Englishwoman began to feel a bit dizzy. To and fro, her
head pivoted as she listened to their tale. First to one friend, then
to the other, like a spectator at a tennis match, she watched as
Dena and Shelby volleyed alternating shots. Their words coming
in quick succession, the pair completed each other's sentences as
they outlined their plan of attack, its execution and outcome, and
the aftermath of a battle well-fought.*

"And, of course, we learned the true meaning of diva."

"Which is...?" *questioned their audience of one.*

"And that a little bit of delusion can change your life forever,"
Shelby continued, ignoring the woman's question.

"And that we have a story to tell..."

*So, over coffee and a Danish...pastry...the trio introduced
themselves, and Dena and Shelby began to satisfy the curiosity
of their new acquaintance, India Wallis, transporting her back to
the maelstrom of events that had unshackled their desires. Long
pent-up desires propelling them on that first spring trip to Italy.*

3

Chapter 1

"**A**AAAHHH! AAAHHHHH!"

Picking up the phone, Dena heard a terrible screeching on the other end. It, along with the near riot coming from the playroom, threatened to puncture her eardrums. Obviously a crazy person on the line, she concluded before slamming the receiver onto its cradle. Just as well it wasn't anyone she needed to talk to. If she didn't find out what her three little darlings were up to, they might annihilate one another.

"Giselle, what's going on down there? Why's Adie screaming?" she yelled to her eldest child. On second thought, Dena decided, trudging down the staircase, she'd better find out for herself what all the ruckus was.

The playroom looked more like a boxing ring as her two younger children rolled around on the floor in a human ball, making it hard to tell where one little hellion left off and the other began. Fighting yet again, each of them landed punches like a prize fighter. Even as little Adie delivered an expert body blow to older Maurice's stomach, she was holding her own injured toe and crying furiously. But she refused to give in. Though she knew she shouldn't, Dena had to admire her youngest's tenacity.

"They're wrestling again, Mom, and I think she broke her toe," Giselle explained in bored tones, eyes never leaving the TV.

"Oh, for gods sakes! Another glorious Christmas vacation," Dena muttered to no one in particular.

A familiar holiday tune came to mind, but in Dena's version, the lyrics were slightly different. Twelve cookie batches a burning. Eleven ornaments broken. Ten hungry relatives. Nine unwanted gifts to return. Eight pounds of leftovers. Seven rooms a mess. Six galoshes dripping. Five more golden days to go. Four rock hard fruitcakes. Three kids a screaming. Two tortured cats. And a husband missing in action.

"Upstairs. All of you. Right now!"

Dingaling. Dingaling. That damn phone again.

"Why'd you hang up on me?" the caller complained.

Oh, it hadn't been a crazy person on the line before, but Dena's best friend, who only sounded crazy.

"He called!" Shelby screamed, not even waiting for a hello from the other end. "Giancarlo called!"

Dena didn't need to see her friend to know she was over the moon. But with ten-year old Adie downstairs wailing as if a grizzly had her in its grip, she was hard pressed to focus on Shelby's news. "Look, Shel, let me call you back after I get the kids settled."

Dena didn't see the ornery pout of Shelby's lips, only heard the usual graceful reply to this maddeningly familiar turn of events...no problem, talk to you later. Dena also didn't hear Shelby's private thoughts...by then, we'll both be silver-haired, and the wrinkles on our faces will look like ten miles of pitted and pot-holed roads.

Waiting for the callback, a pensive Shelby blazed a restless trail back and forth through her tiny apartment. The feel of its quiet coziness had always sheltered her from the insanity of Manhattan below. Shimmering mink brown eyes fell reflectively on a beloved collection of Black memorabilia -- Mammy and Chef cookie jars; framed, dog-eared prints of vintage Cream of Wheat advertisements; and pages from century-old Harper's Weekly newspapers depicting a long-ago era in American history. The furniture was an eclectic mix of old and new, which with the family heirlooms she'd wrestled from her grandmother over the years and modern pieces lovingly chosen, Shelby had made a home here in the six years since meeting Giancarlo on her first trip to *Firenze*...Florence, the birthplace of the Renaissance. Yes, a solitary home, but she had made do. Still, once there had been the promise of so much more.

Six years earlier

Girls Night Out. Shelby and her friends had chosen the popular Florentine nightclub, Full Up.[1] As she relaxed and listened to the smooth music at the piano bar, Shelby was completely unaware of the admiring man at the next table, until he leaned over to inquire where the ladies were from.

"Ahh, two of the most famous cities in the world!" the onyx-eyed stranger replied upon hearing New York and Los Angeles. With practiced ease, he angled himself to the women's table and fixed his sights on Shelby. Likewise, she couldn't take her gaze from him.

Giancarlo, as he introduced himself, was about five feet ten inches tall, slim, and darkly handsome. His black eyes had

---

[1]Full Up, Via d. Vigna Vecchia 25 r , PH 055/29-30-06

retained their boyish sparkle, his olive skin had the patina of burnished copper, and his longish gently wavy black hair wore a glistening touch of gray at the temples. His nearness and the spicy scent of his cologne sent a frisson of excitement through Shelby that she hadn't felt for years. Probably about fifty, she thought, guessing his age. She definitely liked what she saw, but as usual, she remained reserved with only the barest hint of a smile.

Undaunted by Shelby's cool demeanor, the stranger sank down on the seat next to her. "Why you come to Italy?" he wanted to know.

Leaving out the part about being way past college age and using a semester-abroad program as a ruse for an extended vacation, Shelby explained that she and her friends were studying in Florence. Then, she introduced everyone...first, Riley, indicating the pretty young woman seated closest. Next, she aimed her hand across the small round cocktail table and introduced Lisa and Melinda. Her friends said *Buona Sera* in their best Italian and smiled at Shelby knowingly.

With a perfunctory politeness, the Italian acknowledged the other women. Then, his eyes again swiftly caught Shelby's in an intimate dance, their piercing beauty never leaving her face. "How long you will be here?" he asked.

"Two more months," she replied. Before tonight, that had seemed like an eternity. But right now, Shelby had the feeling it would not be anywhere near long enough.

"So you not married then?" He smiled with relief, obviously assuming no woman would leave her husband for so long.

Oh yeah, Junior, Shelby thought to herself. To be quite honest, she guessed she did recall saying "I do" to someone regarding something seven years ago. All right, she supposed she was still married to Junior, as his family had nicknamed William. No use lying.

"Well, I am separated," she admitted to the stranger. Or, at least, it was on the top of her To Do List when she got home.

Giancarlo's eyes filled with sympathy. "I'm sorry," he offered.

"No, it's okay. We both want a divorce," Shelby answered with a quick smile.

Or rather, she had thought they both did. She hated living in the Bed-Stuy section of Brooklyn, and Junior knew it. He'd refused to have children throughout their seven-year marriage. Hell, he'd refused to even talk about having children. And a child was all Shelby had ever really wanted from the time she was a child herself. It didn't take a psychic to see the marriage was toast. So, Shelby had decided to fulfill another dream by coming to Italy for three months.

Then, those damn candy bars had turned up in her luggage. Junior knew they were her favorite. What'd he think? A few Hershey's with Almonds would make everything honky dory?

Okay, to be perfectly honest, maybe she had felt a twinge or two when she found the hidden chocolate bars as she was unpacking her bags in her new Florence apartment. Maybe she had gotten teary-eyed....all right, maybe she'd cried like a blithering idiot. Maybe she had thought about when things between them had been good and wished it had all gone differently, just like Junior apparently had. But painful reminiscing was useless. That horse was out of the barn, and it wasn't returning. The marriage was over.

"Do you like pizza or pasta?" Giancarlo interrupted Shelby's thoughts, dragging her back to the present.

Shelby loved both and said as much.

"Then you must be my guest at my restaurant!" he pronounced with pride.

His restaurant. Sure. He's probably a waiter there. Or better yet, a busboy. And he probably gets a commission for every poor fool he drags in off the street, Shelby theorized cynically. Still, he is kind of cute, she relented.

They talked for another twenty minutes until Giancarlo took a quick glance at his watch. "I must leave now," he said. The regret in his eyes told her he didn't want to. Reaching into his pocket, he fished out a business card and hastily scribbled something on it.

Shelby watched his fingers as he wrote. Nice hands. Lean and tanned. When he lifted her own hand and gently placed the card in it, Shelby noticed a quiver of anticipation at his touch...something else she hadn't felt for years.

"Please call me and come to the restaurant for pasta or pizza, whichever you want."

Eager. That's nice.

The ringing of the telephone jolted Shelby from her instant replay of the past. It was Dena.

"After all these years, he just called out of the blue? How'd he know where to find you?" she asked as if their conversation had never been interrupted.

Shelby cleared her throat, stalling for time. So easy to lie, she thought briefly. So easy to say that Giancarlo had finally realized what a mistake he'd made six years ago. That he had moved heaven and earth to find her again. Easy to lie, but this was Shelby's best friend since they'd met on their first day of high school. The thought of admitting that she had contacted Giancarlo months earlier almost killed her, but admit it Shelby did.

"You wrote him? For what?" Dena screeched. Surprise laced with a hint of disgust dripped from each word.

Shelby's thoughts were racing. Would she believe it if I said that I had just remembered something I'd left at his house and wrote to get it back? Hmm. No, even Dena's not that gullible, Shelby conceded. Unable to come up with a plausible fib on such short notice, a cornered Shelby was forced into a position she usually avoided at all costs, especially if it made her look foolish...telling the truth.

"Well, it was the dawn of a new millennium. It seemed as good a time as any to contact the two of them to bury the hatchet," she began tentatively. No laughing came from the other end of the line, so Shelby continued, even though the words sounded hollow even to her own ears. "You know, to say there were no hard feelings and wish them happiness."

Dena was impressed. "Mmm, mighty mature of you. Don't think I could've done that," she complimented. "And on top of it, wish them happiness? Forget it. I'd have buried the hatchet all right, one in each of their backs!"

Damn, she actually bought that drivel. Shelby laughed silently. Like I really gave a rat's ass if Giancarlo was happy with that woman.

She breathed a sigh of relief at being spared. Telling the complete truth twice in one day could be hazardous to Shelby's personality. No reason whatsoever for dear Dena to know the only reason she'd written that damned letter was to see if the two were still together. That would be Shelby's little secret, best friend or not.

"So, are they happy?" Dena asked.

Dena couldn't see the sly grin stretching across the other woman's face. It wasn't necessary. The almost giddy excitement in Shelby's voice as she recounted her talk with Giancarlo told its own story.

"I tell you, I could barely believe it was his voice over the phone after so many years. I was near tears." The words tumbled from Shelby's lips, like snow freed by the fury of an avalanche, as she launched into the subject with gusto.

With that, she was off and running, regaling Dena with every detail -- the emotional warble in her voice as she spoke to him. The jittery dance of every atom in her body, sizzling and popping like water on a red hot skillet. How even after all these years, her insides still melted like sun-warmed honey at the sound of his voice. With almost instant replay-like precision, Shelby recounted how remaining still as they spoke had been impossible, so instead, she'd frantically paced the length of her tiny kitchen floor. How the conversation had lingered for ages on a million stupid and inconsequential topics - Italy, New York, the weather, work, their families. And how she had been dying to hear the answer to just one question as Giancarlo had rattled on about nothing.

"I was about to jump through the phone line and throttle an answer from his lips." Shelby came to a little halt, almost out of breath, but she wasn't finished. "And then, almost as if he sensed I had about had it with all the pretty little talk, the dolt finally eased the conversation around to more personal things."

Specifically, to her husband Junior.

"Ex-husband, I informed him, emphasis on the ex," Shelby told her friend. "And then, at long last..."

Shelby paused yet again, savoring privately what she knew would surely go down as one of the most delicious moments of her life.

On the other end, Dena was on tenterhooks. But she knew there was no use trying to hurry Shelby, who, every once in a while, was a bit of a drama queen and would spill any beans she had only in her own good time. Still, if it weren't soon, the girl might find herself the victim of someone going for her throat through the phone lines, Dena vowed.

"At long last," Shelby repeated with deep sigh, "he asked if I was still alone!" She let out a tiny scream of excitement as she finished the sentence.

It hadn't been until that moment, when he had asked the question, that Shelby had truly allowed hope to take root. Yes, alone, she'd told him.

It had been only seconds, perhaps, milliseconds even. But the time between her answer and Giancarlo's next words had stretched out like an anxious child's sleepless night before Christmas. Then, he had uttered the words she had been praying to hear for six devastatingly long years.

"They split up three years ago?" Dena repeated her friend's words. She didn't so much laugh as guffaw at what she heard next.

"Of course, I expressed my utmost sympathy at the sad turn of events in his life," Shelby said with almost pious solemnity.

How stupid does she really think I am, Dena asked herself. "Yeah, you sound all broken up about it, Shel. You think you could stop your sobbing long enough to give me the details? Whaddya really say?"

"I'm not kidding. I said *che peccato*...what a shame! I tell you, it was all I could do not to laugh out loud," Shelby answered. A mischievous giggle punctuated her words.

"I bet," Dena agreed.

"Yeah, I had to settle for kicking up my heels and dancing a soft shoe jig on the kitchen floor."

"That sounds more like it!" Dena laughed. A tiny hesitation gripped and held the next words in her throat, but only for a moment. She just had to ask.

"So you told him you were alone, but what about Rick?" Or Dick, as Dena preferred to think of the weasel. She smothered a chuckle.

"What about Rick?" Shelby shot back.

"Did you tell him about Rick, your dream come true?"

Dream come true. That was Rick certainly. Trouble was he was someone else's dream...or nightmare, depending on one's perspective. Handsome, intelligent Rick. Blessed with quick wit, a quirky sense of humor, and a surfeit of charm. On top of it all, he was reliable, relatively mentally stable (if one made allowances for his roughly three-pack-a-day habit), and a good provider. There was just one teensy weensy fly in the ointment of his and Shelby's relationship.

Rick happened to be another woman's dream come true. Whose? Well, actually, the woman he had married almost twenty years earlier. Yes, dear Dick was a good provider. It was just Shelby's bad luck that he was providing for his wife and kids, not her. So, hell no, she hadn't told Giancarlo about Rick.

"Yeah, you're right. Why bother?" Dena agreed. "I suppose being with Rick and being alone are one and the same."

Exasperation was apparent in Shelby's loud sigh. Okay, here we go again. She knew there was no use trying to explain her and Rick for the umpteenth time. Dena would never understand. But no matter what the other woman thought, Rick had been a good friend for more than fifteen years, helping Shelby when she'd started her new job, showing her the ropes. Even knowing it was wasted breath, Shelby tried one more time, but Dena interrupted her midsentence.

"I know, I know! He took you under his...um," Dena began. Play nice, she thought to herself. "Under his wing."

Shelby ignored the sarcasm in her friend's voice and gave up. It was futile repeating that Rick had been there for her after Giancarlo's defection. That when she'd felt like there was no point in going on, Rick had been the longtime friend, familiar, comfortable, and completely non-threatening, in a way no other man could ever have been. Likewise, as no other man could have, he had coaxed Shelby back to the land of the living. And for that, he would always have a special place in her heart. She said none of this to her friend. There was just no convincing Dena.

Knowing Shelby's silence meant the subject was closed, Dena moved on. "Well, what about Rick? Are you going to tell him about Giancarlo's call?"

"Of course. I'm his friend, not a saint," Shelby answered. After all, what harm was there in letting the man worry about her and what she was up to for a change?

Dena gave a silent sigh of relief. At least her friend hadn't lost all common sense.

Just then, Dena heard the back door open and close. Her husband. "Luke's home. I should get off. Call you later."

The Englishwoman raised her eyebrows. "Luke? So, you're still married?" she probed. Her steely gray eyes bore into Dena. "Guess that means there's trouble in paradise..."

"Your plate's in the oven," Dena started. She was talking to Luke's back as he strode past her to the spare bedroom.

Hearing that he'd already stopped in town for dinner didn't surprise her at all. Same thing every night...works late, eats out, and strolls into the house just in time to spend a few minutes with the kids before their bedtime, she fumed silently.

Walking past their bedroom on her way to check on the kids, Dena found him packing a bag. Twenty-four years of living with the man, she knew the drill. Long johns, ski jacket, ski socks. Off to Jiminy Peak. Must be nice! She assumed, on his way out the door, he'd inform her when he'd be back. Her fuming escalated.

"Oh, what a nice surprise! We're going skiing," she said snidely.

"You know you don't like to ski anymore," Luke replied with barely a break in his stride.

Displaying about as much maturity as her youngest child, Dena pulled a face at his back. "Nope, right as usual. I prefer being stuck here in the boonies with three kids, two cats, a gaggle of geese, and the occasional mountain lion come to call."

Again, his response was familiar. In fact, sometimes Dena wondered if he'd had it tape recorded and was merely lip synching the words. Sure, there were slight variations, but basically it always went something like this...stop the pissing and moaning...you don't have to work...you get to stay home with the kids...you have a nice house...no stress like I have at work every day...what more do you want.

What more did she want? How could he ask that question? Didn't Luke want more, too? Their life together certainly had not turned out the way she'd expected, and she refused to believe that it was what he had envisaged either.

They had met when she was nineteen and working her way through college and he a twenty-three year old law student. Their mutual attraction had been instantaneous, and before long, they'd fallen in love. They loved dancing, listening to music, sailing, and traveling, especially to sandy beached, sun-drenched islands. And most of all, Dena remembered Luke's love of telling a good story with infectious good humor and how she loved to hear them. They'd laugh for hours.

But as the years progressed, real life had intruded. Marriage, three kids and their needs, building a law practice, renovating a home. Each had taken its toll on the relationship. Little by little, the laughter had stopped, and Luke was no longer telling Dena his stories.

She had tried. Lord knows she had. And to be fair, so had Luke. But it was no use. Too many hurtful things had been done. Too many angry words had spilled out onto the battlefield of their marriage. For Dena, it was over.

So, when Luke asked what more she wanted, the answer was always achingly similar. This time was no different.

"Hmmm, let me think a second," Dena began. With a sarcastic flourish, she tapped her finger on her chin and cast her eyes upward as if deep in thought. Then, she fastened them on him, her gaze nearly pinning him to the wall.

"How about you taking a different kind of trip? You know, the one I've been asking you to book for three years now?"

Luke's forehead knitted in confusion. "What trip?"

Dena's caramel brown eyes flashed with a mixture of anger and amusement. "The one that involves you, a U-Haul, all your belongings, and a no-return ticket...AKA a divorce. How hard could it be? You're a lawyer."

"Yeah, yeah. Quit bitching about the same old thing. I said I'd move out in October," he threw back.

"Yes, Luke, and how many Octobers have we gone through? Every Halloween, I take the kids out trick-or-treating, hoping I'll come home to discover my spider has found another web. But oh no. Every year, you're still spinning away right here."

A life worth living. That's what more I could want, Dena continued fuming as she watched her husband and all the dreams they'd had bluster out the door.

Okay, Luke was off to Jiminy Peak. The kids' progress on their school projects was checked. They'd had their baths and were finally in bed. At last, a minute to herself. Dena sighed contentedly as she flopped down on the couch. Better seize the moment before one of them wanted water or had a visit from the Bogeyman. Quickly, she picked up the receiver and dialed Shelby.

"It's me again. Luke came home long enough to say hi and bye to the kids and pack a bag. He's off skiing again," she grumbled.

"Alone?" Shelby queried.

"Yeah, alone. Who else would be going?" asked Dena.

Has to be the all the glue she uses making those homemade Christmas ornaments, Shelby laughed to herself. Positively clueless. But if it keeps her sane (make that somewhat sane), who am I to interfere?

"Yeah, you're right. Who else?" Shelby answered, tactfully biting her tongue.

Dena didn't want to discuss Luke again. The friends had spent untold hours doing that, and there was nothing left to say. She wanted to hear about romance and love. "So back to Giancarlo. Do you think you'll ever see him again?" she asked.

Settling back even further into the comfy cushions of the couch, she listened as Shelby lapsed into another blow by blow of their conversation. With a little popcorn, a night at the movies couldn't possibly be any better, Dena thought fleetingly. She gasped upon hearing that Giancarlo had actually invited Shelby to Italy. How romantic! She had to admit to a touch of envy, even as she worried that her friend might get hurt again. Apparently, Shelby had no such qualms.

"I tell you, my heart was racing like wild horses," Shelby exclaimed. "I can't wait to see him again."

"So when are you going?" Dena asked.

"I'm not," came Shelby's surprising reply.

Shocked, Dena was certain her ears were playing tricks on her. For ages, she'd had to endure Shelby's mooning, pining, crying, and practically having a nervous breakdown over Giancarlo. And, now that he wanted to see her again, she wasn't going?

"He was supposed to come here six years ago and never did. Why should I go running there?" Shelby reasoned. A steely determination hardened her voice.

Sure, it had been almost more than her willpower could handle not to leap on his invitation. Nevertheless, something in Shelby balked at traveling to see him instead of the other way around, she explained to Dena. Play it cool...make him come to me, she'd decided.

"So, I invited him to New York instead. Says he's coming in August," Shelby finished her tale.

August! Dena was flabbergasted. Was the girl nuts? This was December, eons away from the summer. Time for Dena's reality check. How should she broach it?

Did she need to dig up the sordid details of six years ago? Remind her friend about Italian men, exactly as Shelby's other friend, Lisa, had done? Must she open the barely healed scab of how less than two months after Shelby had left Italy, Giancarlo was offering another woman pizza or pasta?

Why, by August, he may have fattened up the entire female population of a small Italian hill town. After all, in matters of the heart, the man seemed to have the attention span of a fruit fly. Maybe this wasn't the best approach, Dena conceded, so she said none of it, but she would if she had to.

"You're not really waiting that long, are you?" Dena nearly shrieked in disbelief.

"Well, he can't come before that."

"Shelby! That's the great thing about air travel. Planes go both ways across the Atlantic. Why don't you go there?" Dena countered.

She scrambled off the couch and over to her computer. Practically assaulting the keyboard, she pulled up Travelocity. She typed as she spoke. FROM...she typed in JFK. TO...she punched out Florence, Italy. Number of seats. Two, of course.

For the next five minutes, she listened to all the reasons Shelby thought she shouldn't go. Like annoying flies at a summer picnic, Dena swatted them away. Bap! Bam! But no matter how she disputed the arguments, still Dena heard her friend's defiant refusal. But was it defiance? Or could it be fear in Shelby's voice?

Dena hated taking advantage of her friend in this weakened state, but she had an ace up her sleeve and it was time to use it. Shelby had never stopped loving Giancarlo.

"Do you want to lose him all over again, Shel?" she asked pointedly. "Because if you sit around waiting 'til August, that's exactly what'll happen."

Dena let her words sink in for a few seconds. Then, like a gymnast on the balance beam, she nailed her routine. "If you want, I'll even go with you," she offered, her voice laden with sweet concern.

"Really?" Shelby asked. "You would?" She held the phone away from her ear in midair and stared at it, speechless and more than a little disbelieving.

The other woman never left her kids, not for love or money. Being attached at the hip didn't do this mother-children bond justice, in Shelby's mind. Sometimes, she wondered if her friend was part mammal, part marsupial. Was Dena really willing to leave her three kids just to give her moral support?

"Of course, what are friends for?" Dena answered, breaking into Shelby's thoughts.

I'll tell you what they're for, Dena continued, but only to herself. To get me the hell out of this two-bit horse town, if only for a week. To help me find a bit of freedom. To get me to the most romantic country on earth with the most romantic men on earth, who pray God, might throw a little affection my way. At least, a dance. Perhaps, a kiss. And dare I hope, a light flirtation. Now, that's what friends are for!

And so it was that the women started planning their first trip to Florence.

Chapter 2

*T*he Englishwoman was a bit lost. "So, wait a minute. Back up to six years ago...your very first time in Italy. I take it you did meet the handsome Giancarlo for penis or...oh, sorry. I mean pizza or pasta?" The Englishwoman blushed at her slip of the tongue.

Six years earlier...a few days later

After meeting Giancarlo in the nightclub, Shelby waited a few days before fishing out his business card and calling. He might have been eager, but she was still playing it cool. Besides, she hated calling men and blanched at the thought of his not remembering her, but the pleasure in Giancarlo's voice at hearing from her melted Shelby's unfounded worries away.

"Have you had dinner yet?" he asked.

Within seconds, she found herself accepting his invitation for that very evening. Walking to meet him an hour later, the enormity of what she was doing hit Shelby. Chaotic thoughts whirled in her head. I must be crazy. He's a total stranger, someone I met in a bar. Probably a cad! Turn around. Go home. Forget he exists. But, for once, she didn't heed that sensible part of her brain. Instead, her feet continued on, almost with a will of their own.

The sexy smile on Giancarlo's face upon seeing her laid waste to all Shelby's fears. She had not just imagined it. He really was adorable, and calling him had been the right decision. They met at the *Buca San Giovanni*,[2] a beautiful and historic restaurant in *centro,* Florence's medieval downtown. In centuries past, the restaurant was part of *Il Battistero*, the baptistery, which was dedicated to St. John the Baptist. Built in the sixth or seventh century, the Baptistery is the oldest standing structure in Florence.

With vaulted ceilings of brick, massive centuries-old wood beams, and frescoes attributed to the Renaissance master Giotto's school of art, Buca San Giovanni is under the protection of the Italian government service for the fine arts. Buca means hole, and true to its name, diners descend a narrow staircase

---

[2] Buca San Giovanni, Piazza S. Giovanni 8, PH 055/287612

from street level to enter the subterranean eatery, which is a series of caverns located directly under Florence's historic cathedral, *Il Duomo.*

While she was duly impressed with the Buca, Shelby wouldn't have cared if this handsome Italian had invited her to Burgie, Italy's equivalent of McDonald's. And, in fact, she barely ate a thing. She was totally captivated. And to her utter delight, it seemed so was he.

It didn't matter if he was the waiter. Oh no, wait a minute. That's somebody else's story. It definitely mattered to Shelby. Love being enough was one delusion she had never had. Much to her relief, Giancarlo was not the waiter. As he had intimated when they met, he indeed owned the restaurant, along with an ice cream shop...make that a *gelateria.* Plus, he ran a business consulting firm. Not too shabby.

Throughout dinner, there was never a lull in the conversation as they shared life stories. Shelby learned he was separated with three children, two already grown and one six years old. In turn, she filled him in on her childhood in upstate New York and subsequent escape to the big city. After-dinner drinks drained, Giancarlo made a suggestion.

"I don't want to take you home yet," he told her. "We go somewhere for a drink?"

From the restaurant, he took her on to a club. Upon learning it was closed for remodeling, he refused to be thwarted. And, luckily, when the owners saw it was Giancarlo seeking entrance, they happily ushered him and Shelby in for a drink and more conversation.

Two hours later, both were still loathe to draw the curtain on the evening. "Do you want to come to see my house?" Giancarlo asked boldly.

Shelby hesitated. Her eyebrows rose in skepticism. Reticence shone in her brown eyes, but Giancarlo must have also seen something else...was it a delicious anticipation?

"You will be safe. I take you home the minute you ask," he promised. His voice was warm as molten honey, thawing what little resistance Shelby could muster.

She couldn't put her finger on it, but something in the tone of his voice and the light in his eyes seemed sincere. Shelby wasn't sure how, but she knew this man would not hurt her. So, with gathering excitement, she accepted the invitation.

That evening, he introduced her to Italian singers, including Nino Buonocore, Pino Danielle, and Fabio Concato. The music was romantic and very seductive. Shelby was thoroughly smitten when Giancarlo sat down at his piano and accompanied the CDs. Then, he began to sing, and she was treated to her own private duet concert, part live, part recorded.

With his back to her, Shelby could drink him in unobserved. The movement of his head in time to the tune, the tap of his foot, his total absorption in the music.

She had just begun learning Italian, so she didn't understand a word either the singers or her own private crooner were singing. It didn't matter. As the blend of voice and melody wafted through the room, she leaned back on the couch and let the sensuous strains communicate through feeling.

After a time, Giancarlo rose from the piano. A smile curved his lips as he continued to sing, his eyes on Shelby now. She was reminded of the words of the Wicked Witch in the *Wizard of Oz*. I'm melting...melting!! No, she may not have been shriveling into the ground, but if she didn't watch it, she would lose herself completely in this man's magic.

This isn't my life, Shelby thought to herself. To be sitting in a gorgeous house in Florence, with a handsome Italian stranger, and be treated to her own private concert. She didn't know whose life she'd stolen into, but could I stay, she prayed.

He lowered himself next to her on the couch, taking her in his arms. She went willingly, wanting to feel the touch of his lips on hers, eager to find out if his kisses lived up to the promise of the evening. His mouth was warm and sensual, lightly teasing and gently insistent. His touch threatened to rob her of all sense, but only for a while. Soon, Shelby's innate suspicion of everyone and their motives struggled to the surface.

I'm like Humpty Dumpty. Ten pounds too heavy. Wearing black leggings and a baggy T-shirt. Not even attractive, let alone sexy. What's he after? To see what it's like to have sex with a Black woman? Even as the bitter thought was born, Shelby acknowledged perhaps it wasn't fair. But some wounds never healed.

As a child, Shelby's parents had enrolled her and her sisters in a Catholic school, insisting the education was better. It didn't matter to them that their girls were the only Black students in the whole school. And to be honest, it didn't matter to Shelby. Truth be told, she hadn't even known she was Black until that fateful day in third grade...the history lesson had been on slavery. Still, although the idea of enslaving people had horrified her, and she wondered how anyone could think of doing that to other human beings, eight-year old Shelby had felt no personal connection to the historical events. But that emotional distance hadn't lasted long.

Later that day at lunch recess, the third-grade girls played a game of tag. Shelby was it, and she giggled with triumph as she tagged her best friend Susan. The words "you're it" stuck in her throat as her eyes fell on her own arm. It was skinny. It was bony. It had the ever-present redness of eczema. Nothing new there. What was new for Shelby was the realization that there was brown skin along with that redness. And for the first time in her life, Shelby knew she was different from blonde-haired, blue-eyed Susan and, for that matter, the rest of her classmates. And, from her young vantage point, that difference was not a good thing.

Shelby never discussed her revelation with her family. They didn't talk about such things. But as the years went by and the girls' games of tag turned to secret notes and whispered confidences about boys, Shelby found herself in the hurtful position of being on the inside looking in. Yes, she was included in the giggle-filled admissions and speculations of first crushes and puppy love. Susan likes Michael. Do you think he likes her? Mickey pulled Eileen's ponytail? I bet he likes her. Or does he like Mary...or Bonnie? But never did the speculation focus on Shelby and Mickey or Shelby and Michael, or Shelby with anyone. That wasn't possible.

Not until Charles Jenkins came to St. Mary's School. Then, everyone was asking Shelby if she liked him. No, it had been more than that. They had assumed she liked Charles. Of course, she remembered thinking to herself cynically. I must like him...and he absolutely must like me. He's Black. So it must be so. Or, at least, that's what they expect.

And as the years rolled on, it hadn't gotten better. At school dances, Shelby danced with the other girls, or she didn't dance at all. No boy ever asked her.

Finally, she graduated from high school and went to college. Spelman College, an historically-Black women's school in Atlanta. More importantly, it was just across the street from Morehouse College, its male counterpart. There, Shelby put the pain of her school years behind her, reveling in an environment where she was not different...or, at least, not so different.

In fact, it would be many years, not until she completed law school and entered the working world, that a white man would ever become a romantic possibility. Enter Rick, married and wanting to cheat. Yet another example of a man not wanting anything serious from a woman...only this man was white. Not exactly a ringing endorsement for putting any cream in her coffee.

So, what was she doing here now with this sweet-lipped Casanova, Shelby asked herself as Giancarlo drew her closer. She knew she should put an end to it, before making a complete fool of herself. But it felt so good. Well, maybe just one more kiss.

Notwithstanding the temptation, after that next kiss, Shelby knew it was time to leave. It was two in the morning, and with a little more coaxing on his part, things could get out of hand. Still, when true to his word, Giancarlo rose immediately to take her home, Shelby felt a pang of regret, wishing she could stay.

They stepped out his door onto a very narrow sidewalk that left little room for pedestrians. Just then, a car whizzed past at breakneck speed, nearly running her over. Grabbing her arm, Giancarlo pulled her from harm's way. "*Stai attento*," he ordered. Pay attention. "I want to see you the next two months."

And see each other they did. Giancarlo soon severed any ties with other women in his life, and the two were inseparable. Shelby met his mother, his two grown children, and his adorable six-year old daughter Carmella, whom they often had with them. To the sea, to a festival, meeting for lunch, day trips to ancient Italian towns, late night dessert at a friend's villa in the Italian hills.

Even more wonderful was his interest in her life. Giancarlo wanted to get to know Shelby's friends and suggested a group outing to the sea. Lisa, Riley, and Melinda joined the couple for a picnic at the beach. Lisa's son Francesco was perfect company for Carmella.

Even though it was an unseasonably warm spring day, the beach was sparsely populated. "*Fantastico*," Giancarlo exclaimed. "We have the whole beach for our little party."

After finding the perfect location, the ladies spread beach towels and arranged tablecloths for their lunch. Impatiently, Carmella and Francesco pounced upon a bag, tearing it open in search of their beach toys.

"*Babbo, Babbo!*" Carmella demanded her father's attention. "*Dove sono i giocattoli?*" Her stern little face gave testament to who was boss in this father-daughter relationship. If Giancarlo didn't produce those toys, he might be given a timeout. Still, he seemed thoroughly enchanted by his daughter's pique.

Realizing they had been forgotten in the car, he put his arm affectionately over Shelby's shoulders and placed a tiny kiss on her cheek. "I go back to car for toys and rest of food. You need anything?"

She tingled at the simple touch of his hand, barely hearing what he said, but managing to answer. "No, nothing. Need help carrying anything?" she asked.

For a second, he hesitated. Then, Riley piped up. "I'll go with you," she offered. "Just in case."

"Thanks, Riley," Shelby said, and then turned back to setting their table on the sand.

Over a leisurely lunch, Giancarlo charmed the ladies with one humorous story after another. The trill of the little group's laughter was music to Shelby. As her eyes scanned the happy faces of her friends and Giancarlo getting to know one another, she was overwhelmed with a contentment that she hadn't known for an awfully long time, and she found herself wishing time could stand still.

Too soon, the cheerful group began to scatter. Melinda tempted Francesco and Carmella with a game of Frisbee. Giancarlo stretched out on a blanket for an afternoon nap, as Lisa and Riley helped Shelby clean up the remains of their lunch.

"Think I'm going for a walk. Anybody want to join me?" Lisa suggested to her friends after the cleaning was done.

"Sure, I could use some exercise after all this food," Shelby agreed. She patted her belly. Turning toward Riley, she raised her eyebrows in question. "Coming?"

The pretty redhead shook her head and gave a little yawn. "No, you two go ahead," she answered. "I'll just sit here, be lazy, and watch the waves roll in and out."

As they set off down the beach, the pair stopped to invite Melinda and the kids. Francesco screwed up his nose with decided distaste. Carmella, her little face the picture of concentration as she tried to master the Frisbee, never acknowledged the invitation. Shelby smiled at Lisa, gave a "we tried" shrug, and the two went on their way. They walked in companionable silence along the water's edge, occasionally throwing rocks and watching the ripples.

While Shelby was searching for interesting seashells, Lisa broke the silence. "This was a brilliant idea, especially for Francesco. When I decided to come to Italy for this semester program, I was a little worried about him being here with no friends. Having Carmella is good for him."

A huge smile crept across Shelby's face and lit up her eyes. She nodded her head. "You're right. It has been great," she agreed. The dreamy lilt in her voice was unmistakable.

Lisa looked over at her friend with an amused smile. "Why do I get the distinct impression that you're not talking just about today? The silly grin on your face wouldn't have anything to do with the dashing Giancarlo, would it?"

Blushing, Shelby's smile turned sheepish. "He's wonderful, isn't he? Lisa, I'm so happy, I can't contain it."

"No kidding...you're radiant. He seems happy, too. It's nice to see." Gives hope to the rest of us, Lisa thought to herself.

After a while, the friends backtracked, returning to the group. By then, Melinda and the children were giggling over an elaborate sand castle they were desperately trying to keep upright. Francesco waved them over. "Mom! Shelby! Come and see," he beckoned, an exuberant smile on his face.

The ladies eagerly joined the infectious silliness of the castle-building threesome. While hard at work on a castle spire, Giancarlo's laugh caught Shelby's attention. With a quick glance over her shoulder, she noticed him and Riley engaged in animated conversation. Only Lisa glimpsed the momentary crack in her friend's smile.

Being with Giancarlo exposed Shelby to an Italy a mere tourist would never see. She loved the country and its people, but most of all, she adored Giancarlo. She wanted to be there, with him, for the rest of her life. Still, much as he said he loved her, throughout their time together, her handsome Italian repeatedly stressed that they couldn't decide to be together forever based on two-month's time.

"I know that," she agreed testily each time the subject arose. Maybe he couldn't decide, but Shelby's heart had long ago settled the issue for her. She knew she was a goner from the beginning. And it terrified her. She had to at least try to protect herself.

"Perhaps, we shouldn't see each other so much," she suggested one day. "We're getting too attached. I should go back to my apartment sometimes."

Maybe he would miss her, she hoped. But even as the thought was born, Shelby knew she was fooling herself. She was the one who would be hurt. It was going to kill her when she had to leave Italy. Still, she had to at least try to save herself.

"You right. Maybe you should stay there sometimes," acquiesced Giancarlo, his voice uncertain and sad. And so, she did, even though it was not what either of them wanted.

But fate had different plans for the lovers. Within a few days, Giancarlo's long ailing father died. Shelby was with him the day he got the call. Naturally, assuming he would want to be alone even more, she offered to leave and give him privacy to mourn.

"No!" His answer was visceral, and the desperate sadness in his usually glinting eyes told the story. He needed her. "I want you here. Any time we have left, I want to spend together."

Shelby never moved her belongings from the apartment she shared with Lisa, Francesco, and Riley, but she also never spent another night there. Giancarlo needed her, and she had come to need him desperately. There was no sense denying it or depriving herself. So, she moved in with Giancarlo and increasingly became enveloped in all aspects of his life.

One evening, they met friends of his, a married couple, for dinner. The older pair were delighted to see Giancarlo so happy and in love, and they warmed to Shelby immediately. Over a delicious meal, the foursome laughed and enjoyed one another's company immensely. Shelby felt even more a part of Giancarlo's world.

Later, the lovers strolled through Florence's cobblestone streets arm in arm. She sighed as she looked up at the star-studded sky. An unfamiliar happiness oozed from every pore, and if thoughts of tomorrow and leaving this place, this man, crept into her soul, she banished them, stubbornly refusing to spoil the moment.

"There's something I wanted to ask you." Giancarlo's soft voice cut across her thoughts. He halted their walk, and drew her into his arms. Shelby melted into him willingly, his scent filling her nostrils, urging her closer. Smiling up at him, she waited for his next words.

"But now I forget what it was," he said. Onyx eyes veered heavenward as he tried to recall. "Now what was it?" he drawled in his sexy Italian accent. "Why can't I remember?"

Shelby watched as a mischievous glimmer stole into his eyes. His look was playful and teasing. "Oh, yes, now I remember, Miss," he continued, using the affectionate nickname he had christened her with long ago. But still, he hesitated.

Shelby grew impatient and gave him a playful slap. "Tell me," she demanded with mock anger. "What?"

"Miss, will you marry me?"

An atom bomb detonating at her feet couldn't have felt more earth shattering. The world around her disappeared, receding into nothingness. Her heart didn't just skip a beat. Shelby wasn't sure it would ever beat again. It would be her luck to drop dead at that very moment, just when all her dreams were about to come true.

"Do you mean it?" she hazarded warily, her voice a mere whisper, almost afraid to ask. He couldn't possibly, could he? He was joking.

"Yes, I mean it," he confirmed, placing a tiny kiss on her forehead.

"*Sei certo?* You're serious? You want to get married?" she tried asking it another way. After all, Giancarlo's English was not perfect. It was late. They were both tired. Perhaps, he was confused.

"Yes, marry me. *Sono certo.*" I'm sure.

Shelby couldn't wait to tell her friends. For Lisa and her son, this was especially good news as they were staying in Italy, possibly for good, once the semester program ended. The notion of Shelby returning to America had saddened both mother and son. Now, their buddy would be coming back, and the fun and friendship would continue. Certainly, this happy turn of events called for a celebration.

A potluck dinner. The venue: Giancarlo's house. The guests: all Shelby's friends. He raised his glass in a toast to his new-found love. "To my Miss. Tell me you don't leave in two days. I miss you already."

Tears filled her eyes at the thought of her imminent departure. But she brushed them aside, determined to savor this last evening with all her friends gathered around.

At a quiet moment earlier in the evening, Giancarlo had presented her with a "going away, but coming back" gift. Proudly, she pulled out the buttery-soft, cinnamon-colored suede blazer. Playfully, she swung to and fro, modeling it for everyone.

Lisa smiled indulgently at her friend, pleased to see Shelby so happy. But just then, another scene caught Lisa's attention. Almost unwillingly, she watched Riley and Giancarlo sitting together on the sofa, engrossed in conversation. Lisa couldn't help but remember a similar scene on the beach, and though she wanted to, she couldn't shake off her suspicions.

Shortly thereafter, she found a private moment with Shelby. "You're not really leaving, are you?"

Shelby dismissed her friend's question with a swat of her hand in the air. "Of course, I am. I have a job, an apartment, and family, not to mention a husband. I have things to take care of before I move here."

But what was an open and shut case for Shelby was a very different matter for Lisa. Several times she opened her mouth, then closed it again without uttering a word. Shelby saw she was struggling with something she wanted to say, not knowing quite how. Then, like a bullet firing from a gun, the words burst forth. "Well, I don't think you should. But if you have to go, you'd better get back lickety-split."

The lines in Shelby's forehead twisted into a pretzel-like formation. She gave a tiny, almost imperceptible back and forth shake of her head. She didn't need to ask why Lisa had said this. Her look of confusion asked the question for her.

Lisa raised her hands in undisguised frustration. She didn't want to alarm Shelby. Besides, she could be all wrong. Then, she would have needlessly worried poor Shelby who was so blissful. And what was that saying about shooting the messenger? Still, she had to try, for Shelby's sake. "Look, there's no easy way to put this. Italian men can't be alone long," she said after an interminable hesitation. "Believe me, I know."

It was no secret that Lisa's husband had left her years ago for a beautiful German woman and was now living in Munich. While Lisa professed to be over it, and claimed she only wished he would be a better father to Francesco, Shelby had always wondered.

Shelby let out the breath she'd been holding and smiled. "Oh, is that all?" she asked with obvious relief. "We'll only be apart two months. Then, Giancarlo comes to New York."

Again, Lisa raised her hands, this time in defeat. "Okay, I'm sure you're right," she acquiesced. Even though she knew her words were a lie, she managed a shaky smile and dropped the subject.

Try as they might, Shelby and Giancarlo were powerless to hold back time. Her idyllic stay in Italy was over. With tears and kisses, he saw her off and promised to be in New York in two months. He would stay for a month, see the United States, and meet her friends and family. Then, they would return to Italy to begin their life together.

"So, he came to New York?" The Englishwoman leaned forward, cupping her chin in her hand, training her eyes on Shelby.

Shelby sank back a bit in her seat. To Dena, it almost seemed as if she were trying to free herself from the onslaught of memories. She remembered that time in Shelby's life. It was painful even for Dena to recall it. So, she knew how hard it must be for her friend.

"I think I need another cappuccino," Shelby announced. She stood up, her eagerness revealing her evasion of the question. "How about the two of you?"

Taking their order, she made a hasty exit. But the Englishwoman was not to be thwarted. Inquisitive gray eyes bored into Dena expectantly.

"Did he come? Well, let's see. Where to begin..." Dena picked up the story for her friend.

"Shelby, eez bad, isn't it?" Giancarlo asked. It was their first transatlantic call since her return to New York.

"Yes, sweetie, it's bad," she agreed. It had only been one day, but forever couldn't have seemed longer. The separation had started taking its toll immediately.

Over the next few weeks, they spoke almost daily. Shelby lived to hear his voice. Still, at points, she couldn't hide her sadness during their long conversations. When he heard it, Giancarlo's response was always the same. "You get on a plane and come now," he would encourage tenderly.

How she longed to do just that. Each day seemed interminable, and the nights alone an excruciating torture. The ultra-modern skyscrapers, horn-blowing yellow cabs, disgusting subway stations, and constantly rushing, pushing crowds of New York City seemed to mock her. We know you don't want to be here, know that you long for the quaint medieval gentility of Florence, for the life and love you share with Giancarlo, they taunted. Yes, she ached to ditch it all and hop the next Alitalia flight. But she couldn't. She wouldn't.

Just as his response to her sadness was always the same, her answer was consistently steadfast. "No, that's ridiculous, Giancarlo. You already bought your ticket here and our return tickets back. Besides, I want you to see the U.S. and meet my family. I can make it until July."

Time dragged like molasses in freezing temperatures. By the tenth of July, Shelby was on cloud nine. Just ten more days. Puttering around the apartment she had found for them, she was delighted when the phone rang, and it was Giancarlo.

"I'm so excited. I can't believe you'll be here so soon. Are you packed? Have you seen Lisa and Francesco? How are they?" she rambled on boisterously.

"Shellllbyyy," he sliced into her mini-interrogation. "I can't come."

The words reached her consciousness, but Shelby mentally bounced them away with the deftness of a tennis master, refusing to let the knowledge penetrate. Surely, she was hearing things. "But we just spoke yesterday. You have the tickets. What happened?"

In shock, she listened, but could barely comprehend his words. Something about a new business client...a lot of work...can't come in July...maybe sometime in autumn.

"*So, he did eventually come,*" the Englishwoman pressed.

"*Well, that depends on how one looks at the question. Shelby and I call these DIQ Test Questions, short for* Diva Intelligent Quotient Test Questions," *Dena answered.*

"*DIQ Test Questions? I can tell by the name this will be good. What in the world is a DIQ Test Question?*" the Englishwoman laughed.

"**DIQ Test Question** (dik) n. *a question designed to measure one's intelligence regarding the Divas and their luck,*" Shelby recited encyclopedically. She had overheard the Englishwoman's query as she returned with their drinks. "*What's the question?*" she continued.

Dena raised her eyebrow and smirked. "*It's the same one, Shelby. Did Giancarlo come?*"

"*Oh, this one's priceless. Get the journal,*" Shelby suggested.

As Dena routed through her overstuffed carry-on, the Englishwoman's eyebrow rose. "*Journal?*" she queried.

Dena smiled proudly. "*Yes, for our travel book.*"

"*What travel book?*" asked India.

"*That's our exciting new career...travel writers!*" Dena beamed. She patted the book proudly. "*In here, are all of our notes, DIQ Test Questions included.*"

Shelby ripped the purple, cloth-covered book from her friend's grasp. "*Gimme that. I'll read this one!*"

What do you think happened next?
   A) Giancarlo came in September,
   B) Giancarlo came in six months,
   C) Giancarlo came a year later, or
   D) Giancarlo never came to New York.

Shelby glanced up from reading and looked expectantly at India. "*So, what do you think's the answer?*"

The Brit sat quietly, thinking. Dena stole an amused look Shelby's way. *We've got her.*

Finally, India spoke. "*I haven't the foggiest,*" she admitted.

"*Actually, this is a trick question. No matter which answer you choose, you're correct,*" Dena proffered.

The Englishwoman's gray eyes were skeptical.

"*Giancarlo came...and I do mean CAME,*" Dena emphasized.

India had just raised her cup to her mouth and taken a sip of the hot liquid. PPPHHHHTTTT! Out came the coffee in a spray.

Dena and Shelby jerked back to avoid a second shower of the morning.

"Oh, I get it. You two are a hoot!" India declared. "Came...as in CAME, not traveled!"

"You've got it," Dena confirmed. "Just one small detail. Not with Shelby."

Shelby's face clouded over in bitter remembrance, and her words reflected the same hurt. "But hey, let's not quibble over the details. No, he never did make it to the U.S. to see me."

What little color she had, drained from the Englishwoman's face. "I know what that's like. You must've been devastated."

Shelby rolled over in the bed and looked at the clock. Four in the morning. Please God, don't let me wake up now. I don't want to think about it yet. Just a few more hours of blessed oblivion. But, it was no use. She would never get back to sleep. No sense staying in bed.

At first, the shock had robbed her of all energy. She had been able to sleep endlessly, able to hide from the stinging reality of it all. But the weeks had passed by, and the sweet elixir of sleep was no longer an option. Her body simply wouldn't comply with her wish to remain permanently comatose.

Daylight finally made an appearance. Take a shower...that'll feel good...for a minute. What to wear? Does it really matter? Should put on makeup. Forget it! Okay, I'll comb my hair, but only under protest.

Off to work. The law library. Smile and act normal. Can't.

"I'll be right back," she said to co-workers.

The ladies room. It was private, no one around. Shelby sank to her knees and cried until she couldn't anymore. When is this going to stop? Okay, get up. Cold water. Wipe your eyes. Go back in there and smile. Act normal. Can't.

Five o'clock. It's quitting time. Go home. It's not the home I want. Eat. I'm not hungry. Go to sleep. Yes, that's what I need. Maybe tomorrow will be better.

That tomorrow took its cruel, villainous time showing up. More than a year.

"Well, I didn't eat," Shelby said.

The Englishwoman knew of that malaise all too well. I lost eighteen pounds, India remembered.

"She barely slept," Dena added.

I used pills for that, India thought silently.

As Shelby recounted how she spent most of her waking hours reliving every moment, every conversation with Giancarlo, the Englishwoman was lost in a world of her own. The tale sounded all too eerily familiar. A chill shimmied through her as her own past haunted her. She mentally shook it off. "So, how did you get through it?" their new acquaintance wondered.

"Well," Shelby let out a sigh, "therapy and lots of it. I used to laugh at people needing that kind of crutch, but in the end, the therapist was my lifeline."

Yes, we Brits are supposed to keep a stiff upper lip, and deal with whatever life throws at us, but it's just not that easy. My therapist is my new best friend. Some people can't wait for Thursday night...happy hour. Therapy is my happy hour! I get to lie down on that couch and unload to my therapist. India felt better just thinking about it.

"Oh, and then there was Shelby's sister, a psychiatrist," Dena chimed, "and massive doses of drugs." The friends shared a laugh.

"Just kidding," Shelby clarified. "I might've gone a bit loopy, but my drug of choice was work, and the distraction it gave me. Thank God I never handed in my notice when he proposed."

"And that lesson became our first **Diva Do or Don't** (*Diva Do/n't*)," said Dena with pride.

Diva Do/n't

Even if he asks you to marry, don't be dumb.
Make sure you still have a means of income.

India nodded her head in wholehearted agreement. It was a good rule to live by. But their audience of one was intent on keeping the storytellers on track. It was just getting interesting, and she was impatient to find out what happened when the ladies went back to see Giancarlo six years later. She needed details. "So, go on," she prodded.

Shelby looked at her watch. "We don't have time for anymore talk. Shouldn't we be boarding soon?"

Dena rose and walked over to the flight board. "Oh, we've got time," she contradicted. She called back over her shoulder and pointed up at the board. "Look, the damn flight's been delayed!"

Chapter 3

W hen she and Dena had begun making plans for that first spring trip, Shelby suggested flying Alitalia. That way, they could soak up some Italian culture on the plane, and she would be able to practice her Italian.

"And we'll both be able to drool over dark-haired, olive-skinned Paolos," added Dena. Shelby smiled indulgently as her friend's eyes clouded over dreamily.

And so, April 1st found the best friends on an Alitalia flight bound for Florence. Two April Fools.

Slowly down the aisle the flight attendants made their way with the drink cart. *"Desidera?"* they inquired over and over. What would you like? *Un vino, una birra, l'acqua, un caffe, per favore* came the passengers' varied replies. The lilting Italian, as it rolled off native lips, was music to Shelby's ears. She couldn't wait to show off her best Italian.

"Something to drink, ladies?" the flight attendant said when she got to them.

Darn, so much for using my Italian, Shelby complained to herself. What's the problema here; don't we look Italian? We both have brown eyes. Dena's hair is blonde and out of a bottle...nothing unusual there. Apparently, a lot of Italian women are born blonde these days. She's olive-toned. Granted, not as dark as me, but I've got more of the southern Italian look going on. Okay, okay, so what if my family took a slight detour through sub-Saharan Africa?

Shelby straightened her shoulders, ready to show off. *"Un vino rosso e un'acqua, per favore,"* she responded, compliment-ing herself on her near perfect accent. Red wine and water.

"Here you go." The flight attendant placed Shelby's order on her open tray. "Three dollars, please."

As the flight attendant turned her attention to Dena, Shelby screwed up her nose and shot a nasty look at the woman. Dena caught her friend's childish gesture and knew exactly what had Shelby going. She leaned over to whisper. "Don't worry, Shel. Keep on the lookout for that Paolo or Gianni to practice your Italian with," she offered cheerily.

Just then, the wail of a surly toddler pierced the relative qui-et of the cabin. Turning to see where the offending sound was coming from, Shelby stared straight into the wizened face of an ancient gray-haired woman. The woman was flanked by two snotty-nosed, teary-eyed, and altogether miserable children. Shelby looked in the opposite direction. There sat a young couple obviously in love. They couldn't keep their eyes or hands off each other.

She nudged Dena. "Look around. You see any unattached Paolos or Giannis worth bothering with? Cuz I sure don't."

Dena did as her friend suggested, looking first one way, then the other, eyes deftly scanning the aisles. A few rows back to the right, she spotted a pair of handsome men seated together. Mmm, they looked positively delicious. She patted Shelby's arm, then pointed the men out.

The sarcastic lift of Shelby's eyes puzzled Dena. "Before you get too happy, watch 'em a while," Shelby answered.

Suddenly, a small pocket of turbulence buffeted the plane to and fro. Dena got a sick feeling in the pit of her stomach, but it wasn't from her normal motion sickness. She hadn't taken her eyes off her potential quarry. One of the men leaned over and gave his friend a peck on the cheek and a reassuring squeeze of the hand as the plane did another bob and weave. Dena's spirits did a parallel nosedive.

"I think Gianni and Giuseppe just had a private moment that doesn't call for a Gina," Shelby snickered.

As Dena panned the cabin one more time, it became dismally clear that the Paolos and Giannis of her dreams had missed the flight. But their grandmothers had made it. Not to mention their mothers, aunts and uncles, fathers, grandfathers, great-aunts and great-uncles, and wailing nieces and nephews. Yup, they all had made the flight just fine.

But all was not lost. Shelby and Dena still had the food to look forward to. That would certainly get the travelers into the Italian swing of things, wouldn't it? Once again, down the aisle the flight attendants came, always the same refrain.

"*Pesce o bistecca? Pesce o bistecca*?" Fish or beef...fish or beef.

By the time the attendants got to the ladies, the refrain had changed slightly. "Pesce...pesce," they said. Shelby looked up at the pretty woman. She waited to hear more choices. "Pesce," the attendant repeated.

"...o bistecca? Pesce o bistecca?" Shelby finally added.

"No, just fish. We're out of the beef."

Shelby's eyes widened in dismay. She tried to explain her predicament. "I can't eat fish. Anything else? You must have something," she pleaded in desperation. She hadn't eaten all day, too excited and busy to bother with nourishment. But now she was starving.

The flight attendant shook her head. Nothing.

Dena looked on sympathetically at this unexpected turn of events, knowing all too well her friend's deathly allergic reaction to fish. One morsel and Shelby would blow up like the Goodyear blimp and start gasping for air. They'd have to crash land onto a hospital landing pad.

So, when the woman didn't offer any alternatives, Dena leaped into the fray. "Surely, you have something, anything? She'll drop dead if she eats fish," she elaborated.

Again came that damnable shake of the head. "Pesce," the flight attendant answered unsympathetically.

Dena couldn't believe her ears. Just as she was about to say as much, a low rumble in her stomach signaled her own hunger, diverting her from Shelby's plight. Glancing across the aisle at a gentleman raising a forkful of temptingly seasoned filet to his mouth, her stomach grumbled again.

"Pesce, per favore," she said quickly in case they ran out of fish, too. After all, she wasn't allergic to fish, and there was no sense in both of them going hungry. One of them needed to keep up their strength.

"So, they literally had nothing for you to eat. Not even a roll?" the Englishwoman was incredulous.

"Nope," Shelby confirmed. "I couldn't take a chance it had touched the fish."

"Well, why didn't you request a special meal in advance?" the Englishwoman asked logically.

Doing that had never entered Shelby's mind. In all her years of traveling, she had never been confronted with fish as an airline meal choice. "After all, fish is a pretty common allergy," she pointed out to India.

"Yeah," Dena piped up. "We were wondering if it is only on foreign airlines."

"Whatever. You can bet I won't make that mistake again," said Shelby.

The Englishwoman nodded in agreement. "For sure, that's a good thing to keep in mind...a handy little traveling tidbit."

Traveling Tidbit for the Persnickety Eater: Those who have food allergies, are vegetarian, or are just plain ol' picky, should request special meals in advance. Wait 'til the flight, and you might be out of luck.

When arranging their vacation, the ladies had engaged the services of a knowledgeable travel agent. Available seven days a week, twenty-four hours a day. Efficient and personalized service and itineraries. Offices conveniently located worldwide and in-home consultations available. Guaranteed lowest prices. All at absolutely no charge. The agent's name? Mr. Web. First name...World. Middle initial...W. Agent's full name...World Wide Web, aka the Net.

Dena and Shelby had also done some background research using <u>Fodor's Up Close Italy</u>,[3] which boasts getting more lodging for your buck; <u>Frommer's Italy from $70 a Day</u>,[4] the ultimate guide to comfortable low cost travel; and <u>The Guide to Lodging in Italy's Monasteries</u>,[5] whose title says it all.

So, how did that work for the travelers? Is that the rancid whiff of another Diva Intelligence Quotient Test question in the air?

Where did our travelers end up staying in Florence?
    A)   Grand Hotel Astoria, a luxury 5-star hotel,
    B)   Convento di San Matteo, a convent for those seeking the monastic life,
    C)   Giancarlo's palatial flat in centro, or
    D)   Hotel Aldini, affordable no-star hotel in centro.

The Englishwoman smiled knowingly. She was confident of the answer to this.

"Go ahead, give it a try," Dena coaxed.

"Well," India began analytically, "I think we can rule out the convent."

"Are you sure? After all, we did meet in a Catholic school," Shelby baited.

"Yup, Our Lady of Lourdes High School in Poughkeepsie, New York. First day of our freshman year. Thirty years ago. OUCH!"

---

[3]Reid Bramblett, Shelen Brewer, and Patricia Schultz, <u>Frommer's Italy from $70 a Day</u> (2nd Edition): (New York: MacMillan, 1999)

[4]Nancy Smallvan Itallie, ed., <u>Fodor's Up Close Italy</u> (2nd Edition), (New York: Fodor's Travel Publications, 2000)

[5]Eileen Barish, <u>The Guide to Lodging in Italy's Monasteries</u>, (Scottsdale: Anacapa Press, 2000)

Dena reached down and grabbed her ankle. There'd definitely be a nasty bruise there tomorrow. She shot Shelby a nasty look.

The curl of Shelby's lip and glare in her eyes belied the sugar sweet tone of her voice. "You mean ten years ago, don't you, dear?" she contradicted.

The Englishwoman interrupted. "Catholic school or no, the two of you were here to see men. I hardly think you'd stay in a convent with women who thought they had walked down the aisle to say "I do" to Jesus Christ."

"Okay, one down," Shelby conceded easily.

The wheels grinding round in India's head were almost visible. Shrewd eyes scanned her companions from head to toe. Not a hair out of place, perfect mani-pedis, color-coordinated from head to toe, and hatboxes, no less! This was a no-brainer.

"Then it must be the Grand Hotel Astoria. Only the best for the Divas," she postulated.

Dena gave a hearty chuckle as she recalled her financial planning strategy for their little adventure. Housewives of the world unite! Do you need some extra pin money for clothes, jewelry, a little nip and tuck, or a trip to some exotic locale? Listen and learn.

Ah, the joys of a debit card. The one reason to actually look forward to grocery shopping. As you check out, the cashier asks if you want a little cash back. Your answer? Hell yes, how much can I get? Finally, when your husband remarks on the sudden increase in grocery expenditures, just remind him of the latest drought, crippling strike, civil war, flood, rising cost of production, mad cow disease, or swarming locusts, which has regrettably affected current food prices. Now that you've got the money, how do you account for the surplus funds? With a straight face say, "Why, I redeem bottles. Amazing how fast those nickels add up."

While Dena was patting herself on the back for her resourcefulness, Shelby responded to India's second stab at answering the quiz question.

"A five-star hotel? Are you kidding me?" she crowed, almost spitting out her sip of coffee. "Dena's kids threatened open rebellion if they saw another plate of franks and beans. She relented. But even as we speak, they're probably having Mac and Cheese for dinner."

Dena slipped back into the present, joining the conversation again. "And Shelby's dipped so far into her retirement savings that if Social Security folds, she'll be eating cat food at sixty-five. Meow!" she purred.

"Okay," conceded the Englishwoman. "Luxury hotel, out. So, the two of you stayed with Giancarlo to save money?"

Shelby's entire body seemed to recoil at the thought. "Please!" she spat out as a visible shudder rushed through her. "Do you see an S for Sucker stamped on my forehead? I'd already lost the man to another woman once. I love Dena, but..."

"You don't trust her?" India's words were a question that needed no answer.

Before Shelby could defend herself, Dena leaped into the fray. "Not even her best friend," she revealed, shaking her head in pity. "Isn't that a shame?"

A shade of sorrow flickered in India's eyes. She cast them downward, almost with embarrassment, before looking up and meeting Dena's gaze. Yes, she thought, it is a shame. But, the Englishwoman hesitated, as if struggling for just the right words. Then, haunted eyes quickly turned to a defiant glare. "A shame, but sometimes justified."

Dena caught Shelby's startled look and knew they were having the same reaction. There was a story there, both women were sure. Separately, they speculated on what had happened to India to cause such a response.

"Justified?" Dena questioned with disbelief. "How can someone have a best friend they can't trust completely?"

India, face clouded over even more, was silent, lost in a painful memory...one Dena and Shelby were a bit apprehensive about interrupting.

Finally, the British woman looked up and spoke. "Well, let's face it. Do we ever really know someone's true motivation? Even someone we've known for a lifetime? I know I certainly didn't."

Again, Dena and Shelby shared a quizzical glance. Two sets of eyes trained on India, demanding an explanation.

"It's no deep dark secret," she revealed. "Annabel and I were just like you. Best friends for almost thirty-five years. She meant the world to me, until one day she said something utterly hateful. Something I just couldn't forgive. And I never trusted her again."

Ooh, this sounds juicy, Shelby thought. Obviously, there's more to this woman than meets the eye. "What'd she say?" The words were out of her mouth before she could corral them.

Silently, India berated herself for opening up to total strangers. It was alright for these two nincompoops to provide her with a laugh or two, but damned if she would reciprocate.

"Oh, it happened so long ago, it's not worth talking about," she said, deflecting the question smoothly. "Besides, you haven't finished your story. So, you ended up staying at the Aldini?"

Upon their arrival, Dena and Shelby realized Frommer's Guide couldn't have been more accurate about one thing. The Hotel Aldini,[6] an affordable no-star in centro, was indeed located in a centuries-old, stone *palazzo* right in the shadow of the magnificent cathedral, Il Duomo. The ladies were quite pleased with their choice when they entered the lobby and found beautiful terra cotta floors graced with Persian runners. The room was small, but nicely decorated with floral bedspreads and matching drapes. And even though located on the noisy Piazza del Duomo square, once the double-paned windows were closed, one could almost hear a pin drop. The bathrooms had been recently renovated and were quite modern. All in all, Dena and Shelby were pleased; however, they did make a few observations that might prove helpful.

> **Traveling Tidbit for the Portly Traveler:** Be prepared for the unusually narrow shower stalls and use soap on a rope. Anyone sporting a few extra pounds who drops their soap and bends to retrieve it could become wedged and trapped in the shower.

> **Traveling Tidbit for the Fops and Dandies of the World**: You'll never make it here. The hotel does not provide irons and forbids the use of your own.

> **Traveling Tidbit for Those Wishing Phone Contact with the Outside World:** Buy a calling card and use a pay phone. It's cheaper and less hassle. Using the room phone, poor Dena spent days trying to call the same children she was so glad to be away from, only to find the phone was in need of repair.

Subject to these few caveats, the Hotel Aldini is charming, affordable, and perhaps, just the place to stay.

Within minutes of entering the room, Dena was already arranging her clothes in neat piles and rows in the drawers and closet. Was she planning on moving in, Shelby wondered. "Don't unpack yet," she dissuaded her fastidious friend. "Let's take a walk, and I'll show you something quite spectacular."

Through the bustling streets of the ancient city, they ambled past majestic old buildings standing proud as the Renaissance

---

[6]Hotel Aldini, Via Calzaiuoli 13, PH 055/21-47-52, www.pronet.it/hotelaldini

era from which they were hewn. Click, click tapped their shoes along the cobblestone streets. Stylish Italian designer boutiques shared the byways with *pasticcerie* offering mouthwatering confectioneries, *salumerie* displaying a tempting array of aromatic cheeses, salamis, and prosciutto, and outdoor cafés beckoning passersby to relax and take in the sights and sounds that are Firenze. Crossing the River Arno, which snakes through the metropolis, Shelby led Dena up the tree-lined path of Florence's famed hilltop, Monte alle Croci. Their goal was its summit and Piazzale Michelangelo.

Once there, a bronze copy of Michelangelo's *Davide*, of David and Goliath fame, greets visitors. The statue dominates the center of the square seeming to hold court over the city below. For quite a long time, Dena stood transfixed gawking at the giant's face and his...uh...well...uh uhm...oh, all right...the other manly attributes of this perfect, and perfectly nude, male specimen.

Shelby laughed at her friend's preoccupation. Any minute she was liable to hoist herself up and try to put the boy in a lip lock. Reaching for Dena's arm, Shelby coaxed her along. "Come on, dear. There's something else you should see.

Dena resisted, edging away from her friend's grasp. "Oh, do we have to? This is quite an eyeful right here."

"It's a statue. Get hold of yourself!"

Dena longed to remind her friend that she wasn't the one who'd spent six years pining for a man who'd disappeared into thin air. Hell, she'd had more of a relationship with this statue in two minutes than Shelby had had with Giancarlo in all these years. The words were on the tip of her tongue, but Dena knew if she uttered them, it would spoil their first hours in Italy by opening old wounds. So, she remained silent and reluctantly allowed herself to be pried away.

A hilltop view of the city awaited them. Despite a gloomy shroud of charcoal-gray clouds and a dampness that threatened chilly spring showers, the view of Florence from the hilltop aerie was breathtaking. A potpourri of russet-color tile rooftops seemed to pay homage to Il Duomo, the grand dame in whose shadow other buildings stood. The cathedral's magnificent burnt sienna, tiled dome dominated the skyline. From there, the ladies let their eyes follow the River Arno as it meandered through the heart of the city with graceful bridges connecting the historic city center with *Oltr'arno*, the city's south side. Off in the distance, the Apennine Mountains stood tall and proud, guarding the city.

Not a sound came from Shelby's direction. Is she breathing, Dena wondered. She seemed as still, and dare one say, as stiff as Davide. "Shelby, are you okay?" Dena asked.

But lost in a hazy world of her own reaching back six years, Shelby was unaware of her friend's concern. Snippets of time spent with Giancarlo in this enchanted city reeled through her mind like a video. This was supposed to be my home, she thought wistfully. Our home. I belong here. Remembering a starry night years ago in this very place and how his warm arms enveloped her, Shelby wrapped her own arms around her waist, wishing they were his.

"Shelby?" Dena tried again.

Finally, letting her friend's words penetrate, Shelby shook free of the past. "It's magical, isn't it? If we continue up, you'll see the Church of San Miniato. It's magnificent," she suggested.

As Dena followed her friend a few steps upward, a dewy moustache of perspiration emerged glistening on her upper lip. Feeling as if she might suffocate, she unbuttoned her coat and tore off her scarf. Labored breaths pumped her chest in and out. She needed air, unable to take another step. "If we continue up, we'll be in nosebleed territory," she complained. "At least, let me stop for an espresso before going on."

Over at the little bar, Dena placed her order for an espresso like a true Italian. Shelby turned up her nose at the mere thought, despising the diesel fuel the Italians called coffee.

"*Un cappuccino, per favore*," she requested instead. She waited for the *barrista* to likewise turn his nose up at her order and was not disappointed. Luckily, she didn't care what he thought of her.

"He looked at you as if he'd smelled something quite putrid," Dena whispered.

> **Traveling Tidbit for the Clueless American:** Those tracksuits and sneakers you love so much have American tourist written all over them. Should a savvier friend manage to convince you to leave them home, don't blow it by ordering cappuccino past noon. It's an Italian no-no.

Ignoring the barrista's withering stare, the ladies finished their coffee and headed for the church. Confronted by a steep staircase of crumbling steps carved into the mountainside, Dena blanched. Did Shelby think she was a llama? The walk up to the piazza had been strenuous enough. Still, as she stood at the foot of the stairs, she was entranced by the church's unique mosaic façade.

High up over the main door, Jesus is depicted on a throne between the Virgin Mary and Saint Miniatus, a martyr persecuted in the 3rd century. The green and white marble façade of the impressive thirteenth-century church is typically Florentine. Thank you, Messrs. Fodor and Frommer, for that excellent description.

Inside, the floor of San Miniato boasts an elaborate marble inlay of the zodiac signs and their symbolic animals. Shelby and Dena found their signs, the Bull and the Virgin.

"So much for astrology," Shelby huffed. "I'm not stubborn at all, and you're hardly a virgin."

Dena turned away and rolled her eyes. Oh, I don't know, she mused to herself. Seems pretty accurate to me. Bull, mule, take your pick. Or, how about Shelby the Jackass? Yeah, that's it! And as for me being virginal? Oh well, one out of two ain't bad.

Traveling Tidbit for the Flat of Feet, Short of Breath, or Simply Lazy Traveler: The walk up to Piazzale Michelangelo is not easy. For the big of ducats, hire a limo (and give the ladies a call). For the short of cash, take Bus number 12 or 13 (no need to call the ladies, but they wish you well).

Corollary Traveling Tidbit for the Arthritic, Wheelchair Bound, or Cholesterol-ridden Traveler: You won't make it up the steps of San Miniato alive, so don't try. In fact, by the ladies' best estimate, no place in Italy is wheelchair accessible. So just stay home. Travel our great U.S.of A.

So, the ladies began the long descent. A few steps down and both women picked up their pace, their feet moving so fast, they barely made contact with the steps. Neither wanted to admit that a side trip back to the bar to use its facilities was necessary, until Dena took off in a gallop and Shelby brought up her rear quite convincingly. With advancing age, their bladders had much in common with a milking cow's udders.

"Must be that strong Italian coffee," Dena surmised.

"Exactly, I'm usually able to wait for hours," Shelby nodded in agreement before taking off. This from the woman who limited herself to one cup of tea per morning before setting off for her fifteen-minute commute to work.

Dena looked a bit shell-shocked as she emerged. Having preceded her friend into the restroom, Shelby knew why. "Some bathroom, huh?" she remarked with amusement.

"Is that what they call it?" Dena countered.

Traveling Tidbit for Travelers Needing a Commode Consisting of Slightly More than a Hole in the Ground: Don't stop here. This is quite literally a hole in the ground. Also, don't bother looking for toilet tissue. Bring your own.

It's said that the older one gets, the less sleep one needs, and the ladies were proof of it that day. Operating on sheer adrenaline, they rivaled the Energizer Bunny. Where others might have taken a nap at this point, Shelby and Dena were raring to go. Back at their hotel, Shelby consulted Frommer's for their first dinner in Florence. As she mulled over promising choices, it occurred to her to compare it with Fodor's, so she turned to her friend. "What recommendations does your book make?" she asked.

"I didn't bring it," Dena revealed nonchalantly.

Shelby's brow furrowed quizzically. She didn't say a word, but Dena saw the question in her face and hurried to explain. "Well, you told me not to bring sneakers or jogging suits if I didn't want to look like a tourist. Do ya think a guide book might give 'em a clue?"

"Yeah, but it might have given us a clue, too," Shelby retorted. Shaking her head in disbelief, she returned her gaze to her own guide.

Traveling Tidbit for the Image-Conscious Traveler: Should you be traveling to only a handful of cities, copy the relevant pages from your guide book to avoid looking like a clueless tourist.

Shaking her head and mumbling to herself, Shelby chose a restaurant.

"Aren't we going to take a cab?" Dena asked. "After all, it is nine at night. Is it safe?"

Shelby pooh-poohed the idea, reminding Dena that she had once practically lived in Florence. "It's quite safe at night, and I can find my way around the city blindfolded."

The confidence in her voice should have reassured Dena, and for a moment, it did. However, as she spied her friend stuffing the two-pound Frommer's Guide in her purse, she was a bit perplexed, but decided discretion might be the better part of valor. After all, she was quite hungry. If she angered Shelby, her dinner could easily consist of Tums and the extra peanuts she'd filched from Alitalia.

So off they went through the winding streets of Florence. Dena remembered having heard somewhere, perhaps from Shelby, that the city center was quite small and could be covered on foot quite quickly. Therefore, after a half hour's walk, the thought crossed her mind that they might find the way faster if Shelby were indeed blindfolded. "How much farther," she whined, reminding even herself of her kids.

Reluctantly, Shelby pulled out her Frommer's, searched for light, and studied the map. Even with the lighting of a corner lamp, the page was a blur. Both ladies cursed the gods for this first sign of impending old age, and with the precision of synchronized swimmers, reached for their reading glasses.

A right down this street, a left at the next corner, cross that piazza. The Italian custom of dining late was working in the ladies' favor this particular evening. If they were lucky, they might be eating by midnight.

Fifteen minutes more into their walk and a few more stops for reading light, Dena hazarded another question. "Well, how do you know what street we're on? Where are the street signs?"

And so, Shelby acquainted her with the aesthetically pleasing, but visually challenging, convention of placing plaques or etching street names high on the facades of corner buildings.

The supposedly short stroll to Trattoria Belle Donne[7] restaurant was turning into a search for the Holy Grail. Dena, whose hunger was bordering on an acute medical condition, suggested they ask for directions. Shelby knew it was a waste of time, but loathe to admit it, she approached the first passerby.

"*Scusi, dov'è via delle Belle Donne?*"

"*All'angola girate alla destra su via Brunelleschi, poi andate diritto and gira alla destra su via Strozzi. Diritto fino a via delle*

---

[7]Trattoria Belle Donne, Via d. Belle Donne 16r, PH 055/23826909

Belle Donne." Like bullets from a fully loaded Uzi, the words shot from the kindly Italian gentleman's mouth.

Shelby nodded her head several times in understanding. Neither Dena nor their Good Samaritan saw her eyes glaze over as he spoke. *"Grazie. Ho capito,"* she replied prettily. Thanks. I understand.

"So, which way?" asked Dena.

"He said right," Shelby answered as she marched on.

One right turned into two...which turned into a third. As Shelby was about to make a fourth right, Dena blocked her way. "How many rights did the man say? You do remember four right angles make a rectangle? One more and we'll end up right back where we started!"

Okay, how am I going to get out of this one, Shelby asked herself. Dena really was catching on much too fast these days. Had her brain gotten a recent power surge? Calculatingly, Shelby rolled her eyes and shook her head. Derision dripped from her every movement.

"Dena," she sneered, "they were not right angles. It was one acute angle and two obtuse. Another right would have been a trapezoid, not a rectangle. Therefore, we would not have ended up where we started!" She drew a deep breath before continuing. "Besides, I had no intention of turning right."

And with that, Shelby made a 180-degree spin and took off to the left.

"Trapezoid?!" India spat out. "What difference does the size of the angles make?"

"A big difference!" Shelby blustered. "I'd stay to explain, but all that coffee, you know." With that, she scurried off for the ladies room.

The Englishwoman turned to Dena expectantly.

Dena waved a dismissive hand at her friend's receding back. "Okay, it did take me a few seconds to figure it out. The size of those angles didn't matter at all," Dena admitted.

"Really?" the Englishwoman said. Took a few seconds, huh?

India's uncomplimentary thought was interrupted by Dena. "One thing about Shelby. She hates to admit she's wrong or doesn't know something. The truth is she's pretty good at speaking Italian, but when people speak to her, they may as well be speaking Greek."

India's eyes bugged with disbelief. "But I thought she studied the language?"

"*You're right. But, as Shelby says, she studied the Italian of Dante. You know, scholarly Italian.*"

The Brit allowed herself a loud guffaw. "*And all the Italians? What are they speaking?*"

"*Italian, of course, but Shelby says they really should learn to speak their own language more clearly.*" *Dena flashed a tiny wink toward the Englishwoman.*

India blew out a short exasperated breath. "*And you let her get away with that horse manure of an explanation?*"

Dena conceded the Briton's assessment with an easy shrug of her shoulder, but not without a caveat. "*Sure, that's what friends do, overlook each other's harmless quirks.*"

Again, a stabbing envy seared through India, but she refused to let it take hold, quickly changing the subject. "*So, the restaurant? Did you ever make it there, or did you go to bed hungry?*" *she asked.*

The friends finally stumbled upon Trattoria Belle Donne, tucked away on a street of the same name. For sophisticated elegance, this is not the place. However, for a friendly atmosphere with great food and Chianti by the crockful, it pays to put on one's hiking shoes and carry a compass and possibly a change of clothes to discover this elusive gem. The décor includes homey hand-painted ceramic tops on small wooden tables and a menu written on a blackboard.

> **Traveling Tidbit for the Traveling Drunkards:** For the best bang for your buck, order the house red served in what seems like gallon-size ceramic jugs. It's quite good and enough to satisfy even the local wino.

At the end of their delightful dinner, Dena and Shelby were working their way back to the Hotel Aldini. Lively music and laughter from one bar and restaurant after another spilled out onto the streets.

"Let's not go back to the hotel right away," Dena suggested hopefully. Shelby agreed readily, allowing the magic of Italy (not to mention the lure of beautiful Italian men and just one more glass of wine) to draw them into one watering hole after another. The ladies thoroughly enjoyed time spent mingling with the Florentine locals. Additionally, Shelby was happy to discover that her comprehension of the language seemed to improve with each sip of wine.

Stumbling back to the hotel at four in the morning, Dena had to grant Shelby one small point. No matter the time of day or the sobriety of the poor rube walking the streets of Florence, the city really was a very safe place for single women.

"I'll have to make sure I try out that restaurant when I go to Florence," India interrupted again. She took out a small notebook and a pen. "And the watering holes, too. What were their names?"

Did she just ask us the names of the moons orbiting Jupiter, Dena thought to herself. She turned to her friend for help. But Shelby was lost in thought, remembering that night or trying to anyway.

They'd been up for twenty-four hours by the time they fell into their beds. They'd drunk enough vino to supply a small Roman army. That much she knew. Other than that, it was all pretty much a blur. "Well, we're not quite sure, but if it helps at all, one was an Irish pub somewhere in centro," she answered.[8]

Gently, India recapped her pen and put her notebook back in her purse. "Oh, that makes it crystal clear."

---

[8]On a subsequent trip, the ladies located one of those pubs. JJ Cathedral Pub, Piazza San Giovanni 4r, PH 055/280260, www.jjcathedral.com

Chapter 4

They were dead, weren't they? And based on their roiling stomachs and stabbing head pain, they'd been cast into hell's fires or were on their way. Why, then, were bells ringing?

Surfacing from the depths of an alcohol-induced coma, Shelby realized she hadn't been graced with death. She was still alive, if only technically, and was paying for last night's revelry. The bells? Merely the phone. How to make it stop? Reaching a hand over, she groped frantically for the receiver. If I could move, I'd jump down the throat of whoever this is.

"Hellooooo," she croaked, her voice somewhere between baritone and bass.

"Shelby?" came the lyrical lilt of an Italian male.

Ohmigod...Giancarlo! Okay, she still wanted to jump down the caller's throat, but maybe not in quite the same way.

"Are you awake?" he asked.

She told him no, then could have kicked herself. Damn, too drunk to even come up with a suitable lie. Where was he, she asked.

"Here?!" Shelby rocketed out of the bed. "You mean in my hotel?" she shrieked. Oh hell, my head. Had a cannon just exploded between her eyes? She pressed a palm to her forehead, desperately trying to stem the painful tide of what felt like shrapnel piercing her brain.

This couldn't be happening. Standing beside the bed, Shelby slumped down onto the mattress, simultaneously trembling with horror and excitement.

Six years, six thousand miles, and what had felt like six million hours of daydreaming about this moment. And now, the man she had spent an eternity fantasizing about meeting again was just steps away. Everything in Shelby wanted to sprint down that short hallway and feast her eyes on her Giancarlo at long last. But that was impossible.

Years of fantasizing how beautiful she would look, how she would take his breath away, and here she was with pillow face, bed head, and dragon breath. If that weren't bad enough, if she moved any faster than a snail right now, her stomach would likely serve up last night's menu at his fine Italian leather-clad feet.

"You have to go away. I can't see you now," she wailed.

Giancarlo, knowing a thing or two about women's vanity, gave a throaty chuckle. Still, never one to be thwarted when he wanted something, he insisted on escorting the ladies to lunch. "I'll pick you up at one o'clock," he arranged.

"Fine," Shelby conceded. That gave her four hours to straighten up and fly right. Let's see, that would be about...about twenty-four hours less than she needed.

Shelby spied him from a few hundred yards away as he approached the hotel. He was at once acutely familiar and a total stranger. The loose-limbed, sexy stride was the same. The smoldering black eyes that used to melt her heart hadn't changed. Only now, they weren't looking out from a handsomely chiseled face, but a moon face. And the extra padding in his midsection...that was new. What had happened to her tall, dark, and sleek Italian prince?

"Where do they get it from?" she whispered to no one in particular.

"Who? What?" Dena asked.

"Men. Or at least, Italian men. Haven't you noticed their seeming contentment and confidence with themselves and their place in the world?" Shelby pointed toward Giancarlo with disgust. "Look at him. He's getting fat and losing his hair. If that were us, we'd brick up the door to our house. The world would never see us again."

Oh my Lord. Six years, a river of tears, and a mountain of heartache. And for what? The Pillsbury Dough Boy's stunt double? Okay, so he's minus the chef hat and the apron. Too bad they didn't take his apple cheeks and pot belly, too. Her handsome Italian prince had turned into a pizza chef.

Struggling to disguise her disappointment, Shelby plastered a wooden smile on her face. When Giancarlo reached her, she kissed both Red Delicious cheeks in the European way. Then, she quickly turned to avoid his gaze and introduced Dena.

The hung-over women were grateful that Giancarlo had chosen an eatery only steps away from their hotel. As she sat next to him, a nervous excitement bubbled inside Shelby. No, it wasn't last night's liquor. Or, at least, not totally. It had been so long since they'd seen each other; he had been the love of her life. She could scarcely believe she was sitting next to him, actually able to reach out and touch him if she wanted to.

Yes, there was a bit more of him to touch than she remembered, but looks weren't everything, were they? There had been so much more to Giancarlo than looks. His intelligence, his

sense of humor, his romantic nature, his roving eye. Shelby
shook her head to banish that last thought. Nothing was going
to spoil this reunion.

There was so much they had to catch up on...careers and
families...what a mistake he'd made leaving and how much he'd
missed her...all the things he had planned for them to do for the
next week. Surely, these were uppermost in Giancarlo's mind.

"She...she is very nice woman, but," he lamented to his
lunch companions.

Please, God, don't let him say her name. I can't bear to hear
that name. It will just kill me.

"But she have many problems," he finished.

Though Shelby's prayer had been answered, and the name
hadn't left his lips, an avalanche of thoughts and feelings hurled
her back in time. Problems? Oh, did he mean the obsessive
compulsive hand washing? How about the fact that her apartment room had been about as clean as a landfill? No? Well, then
maybe it was that at thirty-four years of age, the woman still
lived with Mommy and didn't have a job. And still, he had
wanted her.

Shelby nodded in agreement, a feigned sympathy in her
eyes.

"She do nothing. I come home...a mess! She no cook, she no
clean. Nothing!" he revealed.

"Well, yes, I did know that about her," Shelby agreed. Actu-
ally, so had he, she thought, but didn't say. Guess little
Giancarlo, the one-eyed monster, hadn't been looking for Suzy
Homemaker.

"She stay in bed all day, not get dressed. She was very...how
you say," his voice faded away as his mind searched for the
right word. "She was d*epressa*?"

"Oh, depressed," Dena furnished the English word. Her eyes
met Shelby's. She didn't know how her friend could sit there
listening to this.

But sit there Shelby did, taking it all in, simultaneously in-
trigued and repulsed by the intimate details of his life with that
traitorous bitch. "Depressed? Oh, what a shame for her," she
commiserated. Don't blow it. Do try to keep a straight face.

"Everybody must do something. You can't do nothing. She
do nothing. No work for money. No work at home. Nobody can
do nothing!" Giancarlo continued the tirade.

You don't say? As Shelby remembered, the woman was
damned good at doing nothing. But she had heard enough. This
could be filed under more information than she needed to know.

Still, she felt vindicated. But it was time to move on to more important topics... Shelby.

"Giancarlo," she said tentatively, interrupting his tirade. "Dena and I want to get our hair done. Do you know a good hairdresser?"

"Yes," Dena jumped on the change of subject like a drowning man on a life jacket. "The Hotel Aldini recommended Mario's. Have you heard of it?"

After thinking a few seconds, Giancarlo suggested the ladies go to Paolo and Fabrizio's.[9] Reaching into his breast pocket, he retrieved one of his business cards. On the back, he jotted down the name of the salon, but unfortunately, he could not produce an address. So, he gave the ladies directions based on landmarks.

Ohmigod, no address, Dena inwardly groaned. Here we go again. Ms. Magoo, the Sequel. We'll never make it there. What geometrical shape will she blame it on this time, a diamond or a pentagon?

After a sumptuous lunch, they left Giancarlo, but not before he had extracted a promise to meet for dinner the next evening.

"So, where did he take you for this fabulous lunch?" India inquired as she reached for her notebook yet again. Finally, she thought, the name of a place where Florentines actually eat.

"Oh, we don't know. But it doesn't matter because you couldn't get in anyway," Shelby added. "It was a government cafeteria."

Once again, India placed her notebook and pen back in her purse. Okay, so far these would-be travel writers have recommended a restaurant that's about as easy to find as the Lost City of Atlantis, three bars whose names elude them, and a place not open to the general public. Somehow, I don't think Messrs. Frommer and Fodor need to stay awake at night worrying.

"So, did you get your hair done?" she asked.

"Scaling the Himalayas would be faster," Dena groused as she trudged alongside Shelby.

After dinner that evening, the two had set off to find Paolo and Fabrizio's so they would know where to go the next day.

---

[9] Paolo & Fabrizio, Borgo SS. Apostoli,50/52r, PH 055/216007-282444

They had been wandering around in circles for what seemed like hours.

"This is ridiculous. I barely remember what we're looking for anymore," Shelby agreed. "Forget it! We're just going to Mario's tomorrow."

Dena offered no argument. After all, how much of a difference could it make?

And so, in the early morning sunshine, the ladies made their way to Mario's, barely able to contain their excitement.

"We walk in the Ugly Americans...." Shelby said.

"And we emerge Italian bombshells!" Dena finished her friend's thought.

Visions of Sophia Loren, Maria Cucinotta, Gina Lollabrigida, and Isabella Rosellini kaleidoscoped through their minds' eyes. A mere detail that neither one of them had a drop of Italian blood, or that Dena could multiply her cup size by 10, and still not have the breasts to match these women.

"Walk faster," Shelby urged, quickening her pace. "Or we'll be late."

The salon was situated above a cosmetic shop, where the kindly shopkeeper informed the ladies Mario's hadn't opened yet. However, she directed them to an elevator in the rear, where they could go up and wait. With barely concealed anticipation, the friends took seats in the waiting area, anxious for the arrival of Mario and his minions. Thankfully, it wasn't long before the whizzing of the elevator on its upward journey signaled their arrival.

"He's coming," Dena announced excitedly.

Pop! The elevator. Both women's gazes held fast as Crazy Glue to the parting doors. Out marched one little old lady. And then another. And another. Each with various shades of white, blue, silver, silver blue, and the most unnatural red hair color that Dena and Shelby had ever seen. The friends looked at each other a bit befuddled.

Shelby covered her mouth and whispered conspiratorially. "Is Mario the hairdresser to the Italian geriatric set?"

"I wanted Lady Di, not Dinah Shore," Dena groaned.

They gaped in openmouthed wonder as the little old ladies donned baby pink lab coats. Soon, it dawned on the duo that the situation was far graver than even their fertile brains could have imagined. Both pairs of brown eyes widened in horror as reality sunk in.

"Sweet Jesus," Shelby screeched. "They're not clients. They're...." She stopped in mid-sentence, almost afraid to utter the increasingly obvious.

"The hairdressers?" Dena finished for her.

The friends found themselves catapulted back in time, plopped smack in the middle of a Woolworth's beauty salon. They watched aghast as the crones doddered to their stations and proceeded to mix, pour, blend, stir and shake fetid smelling solutions. Not one blow dryer, heat lamp, or aluminum foil strip was in sight. What was? A ship load of tiny pink perm rollers and sponge rollers, blue hair nets, bobby pins, and rat tail tease combs.

Shelby stroked her corkscrew curly locks protectively. She was sure these little old Italian *nonne*...grandmothers...had never dealt with hair like hers before. A woman's hair is her crowning glory. Shelby feared hers would be a crown of thorns if she let them get their hands on it. Within seconds, she decided to cut her losses.

"I don't think I'm going to get my hair done here," she whispered. "I just don't feel they would know what to do with my kind of hair. But, by all means, you go right ahead. I'll wait for you."

A worried Dena stared blankly at Shelby, and then let her gaze stray back to the hairdressers. Try as she might, Dena was hard put to figure out what possible kind of hair these women did have expertise in. Renaissance wigs maybe. She blanched at the idea of what they might do to her. Damned if she was going to be the only one walking out of there looking like Margaret Thatcher.

"Oh, no," Dena disagreed. "I couldn't have you sit here waiting for me all that time. Let's go."

What to do? What to do? Where was a band of marauding kidnappers when one really needed them? Why do emergency phone calls from home only happen when things are going well? It wouldn't take much. One of Dena's children with a low-grade fever or Shelby's mother in a minor traffic accident. Had any of these events befallen the ladies on their way to Mario's this morning? No such luck. And on top of that, their walk to Mario's had been swift and sure, no trouble finding it at all.

So, here sat the sorry friends on the horns of a moral dilemma. To cruelly tell the truth or to try to flee Mario's as quickly and gracefully as possible. But why tell the truth when a lie would do?

Shelby chose the little old lady with the fuchsia bouffant. She looked crazy and would probably believe anything. "Oh!" Shelby gasped loudly in the woman's direction, covering her mouth with one hand and feigning a look of distressed surprise.

"*Abbiamo dimenticato qualcosa! Torniamo subito.*" We forgot something! We'll be right back.

With nary a backward glance, the friends sprinted for the elevator, vowing never to darken Mario's street, never mind doorstep again.

"Now what do we do?" Dena asked when they finally slowed down. She'd really had her heart set on having an authentic Italian hairdresser work his magic.

Were their dreams of new Italian coifs too much to ask? She thought not. If they had to swim the mosquito-infested Arno River to find Paolo and Fabrizio, they'd do it.

By process of elimination, the friends narrowed the possible streets down to one, Borgo S.S. Apostoli. It shouldn't be too hard, they agreed. After all, how many hair salons could there be on one Florentine street?

How high can one count? To the pair's dismay, Borgo S.S. Apostoli turned out to be Florence's Hairdressers Row, with one salon after another studding the street.

Time was running out, and Shelby was getting anxious. She wanted to look beautiful for Giancarlo that evening. Let the man eat his heart out over what he'd lost.

"We'll split up," Dena suggested. "You take the north side of the street, I'll take the south." And off both women went.

Reaching her head into the first salon, Dena inquired, "*C'e Paolo?*" Is Paolo here?

"*No, no, diritto.*" No, keep straight.

"*C'e Paolo?*" Shelby asked across the street.

"*No, diritto,*" came the same answer.

"*C'e Paolo?*"

"*Si, si, signora, sono Paolo!*" Finally, Dena hit pay dirt.

Both women stared in wonderment as they passed through the sleek glass doors. They had found the pearly gates, a little slice of heaven. Paolo and Fabrizio's was a veritable oasis. Now, this was more like it. Electricity, telephones, indoor plumbing. Within seconds, they landed appointments for an hour later, and thanked their lucky stars for Giancarlo's advice.

Back out on the street, they looked at their watches and wondered what to do in the meantime. "Mmm, only 10:00a.m. Too early for a wine break, I take it," Shelby said, testing the waters.

"Oh, my, yes." Though Dena's words were swift and sure, the quaver in her voice was not nearly as unequivocal. Quickly, she shooed the lure of a morning nip away and made an alternative suggestion. "I haven't seen the Duomo yet."

Shelby's eyes brightened at the mere mention of the beautiful cathedral. "Ah, Our Lady of the Flower is not something you just see. She's something you experience. Giancarlo says he's still in awe of the Duomo's majestic beauty even after having lived here practically his whole life."

The embarrassing truth was it was their last day in Florence before departing for the island of Capri, and Dena and Shelby had been inside only one church and nary a museum. Perhaps, it was time to rectify the situation.

Minutes later, the ladies stood before the mammoth green, white, and pink marble structure that is Il Duomo, a sight to behold. Both women focused on the intricate patterns of color and sculpture, which give witness to the genius, the craftsmanship, the absolute dedication, and divine faith that must have inspired Renaissance artists.

"Just look at this place. And it's even more spectacular at night," Shelby mused in wonderment.

"Yeah, overwhelming," Dena agreed. "And you certainly don't need to be religious to be moved by man's ability to create such perfection."

"And that's the last introspective thought for the ladies on this trip," Shelby announced. "Because frankly, I'm not in Florence for reflections. I'm here for erections."

Dena gasped. "Shelby!"

"What?" Shelby gave an innocent shrug of her shoulders. "Of buildings, of course," she amended.

A quick walk back to the beauty salon, and the ladies were promptly whisked away for their consultations. With a combination of testiculations...oops...gesticulations, and Shelby's limited command of the Italian language when sober, they conveyed their preferences to Paolo, Fabrizio, and the quite hot colorist. Truth be told, the friends had never been the recipients of so much male attention since their twenties. Okay, okay. Shelby was not very attractive in her younger years. Oh, alright, she was a dog. This was the most male attention she'd ever had, and that included seven years of marriage.

Three hours later, they were over the moon with the results of their transformations. "Your haircut is smoking," Shelby complimented. "And the hair color is positively inspired. Do you like it?"

The short, spiky style suited Dena's slender face and large, luminous eyes. The extremely, almost baby blonde highlights were striking and gave her an edgy look worthy of a celebrity. "I love it!" she enthused. "They're geniuses. And you? Like what they did to your hair?"

Shelby paused and preened in the mirror one more time. "Yeah, I do," she confirmed, turning her head to and fro to watch her hair swing breezily.

Yes, it had taken three hours, the Herculean efforts of many men...virile Italian men, the ladies might add...and nuclear-powered chemicals to transform them from backwater belles to *belle donne*...beautiful women. And even if they weren't quite ready to conquer the western world, well, Firenze, watch out!

Chapter 5

"*Ladies and Gentleman, may we have your attention please. British Airways Flight 2599....*"

"Oh, bloody hell!" India slammed her hand down on the table. Her words were nearly drowned out by the loud-speaker announcement. "Just when the story's about to get interesting."

"*....has been delayed,*" the disembodied voice continued.

"Good," the Englishwoman said with visible satisfaction. "So, hurry, tell me before they change their minds and start boarding. Are you divas now? Was Giancarlo mesmerized?"

"Nope, not divas yet," Shelby answered. "But we're getting there."

The walk to Giancarlo's ice cream shop. Oops. So sorry, Giancarlo...to Giancarlos's gelateria...was a quick one. Any doubts about Paolo and Fabrizio's talents instantaneously disappeared with the appreciative gleam in their dinner companion's eyes.

"Oh, lucky me to have dinner with two movie stars," gushed Giancarlo, oozing his trademark Italian charm. "You both beautiful."

Shelby toyed with her now straight-as-an-arrow hair. She hadn't been so sure about the stylists' plans to fry the curl out. The heat from the blow dryer had been so hot, she'd been certain P.T. Barnum had loaned the salon a flame thrower to style her hair. Every hair shaft in her scalp was no doubt petrified. Making matters worse, if the humidity level rose even one percent, the jig would be up. All she'd have to do is stick a bow up front, and she'd be certain to win the blue ribbon in any poodle competition.

She got a bit queasy at the thought of paying all that money for something so fleeting. But the admiring flash in Giancarlo's eyes made it worth it. So what if the hair style had the life span of Cinderella's coach and horses? Big deal that it had cost an arm and a leg. Hell, she'd amputate the other arm and leg herself to see Giancarlo look at her like he'd done six years ago, Shelby laughed to herself.

Arm in arm, through the romantic cobblestone streets of Florence, they ambled. Giancarlo seemingly had a trip down memory lane in store for his former love as he led the ladies to the Buca for dinner. Making their way there, he explained he no longer owned the restaurant where he and Shelby had had their first date, but thought it would be fun to revisit it. Compliant as a lemming, Shelby was quite happy to fall in with his plan.

"Ciao, Giancarlo! *Come stai*?" The current owners of the restaurant, brothers Vito and Pasquale, greeted the trio warmly. Like pampered guests, they were presented with flutes of champagne as they stood waiting to be seated in the perennially busy restaurant. Much to Dena and Shelby's delight, Giancarlo scored a choice table in the central dining room, the place to be if one considers people the most important sightseeing tourist attraction. Singer and pianist Vittorio provided an added bonus as he serenaded his audience, periodically including enthusiastic diners in his performance.

Giancarlo ordered dinner for the little group along with the requisite bottle of red wine. Ding a ling a ling! Just then his cell phone rang.

"*Scusi*, ladies," he apologized and left the table. This was no problem since just then the waiter arrived with the Chianti.

Left to their own devices, and under the effects of the champagne, Shelby was feeling a bit devilish. Having given their waiter the once over, she decided to spice things up a bit for her friend. Leaning over, she whispered in Dena's ear. "He's cute!"

Following Shelby's lead, Dena unabashedly ran her eyes over the man from head to toe, and back again. She liked what she saw. Was he on the menu, too? She'd be only too happy to pay for dinner if he was dessert.

"*Comè*?" he said in a deep voice as he poured their wine. A teasing smile and laughter in his eyes signaled his comprehension.

Dena's face reddened with embarrassment. "Ohmigod, he heard you. What does *comè* mean?" she hissed.

"I'm not sure. Probably something like 'What did you say?'"Shelby answered with an unconcerned shrug.

Brown eyes widened with interest. A sexy smile played across the waiter's face. "You American?" he asked.

"From New York," Dena replied.

"Ah, I like to come there someday." Searching eyes bored into Dena's, melting her with their intensity. It was obvious he would have lingered, but the restaurant was busy.

As he walked away, both women's eyes trailed after him. "Cute butt, too," Shelby remarked playfully.

He was not very tall, perhaps 5'8" or so. Lean and toned with an olive complexion, wavy dark hair, and teasing mocha eyes. Nor was he classically handsome, but every movement, every gesture seethed with sensuality, and when he fixed those smoldering eyes on Dena and treated her to a flirtatious smile, she felt her insides quiver like jelly.

It should be noted that waitering is considered a profession in Italy. One must complete formal training. You know, like McDonald's University. Therefore, when Giancarlo again graced the table with his presence in between *telefono* breaks, Operation Get-Dena-A-Date had to go underground. Shelby knew better than to flirt with a waiter in front of Giancarlo. The waiter knew better. The only one who hadn't read the memo, and couldn't have cared less, was Dena.

Still, she took her cue from the well-educated waiter. Overt flirtation became deliciously forbidden, covert intrigue. Each course he served was accompanied by a stolen brush of his hand against hers, a secret wink, an intimate smile.

Tossing back the vino and engaging in flirtatious high jinks, Dena nearly forgot she was there for dinner. Until her hunk arrived with a hunk.

The signature dish of Florence is *Bistecca alla Fiorentina*. It arrived still aflame on a wheeled cart, and Dena's and Shelby's mouths dropped in unconcealed wonder. Never had they seen such a large piece of meat not still attached to its owner. They wished they could ring up the late Clara Peller. Surely, the former Wendy's spokeswoman would want to hear the good news. "We've found the beef. All of it. It's in Italy."

The ladies were curious to find out more about their new dinner companion. What was its name? Where did it live? Did it have its own zip code? It didn't need bath facilities, did it? Because this steak wouldn't fit in their shower stall at the Hotel Aldini.

Okay, this might have been a bit of hyperbole. Still, it was the largest cut of steak either woman had ever seen. Notwithstanding its girth, this Yeti steak was inarguably the most delicious beef they had ever tasted. From the huge white Chianina oxen raised in the Val di Chiana near Arezzo, come melt-in-your-mouth steaks that can easily weigh up to six pounds. They are marinated with good quality olive oil, fresh garlic, and black pepper. During grilling, salt is added. In the hands of the right chef, the diner feasts on the ultimate grilled steak.

Both women were thrilled with the way dinner was progressing. Shelby swooned as Giancarlo crooned a romantic tune along with the piano player. The hypnotic sparkle in his eyes melted her heart, and she finally saw the Giancarlo to whom she'd entrusted that heart six years earlier, not the Pillsbury Doughboy of yesterday.

Meanwhile, Dena's relationship with the waiter was also making headway. The steamy looks between them had advanced to surreptitious caresses, a promising nudge of his leg against hers, an electrifying sweep of his hand up the small of her back. And who knew that the short, spikiness of Fabrizio's haircut would render the unexpected dividend of removing any obstacle to the sensuous glide of his fingertips across the nape of her slender neck? Dena shivered with each delicious touch.

Ding a ling, Ding a ling. Phone attached to his ear, Giancarlo left the table yet again. Sexual tension was building on both fronts, and the friends tossed off their bottle of wine in record time, even for them. Suggesting they order another, Dena raised her hand to signal the waiter.

"No, no," Shelby growled under her breath. "Giancarlo hates pie-eyed women. And I'm not blowing this." She reached across and jerked Dena's hand down, but it was too late.

As the waiter stood looking down at her, his hand stroking her arm, Dena again wished there was more than wine on the menu. She gave her head a little shake to banish the errant thoughts. "Aah, aah. Another bottle of wine, please."

Shelby leaned over Dena in panic. "No, no more wine," she hissed at the waiter. "He'll see it on the bill, and he'll see the bottle."

Putting his higher education to good use, the waiter suggested a half bottle as the perfect solution for all concerned. Finally, Shelby acquiesced. But when he returned with the bottle, she sprung into action.

"Quick. Pour it in the glasses," she squealed. Fumbling in her purse for money, she continued to fire orders like a drill sergeant.

"Now, take the bottle away. Here!" she said, flinging the notes at the poor man. Not until he walked away, did she manage to breathe a sigh of relief. All angles were covered; all evidence removed.

As the friends swilled down their newly purchased wine, Giancarlo returned, but not alone. He had a friend with him. When they saw the new arrival, even Shelby had to thank her lucky stars that they'd ordered wine reinforcements and were well on their way to being crocked. The friend's vital statistics were as follows. Name: Dante. Profession: doctor. Age: young, perhaps late twenties. Style: well dressed European. Build: tall and toned. Miscellaneous: spoke English well and quite entertaining.

India's antennae rose with heightened interest. "Ooohh, a young Italian doctor. I bet you dropped that waiter pronto."

Shelby snorted gleefully. "Yes, India, you and I and perhaps 99.9 percent of the female population on the face of the earth and beyond would have done just that. But not our little Deenie."

"No?" The Englishwoman's mouth dropped in shock.

A sarcastic smile spread over Shelby's face as she shook her head. "Dena's taste in men tends toward the more pedestrian."

Dena, growing tired of being spoken about as if she weren't present, jumped in to defend herself. "Okay, Shelby, let's finish Dante the Doctor's vital statistics. Looks: pasty of skin...," Dena interjected.

"Ferret of face," Shelby admit with a slight shrug.

"Squinty of eye and..."

"Thinning of hair."

Dena offered a smug smile, having made her point. "In short, India, with the addition of a small hump on his back, the dear doctor would have been perfect in the remake of the Hunchback of Notre Dame. So, give me a hunky waiter anytime, thank you very much!" she huffed.

Still, ever the trouper, Dena made the best of the new addition to their party, engaging the doctor in polite conversation. But politeness had its limit, and for Dena that limit kicked in when she noticed the swift retreat of her waiter's attentions. Panic set in at the thought of being saddled with *il dottore* for the evening.

Her only hope was her weak bladder, and she would use it for all it was worth. The plan? On one of her potty runs, she'd corner her quarry and seize the only opportunity she might have. She wished she could play the shy coquette, but time was running out. This was her last night in Florence before heading for the island of Capri, and dinner was fast concluding.

The foursome was ending the meal with some biscotti and *Vin Santo*, a popular dessert wine, whose name Dena learned meant Holy Wine. Quickly, she doused her biscotti with it, took a bite, and offered up a prayer. Then, with slinky precision, she rose, heading to the restroom. Surreptitiously, she sidled up to the waiter, who was standing at the cash register.

A blow-by-blow description of their conversation is hardly necessary. Here are the most salient points: "No, I'm not with Dante. Yes, I'll meet you later. I'm at Hotel Aldini."

At this point, further communication became nearly impossible. Dena's Italian began and ended with *si*...yes. Frustratingly, her waiter's English was little better. Refusing to be foiled, Dena had an idea. Back to the table she sashayed to enlist her friend's aid. Shelby would be her ambassador of love, firming up (excuse the ladies again), finalizing where and at what time she and the waiter would meet.

Just when Dena thought this little dinner was winding down and freedom was near at hand, the men began discussing plans for the remainder of the evening. When Giancarlo presented his brilliant idea of going dancing, Dena nearly choked on her biscotti. She cringed upon hearing Shelby's simpering, "That sounds wonderful."

Wonderful for you, Dena thought to herself, but a disaster for me. Flashes of spending the rest of her evening with Dr. Doolittle, or in this case, Dr. Does Nothing for Me, flooded Dena's mind. With a force similar to the explosion of a champagne cork, her eyes popped wide. She leaned forward, grabbing her throat, gagging, nearly choking on her biscotti. Concerned, Shelby shoved a glass of water to her friend's mouth. After a few gulps, Dena was able to speak.

"So sorry, I'd love to go out dancing, but my head is killing me. Perhaps, it's jetlag."

She hated deserting Shelby and felt a momentary twinge of guilt, but was relieved to see that her friend didn't seem in the least put out. Indeed, things couldn't be shaping up more nicely as far as Shelby was concerned. With Dena out of the way, Dante the Dull would surely bow out, too. She would have Giancarlo all to herself.

As the little group made their way through the Buca, a spine-tingling electricity coursed through Dena when her waiter graced her with a final wink that promised he'd see her soon. Her heartbeat had risen to a fevered pitch, and she was sure that if she could see beneath his neat waiter's apron, something of his had risen also.

Halfway out the door, Giancarlo stopped abruptly, his hand reaching toward the small of his back. A slight groan of pain left his lips. "Shelby, I don't think that I can go dancing."

Dena's aches and pains must have been catching. She'd seemingly infected Giancarlo. Shelby was crestfallen. So much for him wanting to spend time alone with me, she lamented as they headed toward the hotel.

All too soon, the little group was standing at the entrance of the ladies' hotel, saying their goodbyes. It was just then that Giancarlo made a tactical error in his bid for a clean getaway.

"Are you happy?" he asked Shelby. "Are you happy in New York?"

Be careful, old girl, your future could depend on how you respond. The right answer and he could ask you to move to Italy and marry him. What to say? What to say?

"Happy?" she repeated slowly, buying herself some time. "Oh, yes, very happy."

She looked over at Dante and Dena, who'd discreetly moved away to give the former lovers some privacy. No help at diversion from that quarter. So, Shelby pressed on.

"I live in the greatest city on earth, have a good job, a sweet little apartment, good friends," she said, gesturing her head towards Dena. "My family..."

Giancarlo's eyes caught and held her own, and Shelby's voice trailed off into an awkward silence. Lies. All lies. Complete lies. She hadn't known happiness since him, Shelby admitted to herself. Tears welled up in her eyes, blinding her. She tried to brush them away quickly, but it was no use. Behind those first few teardrops lay a torrent that had been waiting six long years to be seen and acknowledged by the only one who mattered. Giancarlo.

"I loved you so much," she let out in a pitiful whimper. With the unintended admission, a great heaving sob racked her body, followed by another, and then, another.

"I loved you so much," she repeated mournfully. Over and over again, came the same sad refrain, Shelby unable to stop herself, to stop the words or the tears. "I loved you so much. I loved you so much. I loved you."

Giancarlo folded her into him, his arms tender with concern. Far beyond the need to keep up appearances, Shelby buried her face in the buttery softness of his leather coat. His hands stroked her hair, offering her comfort. Can I stay here forever? Please don't let me go again. It feels so good...so right. Won't you say something to make the past six years melt away? Please. Say something!? Something I want...no...need to hear.

Dead silence mocked her wordless plea. He continued to hold her to him, but even through her tears, Shelby could see the situation was becoming increasingly awkward. Eventually, with a great deal of effort, she struggled to pull herself together. The tears subsided, and she swatted the last of them away. With great effort, a wooden smile even crept across her lips.

And it was not until then that the invisible cat finally let go of Giancarlo's tongue. Always knowing the right thing to say and completely sensitive to her pain, he tried to console her.

"Maybe one day we dance at each other's weddings."

Did he say our wedding or each other's weddings? I don't think I can breathe. No, no. I distinctly heard an "s" at the end of weddings. Is that a knife I feel plunging into my heart? Please don't say anything else. I feel it twisting, and the edge is jagged. So sorry, I guess I loved you so much was the incorrect answer to the question. And I suppose an imminent transatlantic move is out of the question.

Oh, oh, wait a minute. Don't forget, the man's English leaves a lot to be desired. I'm sure he meant our wedding. Yes, that must be it. It's his English. He definitely said our wedding. Finally, Shelby breathed.

"Aahh, here's where your delusion starts, I guess. Did you really believe the two of you would ever marry?" interjected India.

Shelby stiffened at the question. "Well, possibly. After all, he had called and asked if I'd consider coming back to Italy...said he wanted to see me," she responded.

"Yeah, but seeing you and marrying you are two different things," the Englishwoman refused to concede the point.

"Well, he wanted to marry once," Shelby countered.

India's eyes registered her astonishment at Shelby's naiveté. "And dumped you for your friend!" she pressed.

"Okay! I was delusional about Giancarlo and me," Shelby admitted with a rueful look. Still, she wasn't ready to concede everything to the blasted Brit. "But the possibility of marriage wasn't the delusion."

"Then what was?" demanded India.

But the ladies would not be hurried by their Gestapo interrogator. There was still much more to the story before she would find that out.

While Shelby was busy making a complete fool of herself in Giancarlo's arms, Dena was trying to rapidly rid herself of the doctor. For chrissakes, how long did it take Shelby to say her goodbyes? From across the cobblestones, Dena watched the former lovers. Their tender embrace made a touching tableau, enough to melt the most brittle of hearts. But Dena had no time for sentiment. If she didn't bring down the curtain on her friend's one-act play, Shelby would be taking bows until tomorrow. As Dena saw all of her own exciting plans going up in smoke, tears gathered in her eyes...tears which did not escape the good doctor's notice.

"Oh, how sweet! You cry for your friend's hurt," he said.

He knew the couple's history, Dena realized. And he assumed she wept for Shelby. Dena accepted the handkerchief he graciously offered, and gently dabbed the tears away. Okay, take it and run with it!

"Oh, yes, it's so sad, isn't it?" she said with all the sincerity she could muster. Keep going. Bring it home, girl. She held her head between her hands for effect.

"Ohhhh," she moaned. "It makes my head hurt even more." And she would make sure heads rolled if she missed her date.

Dante became truly concerned. "Shelby," he called, taking the matter into his own hands. "I think Dena needs to rest now. Her headache eez getting worse."

And with that, Dena leapt into action. She grabbed her friend, practically dragging Shelby like a ragdoll through the doors of the Hotel Aldini. "Bye. Thank you for a lovely evening," Dena trilled behind her.

Shelby tried to break free of the grip, but couldn't. "Could you at least slow down a bit, or I'll be billing you for the chiropractic care from the whiplash," she complained.

Dena barely registered a word from Shelby's mouth as she hustled her friend into the elevator. Thank God. If her estimate was correct, she had a hot five minutes to get to their room, console the poor suffering Shelby, freshen her lipstick, and do some stretching exercises to limber up for the night ahead. Limber up for dancing, of course.

Even though she was a bit tipsy, Dena's nerves were on edge. This would be her first date in more than twenty-five years. She let her mind wander back to her last one, remembering how it had felt waiting for Luke to pick her up. She must have tried on ten outfits before settling on one. Her makeup had taken hours to get just right, and still she hadn't been happy with it.

Luke. An uninvited twinge of regret swept over Dena. Just as quickly, she berated herself for allowing the melancholy to invade her heart. That part of her life wasn't just over; it was dead. This certainly was not the time to resurrect the wreckage. This was a new beginning and every bit as exciting as the last beginning. Dena intended to seize it.

Easy to say, but still there was that bubble of nervousness churning in the pit of her stomach. Get over it, Dena admonished herself. No need for the jitters. After all, she loved to dance and was good at it. And what could be a bigger thrill than being squired about Florence by a handsome, young Italian, she asked herself as she hurried out to meet him.

First stop...Yab Yum.[10] Inside the cavernous disco with blaring techno music and blinding strobe lights, gyrating bodies were wall to wall. Dena knew of techno, had even heard some here and there. After all, she was a mother of three. In vain, she struggled to relate to the electronic sounds and high-energy, rhythmic beat that was popular among the pre-teen to mid-twenties age group.

She and her Italian stood on the edge of the dance floor surveying the crowd. Amused by the tentative tapping of her foot in time with the beat of the music, the waiter asked if she wanted to dance. Oh yes, Dena thought, this little black cocktail ensemble and Barbara Bush string of pearls fit right in with the skin tight jeans, low-cut tops, and stiletto heels all around me. What the hell was she thinking wearing such a granny outfit? He was young and good-looking. She should have known they wouldn't end up at the Plaza. Why hadn't she changed into something trendier? Something to fit in? She hated feeling out of place, feeling different. She always had. Still, she let him lead her onto the dance floor.

Attempting to move in sync with the unfamiliar beat was challenge enough for a middle-aged mother from upstate New York whose last spin on the dance floor was during the heyday of polyester leisure suits and platform shoes. Oh no, not the strobe lights, Dena panicked. The flashing bright white lights aggravated her motion sickness. She might have been able to deal with that, but her awkward movements were accentuated. She probably looked like Robocop.

Seeing she was unable to keep time with the music and hadn't mastered the latest contortionist dance steps, her handsome waiter's brow knitted with pity. His head gave an almost imperceptible shake.

"This music not right for you," he concluded. His voice was soft with kindness as he took her hand and walked from the dance floor.

As Dena allowed him to lead her from the floor, she could almost feel other eyes on her...assessing her...finding her wanting. Still, not good enough, she thought. And everybody knew. Still that little girl in fifth grade. And again her thoughts drifted back in time.

St. Peter's Elementary School. Every November, the students organized a food drive to make Thanksgiving baskets for the

---

[10]Yab Yum, Via Sassetti 5r, PH 055/282018

needy. As an added incentive, there was a yearly contest among the grades. The winners received a class trip to a Christmas movie.

Dena was elected to organize and be responsible for the fifth-grade basket. She worked feverishly coordinating the contents and planning the basket decoration. Anxious to win the grand prize, she was quite the little tyrant.

"Tommy, where is your creamed corn? You better bring it tomorrow," she harangued. "Roseanne, you were supposed to draw a Pilgrim, not a pumpkin!"

Finally, the day to assemble the basket arrived. Dena stood back and surveyed the masterpiece. Surely, it would win first prize. Tomorrow the winners would be announced over the school loud speaker. She was giddy with anticipation.

"And, first prize goes to Sister Mary Immaculate's eighth grade. Congratulations, Eighth Grade, you're going to the Christmas movie!"

Although she was disappointed, Dena tried not to take the loss personally. And, as with most ten-year olds, her defeat was soon practically forgotten.

"Mommy, Mommy," she yelled, bounding through the back door after school a few days later. "I got 100 on my math tes..." she started.

Then, her voice trailed off, and she stopped dead in her tracks, eyes fixated on the kitchen table. What was Roseanne's Pilgrim doing in her house? And was that Tommy's creamed corn? There, in the middle of the table, was the basket her class had made.

The blood drained from Dena's face. Her stomach got a sick, queasy feeling as a million thoughts ran through her mind. Okay, okay, she knew her family didn't buy food with money, like other people, but neither did the Queen of England, did she? And, those handmade mittens and hats delivered every Christmas by the Salvation Army. Well, didn't everybody with five brothers and sisters get those? She wasn't stupid. She knew they weren't rich. But the Thanksgiving Day basket? That was for the poor people. The needy. You know, the people who lived downtown on Main Street.

Dena picked up the can of Campbell's Baked Beans she had proudly donated. Like a firecracker exploding, the can seemed fire hot, almost searing her skin. It dropped with a loud thud onto the kitchen floor. As she stood there looking down at it, the circumstances of her life came into focus.

She was the poor people. And everybody knew it.

"Theees eez better, si?" her waiter asked. He pressed her even closer to him. The touch of his hands, the scent of his cologne, the sexy rumble of his voice drew Dena back from the past.

"Si," she said, melting into his arms. "You have no idea how much better."

Her body turned soft and pliant as putty under his insistent touch. Beneath the convenient cover of her red leather coat, lean fingers skimmed daringly over her curves, at once teasing and promising. Soon, the blaring music and crowded dance floor receded into nothingness. All that remained was this man, this moment and this feeling; it was a feeling she hadn't had in years, the thrill of a first date.

First date. My, how the brain works to protect the soul. First date: a social engagement between two people to discover their likes and dislikes, political beliefs, wants and desires, and religious beliefs. Perhaps, it should have dawned on Dena that when a gentleman picks a lady up for their first date, the parties usually know each other's names already. However, she merely glossed over this telling detail. Besides, this man did want to know all about her...her likes and dislikes, political beliefs, wants and desires, and religious beliefs.

"You like Italian men, si? "You like *panna montata?*" Whipped cream?

"You believe sex in public places should be illegal?"

"You desire me, si?"

"You think sex is a sin?

Oh all right, perhaps these weren't quite the questions her Italian Don Juan fired at Dena. And maybe, it does strain even the brain dead's credulity to suggest that she hadn't yet the slightest inkling that this wasn't shaping up to be the romantic date of her teenage dreams. And, if Dena had been perfectly honest with herself, she did get a huge clue when his expert hands made their seductive way under her blouse.

Soon, Nicola suggested...oh yes, the two finally got around to exchanging names...suggested they go somewhere else. Dena readily agreed, quite happy to leave the mocking crowd behind and head for more intimate quarters.

The date, or whatever one chooses to term this span of time, ended in the most genteel of venues. A real Italian's apartment? A swanky hotel room? A lovers' lane? Heavens no. This Italian waiter had someplace really special in mind for his American love. The side alley of the Hotel Aldini, a choice not to be dismissed out of hand. Consider its attributes: a private idyll underneath the starlit night sky of Florence that is quiet and quite reasonable in price.

Dena's handsome Italian drew her into the narrow confines of the alleyway and leaned her gently against the ancient stone wall. Eager hands slipped under her coat, finding the space between her skirt and her blouse. Sleekly, those practiced hands skimmed over her body toward the slimness of her back. Locating the hook of her lacy black bra, he released it, and something primal within Dena burst forth simultaneously.

If she had had any thoughts of objecting, they skittered from her fevered brain when Nicola caught and fondled one soft breast. Her lips searched for his and drank in the sweet male taste of him. The hard curves of his body pressed against her, making her want more, and soon Dena's hands began an expedition of their own, frantically unbuttoning his shirt and gliding over the hard planes of his chest and stomach.

It seemed impossible, but he gathered her closer to him. A hand swept under her silky skirt and teased the heated skin of her quivering thigh. With expert precision, he lifted her, then raised and snaked one shapely leg around his waist and settled into Dena's body more closely. Thin and silky as they were, every piece of clothing Dena wore became a maddening impediment. She longed to feel every inch of this man against her.

All too soon, he led her around the building to the hotel entrance. And with a sweet kiss goodbye, Dena floated up the elevator with dreams of Nicola to keep her warm.

The next morning our travelers awoke and set off for the isle of Capri.

"Oh, no you don't!" shrieked India. She leaned across the table as if she might turn Dena on her head and shake the words out if they weren't willingly offered. "No way you're going to leave me hanging like that. Forget Capri. I want details. What happened in that alley? What was he like?"

Dena took a sip of her coffee, buying time as she considered how much of the Englishwoman's prurient interest she wished to satisfy. Her eyes pleaded with Shelby for help.

"Don't look at me. I'm sure I don't know what happened in that alleyway," Shelby said, leaving her friend swinging.

"To tell the truth, I was plastered. To this day, I'm not sure I even know exactly what took place," Dena said warily. "It's all such a haze really."

India stared Dena squarely in the eyes. "A haze doesn't make someone return to the scene of the crime twice in six months," she countered. "You must remember something."

Dena's mind wandered back to that night with Nicola. Yes, she remembered, but those memories were hers and were staying hers.

"Well, India, as for romantic trysts against a hard stone wall, I say don't knock verticality 'til you've tried it, my friend. And, after he peeled me off that wall, he did show genuine concern."

"Really?" India questioned.

"Oh, yes," Dena confirmed with an amused grin. "He spun me around and inspected my red leather coat for damage."

The Englishwoman smacked her knee in astonishment. "He was worried about the coat? Your back might have needed traction after that little episode, and he's worried about the coat? What a prince."

If I were these two, I'd gloss over this part and move on to Capri also, India thought to herself.

The first leg of a trip from Florence to Capri entails a train ride to Naples. For the ladies, they might as well have boarded a train to Siberia. Sitting across from each other, the friends were like strangers.

Dena stared out the window, lost in her own thoughts. Every nerve ending in her body was charged with sexual excitement. If she didn't do something about it, she wouldn't be able to eat, sleep, or think straight. She'd start to totter like a cat on hot bricks. People would know. They'd think to themselves—there she goes, poor thing. Hasn't been right since she was peeled off that wall in Florence.

Across from her, Shelby had closed her eyes in feigned sleep, but her mind was abuzz with the events of the night before. Dance at his wedding!? Humph, I'll dance on his grave before I dance at any nuptials of his that don't involve me. I must learn the tarantella. No, too tame. The Mexican Hat Dance. Yes, that's it, complete with mariachis. He did say wedding singular, didn't he?

When making their travel plans, Shelby had been quite looking forward to seeing Capri. Now, after her time with Giancarlo, she really didn't care if she ever laid eyes on the godforsaken little island.

Dena's next words confirmed a twin emotion about their planned itinerary. "Do you really want to go on to Rome after Capri?" she asked tentatively.

Shelby shrugged her shoulders noncommittally. "You've never been. You really should see the Eternal City," she responded dully, hard pressed to summon any enthusiasm.

Dena was hardly convinced. If it was eternal, it'd be there next year or in ten years. But who knew where Nicola would be ten minutes from now, Dena thought to herself. She was determined not to miss her opportunity.

"Yes, but I really haven't seen much of Florence either. I'm so disappointed not to have seen the Uffizi or Pitti Palace," Dena rationalized. Yeah, right. And anyone believing that has a straight jacket calling them.

Shelby tried to squelch the exuberance bubbling up inside her. Like taking candy from a baby. She could get back to Florence, not only with dignity intact, but actually looking like a solicitous friend. Dena really should stop making it so easy for me, she thought smugly.

"Oh, I don't know," Shelby hesitated. "There's so much in Rome I want to see. But," she hesitated with a conciliatory nod of her head, "I've been there before. I'm happy to do whatever you want."

A smile blended of triumph and confusion flashed across Dena's face. She knew there was something wrong here. She was getting her way. But she had no intention of looking this gift horse in the mouth.

Once off the train, Dena sprang into action, a woman on a mission. The Italian public phone system isn't known for its user friendliness, but Dena would have fashioned two cans on a string if she'd had to.

With lightening speed that belied her lack of Italian, she purchased a phone card and dialed Nicola at the only phone number she had for him, the Buca. Her body tingled at his voice and the knowledge that her call brought him pleasure. "Dena, you come to the Buca tonight?"

"No, I'm going to Capri. But I'm coming back."

"To see me?" her Italian asked hopefully. She swooned at his enthusiasm.

"*Si, si, due giorni.*" Within seconds she had closed the deal. She would return to Florence and Nicola in two days time.

"Here's the calling card," she offered her friend. "Aren't you going to call Giancarlo?"

Shelby demurred. Let him miss me for a little while.

"*So, it's obvious why Dena wanted to return to Florence,*" *India interjected. "But you've got to help me here." Her eyes lasered into Shelby, scorching her. "Why in the world would you want to see Giancarlo after what he'd said?"*

"We..we..well," Shelby stammered. "The man was sending mixed messages."

"Mixed?" India repeated. As far as the Englishwoman could tell, the only thing mixed were the brains of these two boobs. Scrambled, to be exact.

"And you," she turned to Dena with an accusatory stare. "You didn't try to dissuade her?"

Now it was Dena's turn to stumble over her words. "Th...this is the first I'm hearing the story, too. I didn't know anything about any weddings with an S," she defended herself. "As far as I could tell, he had flirted with her throughout dinner and seemed as captivated as Shelby. Why not go back?"

There's a damn good reason why travelers purchase guide books for their trips. Quite simply, it helps avoid traveling pitfalls. Having consulted both Frommer's and Fodor's before leaving home, the ladies found that both suggested catching the hydrofoil ferry from Naples to Capri. To the best of their knowledge, neither book ever mentioned Guido, the Crooked Cabbie of Naples.

Within seconds of Dena's completing her call to Nicola, Guido slithered up to the unsuspecting friends. "You need taxi?" he hissed, slightly reminiscent of a snake.

Shelby looked at him just long enough to take in the squat body, leathery face, and sly smile. "No, no," she answered dismissively.

But Dena wasn't so quick. While Shelby scanned the station for the information desk, Guido pressed her gullible friend further. "Where you go?"

"Capri?" he repeated Dena's answer. "I take you. I have nice air-conditioned Mercedes."

Dena's ears practically stood at attention now. But Shelby, only half listening and wholly unimpressed, walked away in search of the information desk. Still, Dena lingered.

"I take you to Pompeii, and then to Sorrento. Then, I take you to the boat to Capri. It not cost you much."

"How much?" Dena couldn't resist asking.

About 125 dollars. Not bad, Dena thought.

"I don't know," she hesitated, sure that Shelby the Skinflint would balk.

"You love Pompeii and Sorrento. Eez beautiful with many rich peoples," Guido tempted her.

Dena ran after Shelby's back. "Shelby, Shelby, I think we should let him take us. It sounds like a good deal," she urged her friend.

Now, usually Shelby vetoed most of Dena's bright ideas. No explanations offered. Simply, nope, I'm not doing that, but you go right ahead if you want. However, on this particular day, Shelby's con artist antennae must have been on the blink.

She could hardly believe it, but Dena was making sense. What Guido was offering seemed like the deal of the century. A couple hours of sightseeing in Sorrento, a veritable jewel on the Italian coast; a few hours in the lost civilization of Pompeii; and tickets for the hydrofoil ferry to Capri included. And, the ladies' tour would be from the comfort of his Mercedes Benz. All this for the incredible price of $125. Even Shelby's penny-pinching mom would have said yes.

First stop, Pompeii. In the car, Guido explained that the lost city was very famous for its cameos and suggested they begin their sightseeing with a tour of the cameo factory. Lured by the opportunity to learn about the art form of carving intricate figures on seashells, the friends happily concurred. So, Guido left the ladies at the entrance to the factory promising to be right there when they returned.

The tour was progressing quite nicely for, let's see...oh, roughly five minutes. Then, to the ladies' complete surprise, the pretty tour guide took a sudden sharp turn to the left and down a narrow stairway.

"Oh, wonder what's down here?" Shelby pondered excitedly.

Anxious not to miss a thing, Dena reached into her bag for her camera. "Maybe I should take some pictures."

"Get prepared, India. Yes, yes another DIQ Test question is at hand," Shelby announced.

> Where do you think the ladies found themselves when they got to the bottom of that staircase?
> A) In a museum filled with antique jewelry and ancient jewelry-making tools,
> B) In a classroom of apprentices learning the art of cameo making,
> C) In a wing of the factory where master craftsmen were hard at work, or
> D) In a large well-lit room filled with display cases of jewelry for sale.

"I'm almost scared to find out," India chuckled. "You two don't seem to have much luck."

"Oh, we have plenty," countered Shelby. "It's just piss poor."

The Englishwoman nodded her head in agreement. "Given that and the fact that Guido was involved, I'd have to pick Answer D again."

"Quite correct!" Dena congratulated her. "One hour, one bracelet, one pair of earrings, and $1400 later, we exited the factory."

It was impossible for India to stifle a giggle. "And I'm sure dear Guido got a nice little kickback for delivering you two easy marks," she concluded.

The two friends looked over at each other and shared a disbelieving glance. "You really think so?" Shelby asked.

"Well, maybe not," India retreated. These two really shouldn't be let out in the world alone.

When the ladies exited the factory, eager to move on to the ruins of Pompeii, they found Guido sputtering and spitting like a steam engine ready to blow. "You must hurry," he said with impatient aggressiveness, shooing them along. "We leave here in forty-five minutes."

"Hurry? What are you talking about?" The ladies were dumbfounded.

"The last boat to Capri...it leave 6:00pm," he informed them.

"You didn't tell us that! What about Sorrento?" Shelby asked sharply.

"Sorrento? No time, no time. Too late, forty-five minutes here, then the boat," Guido decreed.

The sightseers sprinted to the ticket booth for entrance to the Lost City of Pompeii, where the ticket clerk was reluctant to sell them tickets. "We close in forty-five minutes," she informed them.

"Si, si, va bene." That's okay.

"But you need four or five hours!" the clerk said with exasperation in her voice.

Heedless of the woman's warning, Dena and Shelby threw their money at her, grabbed their tickets, and galloped uphill. For the next thirty minutes, the suckered sightseers scurried like rats through a maze, snapping one picture after another of sights they would barely remember afterward.

While the individual wonders of the Lost City would always be a blur in the ditzy duo's memories, the majesty of Pompeii was far from lost on them. So haunting is its beauty, careful listeners might swear they hear the hustle and bustle of the once thriving city that was forever silenced by the eruption of Mt. Vesuvius two thousand years ago. The ruins give testament to the amazing development of a community of twenty thousand inhabitants who enjoyed outdoor theaters, banks, bars, public baths, health clinics and brothels. Unfortunately, many of the city's treasures have been moved to the *Museo Archeologico Nazionale* in Naples for safekeeping. Nonetheless, Pompeii is a treasure to behold.

Dena glanced at her watch. "We gotta go!"

Shelby was reluctant to leave so soon, but knew her friend was right. If they didn't meet Guido at the appointed time, their devil driver was liable to slink away, luggage and all, without them.

He drove like a madman, careening around winding roads with a crazy grin on his face. Sadly, they sped through Sorrento without the ladies' dainty feet ever touching that beautiful town's soil. And while some might have realized far sooner than the two dupes, it finally became quite apparent to Dena and Shelby that they hadn't been offered a ride by the cabbie, so much as taken for one.

An hour later, Slick-as-Olive-Oil Guido deposited the ladies at the dock and purchased their hydrofoil tickets for them. As they were about to say *arrivederci* and escape his clutches, the cunning cabbie took it upon himself to give the women a lesson in Italian etiquette.

Beady, avaricious eyes gleamed out at the women, and a slimy smile sliced across his lips. "Eez customary to give tip," he said with visible anticipation.

As Dena pondered whether to reach into her purse for a few more bills, Shelby became apoplectic. She turned to Guido with icy anger. "*Sei pazzo?*" Are you crazy? "Do we look like stupido and more stupido?"

And with that, Dena nimbly removed her hand from her purse and mumbled something about looking for a piece of gum as they left the Crooked Cabbie of Napoli to find his next prey.

From a distance, the island of Capri rises from the bay, at night a colossal Christmas tree resplendent with thousands of twinkling fairy lights. Its beauty worked like a magic charm, mesmerizing the ladies and lifting their spirits immediately.

However, a touch of disappointment settled over both women when greeted by a chilling rainfall as they alighted the boat. Left off at the main port of Marina Grande, Shelby and Dena promptly searched for transportation to their hotel. Ever the eagle eye, Dena quickly spotted a van emblazoned with the words "Hotel Weber Ambassador."[11] "That's our hotel, isn't it?" she pointed.

Traveling Tidbit for the Non-Hikers among us: The guide books would have you think that one could walk from Marina Grande to Capri Town and the hotels. The ladies' opinion? No problem if you are a mountain goat.

The Hotel Weber Ambassador is a lemon-colored gem perched high on the cliffs of Capri. It boasts a magnificent view of the Marina Piccola beach with its crystal clear waters and *i Faraglioni*, a spectacular geological formation in which high sheer cliffs have been sea- and wind-eroded to the point that sections now remain isolated from the mainland.

Guests enter a pristine, white-tiled lobby surrounded by a wall of glass doors that are opened in fair weather. On this evening, as is done every evening, a complimentary buffet of light hors d'oeuvres had been set out for the guests. Shelby tried to hold Dena back as she leapt toward the table. But it was impossible, and she almost lost a nail as Dena's blouse eluded her grasp. Realizing it was hopeless, Shelby proceeded to the reservation desk to check in.

After the Hotel Aldini, this room could only be termed a palace. Panoramic windows offered a view of the Tyrrhenian Sea. A colorful floral motif and light furniture with simple lines suffused the room with a welcoming tropical atmosphere, a delightful contrast to the dreary cold weather. The ladies almost achieved spontaneous orgasm entering the bathroom. It was simple but elegant, and much to their delight, there was a bathtub. True, they would never use it, but it gave the Americans great comfort just knowing it was there.

Having satisfied her immediate hunger at the lobby buffet, Dena was ready to work on the second. She trapped her friend in the room.

"You're not getting out to see any of Capri. Remember I've eaten; you haven't. And you won't until you find us a room to return to in Florence!"

Unused to such ferocity in her friend, an unnerved Shelby set to work. Scanning her guide book for hotels, she picked up

---

[11]Hotel Weber Ambassador, Via Marina Piccola, PH 081/8370141

the phone and dialed. *"C'e una camera doppia?"* Do you have a double room?

One after another Florentine hotel replied in the negative. A discouraged Shelby was about to give up. She was tired; she was hungry. Remembering a candy bar she'd bought earlier, she reached into her purse for it. But just as she made to rip it open, Dena snatched it from her hands.

"I told you. You eat after you've gotten us a room," she decreed.

Shelby was getting a little worried. She'd never seen such a feral look in Dena's eyes. One night in an alley with an Italian waiter had unhinged the girl. Wearily, Shelby picked up the phone again.

Finally, countless phone calls later, she managed to snag two singles, albeit without private baths. A quick phone call to cancel their room in Rome, another to inform Nicola that the love of his life would be returning to his arms on Friday, and Dena finally freed Shelby to forage for food.

On such a cold, rainy evening, the women were glad to take the dining advice of the hotel staff. They were doubly glad they did so when the hotel graciously ferried them to an unpretentious and welcoming trattoria, *Ristorante Pizzeria Longano.*[12] For a fixed price, which Dena and Shelby believe was all of twelve dollars, the women were served soup, salad, entrée, dessert and coffee. Wine was extra, but still equally reasonable, or in this case, unreasonable. This was a cheap dinner.

"Even in April, the salad is fresh and flavorful," Dena said, savoring the greens.

"And the fried calamari cooked to perfection and tender enough to melt in your mouth!" Shelby murmured as she greedily popped another crispy ring into her mouth.

The next morning they awoke to the raucous din of hailstones pelting against their windows. "Guess we won't be needing our bikinis," Dena said glumly. She hugged her blanket closer, trying to quiet the chatter of her teeth. "More like a winter coat."

They had planned a full itinerary; however, the inclement weather vetoed swimming or sunning. Also nixed was a tour of the famed Blue Grotto, one of the world's most famous caves

---

[12]Ristorante Pizzeria Longano, Via Longano, PH 081/8370187

where blue light shines through the salt water of the Mediterranean and fills the cave with otherworldly azure reflections. Their planned hike along Capri's trails dotted with Roman ruins would be more like a walk through a swamp. And, though no trip to Capri is complete without a trip on the Funicular, a train bringing passengers to the apex of Capri and offering breathtaking views, the rain and windswept landscape didn't exactly inspire the two to make the trip.

"*Che peccato!*" exclaimed Shelby. What a shame!

"I know," agreed Dena conspiratorially. "Nothing left to do but..."

"Shop," the women declared in melodic unison.

Piazza Umberto I dominates Capri Town with brick-colored streets that overlook the water. From the piazza, narrow, upwardly winding roads radiate in all directions, each one leading to one expensive shop after another. And spend their money the women did. Brilliant sunshine (yes, the sun came out in time for shopping), the smell of jasmine in the air, a profusion of gaily potted flowers, scores of beautiful people, and enticing shops went to the ladies' heads like a fine liqueur, giving them a dangerously false sense of wealth.

Traveling Tidbit for the Shopaholic Traveler: Capri's stores are seductive. Leave your credit cards home and empty your pockets before setting foot on the island. Walk fast past the Western Union lest you be tempted to wire home for money.

"Oh, look," Shelby gasped, pointing across the street.

A lightning bolt of fear pierced Dena. She ducked behind her friend, bulging eyes darting to and fro. "What? Who? Is it Guido?"

"No, no," her friend soothed her. "Look at that pair of Black Mammy and Chef cookie jars!"

"Where?" Dena asked, looking around. But she was talking to Shelby's back. Her friend was already across the street and entering the little shop's threshold. When Dena caught up, she was surprised to find the almost terminally cheap Shelby plopping down over a hundred dollars apiece for the set.

Cookie jars might have been fine for Shelby, but Dena had other appetites to satisfy. Determinedly, she whisked Shelby out of the gift shop and headed for a clothing boutique across the way.

"An outfit to drive Nicola wild," she announced. And, she thought to herself, something so she didn't stick out like a sore thumb in a nightclub.

Intimissimi was just the ticket. With outlets all over Italy, this lingerie chain can't and shouldn't be missed. From crystal clear windows peek sheer, lacy, strappy confections that make a woman feel like a woman....and a man want to feel a woman.

Even cheapskate Shelby was lured by the tempting lingerie of Italy's answer to Victoria's Secret. Within minutes, the ladies nearly cleaned the shop out and were on their way to another. A couple of hours later, as they strolled the piazza, the rogue shoppers felt more glamorous than Julia Roberts cruising Rodeo Drive in Pretty Woman, their dresses, shoes, purses, perfumes safely stowed in eye-catching shopping bags dangling from their hands.

Corollary Traveling Tidbit for the Fellow Shopaholic Traveler: If you do bring credit cards, use them for larger purchases, in particular for those being shipped home, in case they don't arrive safely. More on this later.

Final Traveling Tidbit for the Fellow Shopaholic Traveler: Capri and the surrounding region are known for the lemony liqueur, *Limoncello*. Dena had grown quite fond of it. Do not do as she and go shopping while under its influence. While not necessarily hazardous to your health, it can be disastrous to your retirement fund.

India, having heard that Capri was simply exquisite, was eager to hear more. "Hmmm, Capri," she murmured with dreamy eyes. "I've always wanted to see it. Tell me; what did you do besides shop?" she asked. "How was the Blue Grotto? Heard it is magnificent."

"Oh, we never made it," Shelby said.

"Well, what about the Funicular?" India pressed. "Are the views as spectacular as billed?"

What is this, a college entrance exam, Dena wondered as she struggled to keep her irritation to herself. "No idea," she answered. "We never took the ride."

This was too much for the British woman. "Might I ask you two a question?" India asked.

Both ladies nodded their heads.

"This travel guide you plan doesn't seem too feasible. I mean, half the time you don't know the names of where you've been, and the other half..." she hesitated.

"Go on," Shelby encouraged, though she wanted to squash the supercilious woman like a bug.

"Well, the other half of the time, you've not set foot in places most people would want to know about, or you've been too tipsy to remember them. How are you going to get around that?"

"Oh, we have a plan," Shelby smiled triumphantly. "We'll just ask our readers to write in with their descriptions."

Dena smiled proudly as her friend revealed their genius. "Which we'll include in our revised edition!" she added.

The Englishwoman nodded her head slowly, a blank stare on her face. Too bad the mothers of these two dimwits hadn't turned them in for revised editions.

Chapter 6

*T*rain travel in Italy is economical and can be quite pleas-ant...well, if one doesn't mind the occasional Roma (that's politically correct for Gypsy) begging for money, the lack of air-conditioning on some local trains, or the ever-present threat of *uno sciopero* – the dreaded transit strike.

Our two sad sacks hadn't been in any real hurry to get to Naples, so they had traveled on the InterCity train, a modern, air-conditioned conveyance making limited stops. However, their return trip to Florence was a horse of a different stripe. Dena had seriously considered hijacking an airplane, but her only available weapons would have been her panties as a slingshot, aerosol hair products to stun, and a matching bra as a blind-fold. She could employ Shelby to provide the diversionary tactic...a lit match to her make-up case and all those heated chemicals would surely have the explosive power of a small hand grenade. However, visions of languishing in a Neapolitan jail quickly snapped the would-be hijackers to their senses.

And so, the ladies hunted for the speediest train available. "Let's take the *rapido* or the *diretto*," Dena urged. "Those will get us there in a hurry."

"No," Shelby contradicted. "Don't be fooled by the names. The rapido is not rapid, and the diretto is hardly direct."

So, they opted for the Eurostar, the sleek, ultramodern speeding bullet of the European rail system. It pays to book a seat in advance, lest you find yourself on the train tracks begging the conductor for a seat, as the ladies were forced to do.

Smoking car only, he informed them. Shelby hesitated, even the thought of smoke constricting her asthmatic airways. The real thing could trigger an attack.

"Take it!" Dena hissed. "If the smoke gets too bad, stick your head out the window like Lassie."

As they made their way to their assigned train car, it was Dena's turn to waver when it suddenly dawned on her that their seats might be facing in the wrong direction. She wondered aloud what she would do if her seat faced backwards. She'd surely be sick as a dog.

Shelby displayed little sympathy. "Oh, when there was a possibility that I couldn't breathe, that was honky dory. Well, if I can be Lassie, you can be Ol' Yeller. Or better yet, Ol' Greenie. Stick your head out the window and face in the right direction."

As it turned out, the head-out-the-window option was no option at all. Windows in the Eurostar are sealed shut. Aware this trip wouldn't be a smooth one, the only solution left to the sick sisters was drugs. No, not those of the illegal variety, though the ladies might have resorted to them had their lives depended on it.

The air was heavy with smoke from the outset. Like a mad-woman, Shelby rummaged through her purse desperate for her inhaler. In a similar panic, Dena popped another Dramamine, hoping to keep the contents of her stomach...well...in her stomach.

The friends were not on a first name basis with Lady Luck. Now, Bad Luck...he was practically family. So it was no surprise to them that both seats were facing in the opposite direction the train would be traveling.

Beads of sweat broke out on Dena's forehead and upper lip as they approached their row. There was that unhinged look again, Shelby noticed. One by one, Italians backed away as Dena approached them, pleading in a gauche mix of English and Italian for someone to exchange seats with her. *Pazza*...crazy, she heard being whispered behind her as she continued her quest. Finally, she happened upon a courtly, elderly gentleman.

"Si, si," he agreed, recognizing her distress.

Relieved, Dena settled in, and discreetly mopped her face. She scrambled through her purse, pulled out a cigarette, and lit it before turning to Shelby and giving her the thumbs up. "I'm okay, how about you?" she asked.

"Just peachy," her friend answered as she reached for her inhaler again and practically swallowed it whole.

For two hours, Dena was happy as a clam while the wheez-ing and whistling of Shelby's struggling lungs provided musical diversion for her and nearby passengers. Then, the courtly gentleman spoke up again. "The train change directions now. We change seats again," he offered.

Dena panicked. Where was the train changing directions to? Back south to Naples or off to some unknown Italian town. "This is going to Florence?" she asked with nervous tension in her eyes.

Normally, she might not mind a little side trip, but if this blasted train didn't chugalug her back to Nicola and their private alleyway, she wouldn't be responsible for her actions.

"Si, si," the gentleman reassured her. "We go to Firenze." And sure enough, just as he'd predicted, the train started traveling in the exact opposite direction.

To this day, our traveling companions still scratch their heads in wonderment, having absolutely no idea how a train traveling north at the outset could change directions midstream, proceed in the opposite direction, and still end up in a destination even farther north.[13]

Once in Florence, the ladies proceeded to the Hotel Boston.[14] Check-in was a breeze, and they made their way to their rooms. Shelby stopped dead in her tracks when she let herself into her room with the key.

"I can see why this place had rooms available," she whispered to Dena. "Dear Mr. Frommer must have been tanked the day he stayed here."

True, the lower two floors have beautiful exposed wood beams that lend a rustic charm to the establishment. Also, the breakfast room has attractive Renaissance frescoes on the wall. Too bad guests couldn't sleep in there.

Likewise, the two rooms allotted to Dena and Shelby were from a bygone era. Alas, the proprietors of the Hotel Boston hadn't been informed that no one wanted to return to that particular period in time. Like something from a 50's sitcom, the rooms were decorated with nondescript, built-in Formica furniture. Admittedly, they were quite clean. But neither woman would have been surprised if the Beaver or Wally jumped out of the closet, along with Mrs. Cleaver.

"If they unbolt the furniture from the walls, maybe someone will do them a favor and cart it away," Shelby laughed.

While they had to share a hallway bathroom, each room sported a sink and mirror. At least, they would not be forced to greet the public with an unwashed face and a case of severe morning breath.

Truthfully, Dena couldn't have cared less about the room furnishings. If the rooms had been bed-less, it wouldn't have worried her. She didn't plan on sleeping there anyway, and Shelby would just have to live with it. She's always complaining about a bad back. If the beds are not to her liking, a nice hard floor would do her a world of good, Dena rationalized.

Truthfully, the only thing Dena worried about was the phone situation. Entering her room, she eagerly scrambled to lift the receiver and listen, only to be met with silence. No dial tone, no

---

[13]Should any reader have the answer, please do write in. Yes, you've got it. The revised edition, of course.

[14]Hotel Boston, Via Guelfo 68, PH 055/49-67-47

buzzing. In a panic that she would miss Nicola's phone call, she bee-lined it back to Shelby's room.

"Nope, mine's working just fine. I've got a dial tone," Shelby said.

As her friend attempted to replace the receiver in its cradle, Dena ripped it from her grasp. "Give me that. I'm calling the front desk."

Her conversation with the front desk was short and sweet. She slammed down the phone. "Can you believe it? They're sending someone up to teach me how to use a phone."

Shelby shook her head in amazement. What was it with staff of Italian hotels? First, the Hotel Aldini and now this one. Did they think all Americans were telephone-challenged? Well, who could blame them? Yes, an American had invented the telephone. True, the United States had phone service before the rest of the world. But phones are very different in Italy. Everybody knew that, didn't they? One doesn't just pick up the phone in Italy and say hello. No, it's much harder in Italy, and it's very difficult for Americans to adapt. One has to pick up the receiver and say *"Pronto!"* And that pronto must be why Italian hotel staff think Americans have no clue about Italian phone service.

Within minutes, a hotel employee rapped on Dena's door. "It's dead," he concluded.

The telephone company should hire him. He's good, she thought. "Can it be fixed?" Dena pleaded.

"Certo." Certainly. And she breathed a sigh of relief. "In a couple of days," he added.

"Well, if I can't reach him by phone, we'll just have to show up," she informed Shelby.

Destination---Buca San Giovanni for another sumptuous meal served up by the scrumptiously delicious Nicola. Her legs were shaky and her palms clammy as Dena descended the restaurant's staircase. She wondered if he would be pleased to see her. Would his eyes light up in remembrance of their romantic night together? Yes, maybe romantic was stretching it a bit. And granted, a few minutes against an alley wall hardly constituted a night together. Okay, could his eyes at least register some sign of recognition when he sees me?

Once inside the restaurant, she hungrily scanned the room for him. No luck. Instead, the diminutive co-owner Pasquale strode up to greet the ladies. "Ah, the two beautiful American ladies," he said. An appreciative smile came to his lips. *"Benvenuti!"* Welcome.

Dena plastered a reciprocally fake smile on her face, trying to hide her disappointment. Yeah, yeah, yeah. Yadda yadda yadda. Nice to see you, too. Now where's my man? As she allowed the restaurant proprietor to kiss both cheeks in the European fashion, her eyes surveyed the dining room again. Where the hell was he? If he wasn't working that night, she'd die. Even the flute of bubbling champagne Pasquale proffered failed to appease.

Shelby couldn't help but see the almost wild look of longing in her friend's eyes. As he led them to their table, she noticed a hand reaching up, about to cuff poor little Pasquale around the neck. My God, she'll rip out the man's throat if he doesn't produce Nicola. Shelby caught her arm in midair.

"Control yourself!" she hissed. "He's here. Right behind us."

"What's the matter with you? I was only going to wave to Vittorio," Dena snapped, snatching her arm back. Still, calmed by the knowledge that Nicola was there, she stopped in mid-stride and whipped around.

Cocoa brown eyes traveled the length of her body, taking in everything. She met his admiring gaze with a swift, but thorough, appraisal of her own. Then, he walked toward both ladies in slow, deliberate strides, lithe and lethal as a jaguar. His arms embraced them both, and he gave each the obligatory Italian kiss on both cheeks.

Hypnotizing fingers discreetly stroked the nape of Dena's neck. Hearts really do skip a beat, she thought. And then, they race like the wind. With Herculean effort, she pulled herself from him and floated on air as she followed Pasquale to their seats. Seeing Nicola again was all she'd hoped for. He was gorgeous. Seeing her again had obviously warmed the cock...cock...cock...so sorry...cockles of his heart.

When she saw their table, Dena complained under her breath. "Do we look like sardines?"

It wasn't bad enough that Pasquale had led them to one of the side dining rooms, the restaurant's equivalent to Siberia. The little man looked so proud as he offered them a tiny table sandwiched between two others.

Shelby turned sideways and sucked in every possible part of her body as she slithered between the tables to take her seat. "It'd be easier if they hired a crane and lowered me in."

"Didn't know we were meeting friends for dinner?" Dena laughed. So close were they to their neighbors, their seating more accurately resembled a table for six.

They smiled at the elderly couple to their left. Probably born around the time that man discovered fire, Shelby thought. And to their right, were two gorgeous, middle-aged, and obviously wealthy Italian gentlemen who couldn't keep their admiring eyes off the ladies. Please! You didn't fall for that, did you? If that were true, the ladies might have offered to sit on the men's laps.

No, as luck would have it, seated to our ladies' right were two decidedly young, quite beautiful women. Shelby's shrewd eyes gave them an assessing once over. Mmmm, cascading blonde hair, aquamarine eyes, no makeup. What for? They didn't need it.

What Shelby missed, Dena didn't. Thin, toned, tanned, and poured into body-hugging clothes showing off every sensuous curve.

"Who could ask for anything more," Shelby whispered leaning across the table, "than to be seated next to two blonde bombshells?"

Dena patted her friend's hand consolingly. "Well, we could get that kind of attention, too," she began, "if we wanted to be so obvious and show our cleavage to the world."

Shelby practically snorted. "Please, if we show our cleavage, people will be looking at our feet."

Luckily, their displeasure with their seating location was to be short lived. Within seconds of depositing Dena and Shelby in the hinterlands, Pasquale returned and shepherded them back to the front dining room.

Now this was more like it. After all, would one place a Botticelli masterpiece in a broom closet, depriving the world of all that beauty? Shelby and Dena thought they deserved a proper setting, and Pasquale must have agreed. With their new table, they were practically on piano man Vittorio's lap.

The huge grin on Vittorio's face signaled the entertainer's delight in having the ladies positioned so close to his makeshift stage. And when he immediately struck up Frank Sinatra's signature tune, *New York, New York*, the women felt like honored guests. With the self-satisfied grin of a cat that had just lapped up a bowl of cream, Dena turned to her friend with a triumphant smile.

"That's my man. Nicola got us moved," she beamed.

"Yes, dear, it pays to know men in high places," Shelby said patronizingly.

Dena nodded her head in agreement, totally oblivious to the sarcasm. For once, Shelby decided to let it go. She really did love her friend, so why burst the child's bubble? If Dena was daft enough to believe their relocation had anything to do with the admittedly dishy Nicola, let her continue to dwell in blissful ignorance. Nevertheless, it was getting harder and harder to see how the poor girl made it through the day unscathed.

As she looked across the table, Shelby saw her friend almost devouring Nicola's every move, completely captivated by him. How foolish I've been, Shelby thought snidely. All along, what I've needed is a man whose idea of the perfect first date is groping in an alleyway.

Dinner was fabulous. The ladies would wholeheartedly recommend their menu choices if the two (maybe three) bottles of Chianti with which they plied themselves had left them with even the faintest glimmer of memory.

They'd have to rip out my tongue and surgically stitch my lips shut before I could let this go by, thought the Englishwoman. "You're telling me you have absolutely no recollection of what you ate that night, yet you plan on recommending the place in this book of yours?"

"Yup," Dena acknowledged. "We'll tell people to write in if they were there and remember us and what we..."

"Oh yeah, how could I have forgotten?" India interrupted. "The revised edition."

"Of course, we'll thank them in advance," Shelby offered.

"Oh, well, that will fix everything, I'm sure," smirked India.

However clueless Dena and Shelby might be as to what they ate, this night would no doubt prove to be one of the most memorable in their lives. Seated to the ladies' right, an Italian family was celebrating the mother's birthday. The whole restaurant joined in to sing *Tanti Auguri*, Italy's equivalent of Happy Birthday. From that moment, the Buca became Party Central. Vittorio solicited requests from the audience, and people sang along with him. Others rose to dance in the tiny dining room. Restaurant patrons who had come to enjoy a quiet dinner were caught up in a raucous party atmosphere. Total strangers were talking, laughing, and dancing with one another.

At one point, Vittorio decided to sing *New York, New York* again. But this time, looking for a partner, he beckoned Shelby to join him on stage. "No, no," she squawked, waving her hand in refusal.

"Go on, do it," Dena urged.

Shelby shot a withering stare at her friend. "I am not going up there and making a fool of myself," she said. But, a touch of regret lurked just beneath her indignation.

"The beautiful lady from New York, you please sing with me," Vittorio begged over his microphone.

Still, Shelby remained firmly planted in her seat. Oh, it *would* be such fun, she admitted to herself. But she just couldn't do it. Though she desperately wanted to, her legs were like lead, stiff and unmoving.

"You're scared?!" Dena taunted. She could see the warring emotions playing across her friend's face. Incredulity and bemusement accompanied her accusation. "You? Who's never afraid of anything."

"Am not," Shelby denied with childlike fervor. Terrified, but she'd never tell her friend.

Finally, the wine coursing through her, and her own hitherto entombed desire to be in the spotlight, won out. Shelby joined Vittorio onstage. Looking out at the expectant audience, she felt faint. Vultures, ready to swoop and feast on her charred remains after she crashed and burned.

"If you can make it there, you'll make..." she started tentatively, her voice barely a whisper. Her legs shook like leaves tossing in an autumn wind. But she continued on. The whisper soon became a warble, and with each successive note, her confidence grew. Jeez, this is fun, she realized. Within minutes, she and Vittorio were an instant sensation as they sang a duet.

Meanwhile, the birthday family took pity on a solitary Dena, inviting her to join them. She was sure they were very nice, and under ordinary circumstances, she'd welcome the chance to interact with Italians. It was one of the best parts of being in a foreign country. But right now, Dena was interested in an interaction with one particular Italian. If she joined the party table, how would Nicola be able to pass by and occasionally bless her with soft, secret touches? "*Grazie, Grazie.* But no," she declined.

However, no was not an option. Before she knew what was happening, two men swooped down and airlifted Dena, chair and all, refusing to put her down until they deposited her at the other table. There, champagne flowed free as a babbling brook, and Dena raised her flute in toast after toast to the birthday girl before tossing back glass after glass of the bubbly.

As Dena partied with her new friends, Shelby's world debut was in full swing. In English and Italian, she belted out, really massacred, song after song. Notwithstanding a voice that resembled a croaking frog, Shelby whipped her adoring audience into a frenzy and turned the intimate restaurant into an Italian Disco Fever. She was heady with success. They loved her.

Maybe she should move to Italy. Vittorio and she could start a group. She'd be the female lead.

Just when she had really hit her stride, Vittorio decided to take a brief break. Reluctantly, Shelby left the spotlight and joined Dena at the table. "This is great. I'm pretty good at it. My father used to say I couldn't sing. That I was a disgrace to my race. Guess he was wrong. They really like me!"

Dena wondered if someone had laced Shelby's drink with a hallucinogenic. How could the girl possibly believe she had a singing voice? "Oh yes, Shelby, you're a diva. The next Diana Ross, for sure."

More like the next Tiny Tim, and that is an insult to poor Tiny. But Dena could never say that to her friend. "And your moves? Well, Tina Turner could learn a thing or two from you." The girl is as uncoordinated as Joe Cock...cock...cock... Joe Cocker.

Dena waited for her friend to laugh at the suggestion. Okay, a little smile of amusement. That would be enough.

"I know. I'm a hit." Shelby swept her arm panoramically around the room. "Look around," she urged an incredulous Dena. Then, she ran back to the stage.

Dena watched, shaking her head in amazement. She was serious. There must have been more Chianti than blood running through her veins. Dena knew she had created a monster. She couldn't help but notice a very different Shelby up on stage, a very changed person from the friend she knew and loved. Ever conscious of her image and always maintaining a dignified air, Shelby had done a 180-degree turn and lost all inhibition. As she and Vittorio sang, she gyrated to the music, practically treating a gleeful Vittorio to a lap dance. The man was absolutely captivated.

Just then, Nicola approached Dena. With him was a friend he introduced as his cousin Nicola. "Heez name Nicola, too."

"Oh, your cousin!" Dena parroted him again. Then, she turned to the newcomer, smiling and offering her hand.

"Are you visiting Nicola?" Dena inquired.

"No."

"So, you live in Firenze?" she prompted.

"Si."

Another one word answer. Okay, work with me here. I'm trying to keep up my end of the conversation. Dena tried again.

"Where do you work?" she asked, making another stab at it. An awkward silence greeted her question. What was he looking at, she wondered, anger rising at being completely ignored.

Something on the stage seemed to have the man in a trance. Dena followed his gaze.

"Do you know Vittorio?" she trudged on.

"*Scusi?*" He brought his attention back to Dena, his brow furrowed in confusion. "What you say?"

"I ask..."

He interrupted her midstream. "Your friend, she *una bella donna*. She very beautiful."

"Yes, she..."

"And she have *una voce comé un'angelo*," he prattled on. He was talking to Dena, but his eyes were searing Shelby.

Dena smiled in amusement. She turned to her Nicola. "What did he say?" she queried.

"He say Shelby have a voice like angel," Nicola translated with an amused smile.

Yeah, the angel of death. That voice was enough to wake the dead. But apparently that didn't matter to the men. Dena swung her head in either direction. They were like bees to honey....no, no, nothing sweet about that voice. More like vultures circling a rotting carcass.

And the women? A group of single females to her left had their heads together in deep conversation, their eyes trained with venomous curiosity on Shelby. And, the women who were with men? A caress here, a stroke there, all designed to mark their possession. Still, just like the single women, a lethal poison darkened their eyes as they looked toward the stage and Shelby.

Dena couldn't help thinking that perhaps her friend was right. No, not about her singing. Shelby's father had been dead right about that. She really was a disgrace to her race. Actually, that voice was a disgrace to the entire human race. The only way someone could listen to singing so criminally off key was with the aid of earplugs or massive amounts of liquor.

But Shelby's singing wasn't the issue. Right there, right then, every man wanted her and every woman wanted to be her, Dena concluded. She really was a diva, the center of attention.

But the diva was having a bit of a meltdown on stage. With each note, Shelby's chest was getting tighter. She fought for each breath of air, each inhalation becoming increasingly labored. Damned asthma!

"Be right back," she whispered to Vittorio, patting his arm reassuringly. Back at the table, she grabbed her inhaler. Whhhhh! Whhhhhh! With each puff, her breathing gradually came back to normal.

"Well, so much for my great escape from library hell," Shelby lamented. Sadness shadowed her brown eyes. "Unless an oxygen tank can double as a musical instrument, my visions of stardom are over. Some diva, huh?"

"Don't worry, Shelby. There are all kinds of divas. One day, you'll leave that library for bigger and better."

A glance across the crowded makeshift dance floor brought Dena's train of thought to an abrupt end. Only a few yards away, there was her dear Nicola involved in a conversation with the two blonde bombshells. Funny thing was, this conversation involved hands and butts. His hands and their butts. More precisely, his hands on their butts.

"Look at him, look at him!" she hissed at Shelby. Her fingernails were practically digging a canal in her friend's arm.

"Who?" Shelby squealed as she jerked her arm from the death grip.

"At Nicola and those blondes. What's he doing patting their butts?" Dena was almost hyperventilating. The veins in her neck pulsated against her skin.

Was she kidding, Shelby asked herself. She didn't have time for this. She was on fire on that stage. A hit of her drugs, and she was ready to go back and wow the crowd. Her fans were getting restless. What could she say to appease Dena?

"Calm down. That's the way they do things in Italy. You know Italians always talk with their hands. Maybe that's how they say thank you, please come again," Shelby tried to allay her friend's fears.

"Oh, he's saying come again, alright. And it has nothing to do with returning to the restaurant," Dena retorted.

Mmmm, Shelby thought, she's not as stupid or as drunk as I thought. This might be a little harder than I expected. Okay, best to go with Plan B - the truth. Shelby looked her friend squarely in the eye. "Look, have you lost your mind? You just met the man two days ago. He's a waiter, and he's ten years younger than you. This is hardly a fairy tale. What did you think, that this was going to lead to happily ever after?"

"No, but I demand more respect than him flirting with other women right under my nose," Dena said haughtily.

Shelby couldn't believe what she was hearing. My God, she was serious. Respect? This from a woman who had just done the Hokey Pokey in an alleyway with the man. Shelby wasn't prepared to waste anymore time. The stage was calling her.

"You're right, Dena. You go give him hell. See where that gets you." And with a warning look, she returned to the mike.

Some of what Shelby said actually penetrated. Not to mention, countless years and thousands of dollars in therapy hadn't been totally for naught. Dena lifted her head, squared her shoulders, and stuck out what little chest she had. Scanning the crowd, she corralled the dishiest man she could find, determined to have a high old time singing and dancing.

But no matter which way she twisted or turned, her eyes never left Nicola. Within seconds, there it was again. Her Italian waiter talking with hands and another pat on the butts. From afar, Shelby could see sweat beading on her friend's brow, the veins in her neck protruding, her eyes bugging wildly, and her head jerking uncontrollably.

"Quick, Vittorio, let's sing *New York, New York* again," she bade the entertainer, certain the song would help to calm her friend down and change her mood. Gradually the cheery tune began to work its magic. The veins in Dena's neck relaxed, and her jerks became fluid movement. Now if only those blowfish eyes would return to their sockets.

The song was good, but it was no miracle worker. When the blonde bombshells finally took their leave, and Nicola made his way back to Dena, her jealousy again bubbled to the surface and gushed.

"What were you doing touching those girls' butts? Who are they?" she grilled. How dared he? Why, they were practically engaged.

"Eez nothing," he said with easy smoothness, gently stroking Dena's neck. "They friends of my friend. That eez how we do our custom here."

Then, he flashed a sexy smile and let his smoldering eyes travel the length of her with obvious appreciation. Dena swooned at his cute Italian accent and endearing use of English, not to mention his touch, which threatened to send her into a hypnotic trance.

Of course, Shelby was right, she reasoned. It really was just a quaint Italian custom, nothing more. On with the wedding plans for next June.

India let out a sigh that sounded more like a bleating sheep. "Ladies, I wonder...," she began and stopped herself. Shifting in her seat uncomfortably, she tried again.

"Dena, did you..." Again the Briton's words trailed off midstream. She cleared her throat, stalling for time.

"Shelby, did it never occur to you that..." she tried anew and hesitated once more.

"What?" Dena and Shelby asked simultaneously.

"Well, two things really," India got out. How could she word this without insulting these two dumbos?

"Just ask us," Dena said, trying to hide any impatience.

"Okay, here goes." India took another deep breath before proceeding. "Dena, you're still married, right?"

Dena nodded her head affirmatively.

"With three kids still at home? Correct?" India grilled.

Now it was Dena's turn to squirm in her seat. "Yeeesss," she let out slowly, almost fearfully. Suddenly, she wished she hadn't encouraged the blasted woman.

"Then, tell me something. Did you really think that marriage to a waiter living in Italy was even viable, never mind an answer to your apparent unhappiness?"

Dena blanched, taken aback by the candor of the question. "We...we...well...," she stammered.

Sensing her friend's difficulty, Shelby jumped in. "It didn't have a thing to do with thinking, India, but feeling. After years of feeling nothing but extreme loneliness..."

"Exactly," Dena concurred. She flashed her friend a look of gratitude, but now she was able to speak for herself. "For the first time in years, I felt desired and desirable. Was there really anything to think about?"

"Still, marriage to Nicola?" India remained unconvinced.

Dena raised her eyes and gave a concessionary shake of her head. "Okay, okay, I admit it. The idea of marriage was a bit off the wall."

There's hope after all, the Englishwoman thought.

"But maybe living together?" Dena proffered.

India turned to Shelby, eyebrow raised. The British woman's shoulder shrug said it all. How are you going to help her now?

Shelby sat motionless as a dummy without its ventriloquist. She'd done her best to help Dena, but now even she was shocked.

"In the United States, of course!" Dena continued, trying to extricate herself from the embarrassing situation. "That was possible, wasn't it?"

Try as she might, Shelby couldn't stifle a derisive snort. "Don't waste your time, India. I've tried. It's hopeless. You had another question for us?"

Thank God, one of them is still on planet Earth. "Yes I did. It's about those blonde bombshells and why your table got moved."

Shelby smiled knowingly, and raised her hand to halt India midstream. "Say no more, I know exactly where you're going with this one."

"Really?" the Englishwoman prompted.

"Of course, any fool knows getting a better table had nothing to do with Nicola. It was Giancarlo," Shelby answered. There was a smug confidence in her voice as she went on. "After all, he is quite an important person in Firenze," she preened.

Dena swatted her friend's arm. "Shelby, Giancarlo wasn't even there. It had to be Nicola," she contradicted.

"You really do need help," Shelby argued. "Are you truly that out of touch with reality? Do you sincerely believe..."

"Ladies, ladies," India interrupted. Like a referee in a football game, the Englishwoman raised her hand to calm the situation. "Did it ever occur to either of you that maybe, just maybe, Nicola was diddling one or both of those blonde bombshells and having you sit so close to them was inconvenient, to say the least?"

They both looked at their companion as if she'd sprouted an extra head. Then, they turned to each other. Could it be true, Dena asked herself. Immediately, she dismissed the possibility. Not a chance! How could dear Nicola possibly have wanted those two, young, nubile beauties when he had me? Of course, he didn't. Those pats on the butt really were just an Italian custom to say goodbye. Shelby said so, and she should know. Why, she's practically Italian.

Shelby was simultaneously lost in thought. Well, Nicola the Whack-off Waiter diddling the bombshells may very well be true. Who cares, really? But it's certainly not why our seats were changed. Only a fool wouldn't realize that my relationship with Giancarlo got us moved.

In unison, the two shook their heads. "Naaahhhh," they agreed.

"Out of the question," Shelby spoke for both of them.

"Maybe you're right," the Englishwoman relented. Out of the question? I'll tell you what's out of the question...that if Darwin had encountered life forms this dull, he would ever have theorized that only the fittest survive.

"Of course we're right," Dena reiterated.

Ah, the sweet blanket of denial, cozily wrapping these dizzy dreamers in their cocoon of delusion. By their own admission, this wasn't the first time, and most likely, for these two, it wouldn't be the last, the Englishwoman concluded. "So, how did the evening end?" she asked, changing the subject.

That evening, Dena had dressed for success, wearing a stunning black outfit she'd purchased in Capri especially for the occasion. The silken material of the long skirt and the sleeveless shell gently hugged the curves of her body. To the casual observer, the ensemble was the epitome of understated elegance. However, upon further inspection, one couldn't miss the strategically placed slit nearly rising to the heavens and threatening to reveal Dena's celestial body.

Many of the Buca's employees were planning to continue the party at an area nightclub. With the impromptu party at the restaurant winding down, Nicola dashed into the waiters' dressing room to change into his dance duds for the evening ahead. Proud as a peacock, he strutted through the crowd, making his way towards Dena and Shelby.

"My Lord," Shelby shrieked. Her mouth was agape as he emerged. "As Daddy would say, where in tarnation was he when God was handing out fashion genes?"

"Sleeping?" Dena offered.

Earlier in the day, Nicola had been on his own little shopping spree. His proud purchase was the most hideous pair of green plaid pants ever made. John Travolta's polyester-clad character in Saturday Night Fever had nothing on Nicola.

With all her might, Shelby tried to force her eyes upward. But it was beyond her capability. Big and bright as a neon sign, the plaid fabric seized and held her gaze. And to make matters worse, they clung to the boy's body as if they'd been spray painted on.

Now, the Italian sense of style and love of clothes is universally known. So, the ladies were a bit taken aback at this sight. Dena was at a loss for words. "Oh, oh, your pants," she sputtered with a sickly smile pasted on her face.

"You like? I buy for tonight," Nicola beamed, obviously quite pleased.

"Oh, yes, they're nice," she lied facilely. You really shouldn't have, she thought. Please, go put your work clothes back on. I always did love a man in uniform and black is perfect for every occasion.

Of course, Dena said none of this because, in the end, did the pants really make the man? Did it matter what he had on? Of course not. It was the inner man that made the man. Okay, okay...the lower half of the inner man made the man. Correction...what was in the pants on the lower half of the inner man made the man. Suffice it to say, she didn't care what Nicola was wearing. It was time to go dancing with her handsome Italian and to squirrel away another new, exciting experience.

Years earlier, in order to protect the art treasures of Florence from pollution, the government restricted car travel in historic centro. Consequently, Florentines tool around town on small motorbikes called *motorini*, flying through the streets like Evil Kneivel's apprentices, each one spewing more noxious exhaust fumes than ten cars combined.

This night would be Dena's first ride on a motorino. Initially, she was a bit apprehensive, but with a little coaxing from Nicola, she quickly straddled the leather seat like a pro, with the slit in her skirt proving to be both form and function. Gratefully, she donned his helmet and hung on for dear life.

Shelby and Vittorio traveled together, taking their singing act on the rode through the streets of Florence. Unlike Dena, Shelby's first ride on a motorino had been six years earlier with Giancarlo. She had also been leery of the motorized bikes. But once she'd tried it, she was hooked. Happily, riding with Vittorio brought back wonderful, carefree memories.

> **Traveling Tidbit for the Daring Traveler:** Motorini can be a trifle frightening for the uninitiated. But if one has the opportunity, don't pass it up, particularly if the ride includes straddling the backside of a sexy Italian.

Unbeknownst to the ladies, the group was en route to Full Up, where Shelby had met Giancarlo six years earlier, and even in her Chianti-induced haze, the memories of the first time she'd set eyes on him were vivid.

"Speaking of Giancarlo, did you ever call him?" India inquired.
Shelby fumed inwardly. Jesus, Mary, and Joseph! Is she an Interpol operative? A proctologist probes less than this woman. "Yeah, I did," she answered reluctantly.

The words echoed nonstop through her mind. Dance...we'll dance at...wedding...not weddings. Damn it all...wedding. Of course, he said wedding. Wedding. Wedding!

Shelby knew it appeared a trifle odd that she hadn't called Giancarlo as soon as she and Dena had made the decision to ditch Rome and return to Florence. She had put it off as long as she could; it was now or never.

"Ciao, Giancarlo, guess where I am?" she asked. Her voice wore a false high-pitched gaiety.

"New York?" he posited.

That couldn't be hopefulness in his voice, could it? Ignore it, she told herself. "No, no, we're back in Firenze."

"*Che peccato*, I in Grossetto at my villa," Giancarlo answered.

"Grosetto, how nice. I've never been there and always wanted to. Is it pretty this time of year?" she prodded.

"Today eez very cold. Not nice." His answer came quickly, a little too quickly.

"Oh, I'm sure it's wonderful. I'd love to see it," Shelby disagreed. A deafening silence spanned the telephone lines. Okay, then. Maybe not this trip.

"No surprises here. He didn't invite you, did he?" the Englishwoman chortled.

I do believe she's enjoying this, Shelby thought. The woman probably pulls the wings off flies.

"Gee, what gave you your first clue, India? The fact that I was tooling around town with Dena and a host of waiters?" Shelby countered.

Undeterred by the sarcasm, India pressed on. "So, let me get this straight. You traveled six thousand miles to see this man, changed your plans and returned to Florence, and were going home in two days when you called him?" she catalogued, laying out the situation in graphic detail.

Shelby's eyes gave a protracted blink, almost trying to hide from the truth. "Yes," she admitted with great effort.

"Oh, and I forgot. His little wedding remark," the Englishwoman resurrected the touchy subject.

Shelby shrank inside. And the British think they're so damned proper. This one's proper all right. A right and proper bitch. "I told you his English wasn't that good. He might've meant that we'd dance at our wedding," Shelby huffed.

Unconvinced, the Englishwoman looked at Dena with a raised eyebrow. Dena could almost see the question forming in her mind. Had Shelby's mother used her as a bowling ball as an infant?

Thankfully, India decided to let the question hang in the air unsaid. "Back to Full Up," she continued.

Notwithstanding the rather embarrassing outcome of her phone call, Shelby still had high hopes for her future with dear Giancarlo. But that evening, he wasn't there. And the party really had to go on. Since more than one suitor was trying to fill her...uhm, fill her dance card, it was proving to be quite a bit of fun. Shooting down would-be lovers was just the sort of sport Shelby loved. Vittorio was absolutely smitten with her and used everything in his Italian lover's bag of tricks to woo her.

"Why you no let me kiss you? You no like me?" he pressed.

"Oh, Vittorio, I do like you. You're a very nice man, but I am seeing someone here in Firenze," Shelby explained.

When it became abundantly clear that their duet began and ended on the stage, Vittorio quickly exited stage left and went home. Next!

Second up at bat was Nicola's cousin, whom Shelby was just meeting. "Shelby, thees my cousin. He is Nicola, too," Nicola introduced.

"Nicola two?" Shelby was confused. "You mean you actually call him Nicola *Due*?"

"No, no. Not Nicola two, he is named Nicola also," Dena clarified.

Regardless, the ladies dubbed him Nicola *Due*, which means Nicola the Second. "*Due* for short," Dena decreed. So, henceforth that was his name. *Due*. Pronounced doo-ay.

How to describe *Due*? Well, let's just say if Nicola was absent on the day God was passing out fashion genes, *Due* must have been comatose when the looks genes were being doled out. His most prominent feature was his nose, and Shelby couldn't help thinking that if its size was any indication of another bodily appendage, the boy's reputation must have been legendary among the ladies of Italy. Notwithstanding this intriguing possibility, and the fact that he was quite possibly the only true gentleman the ladies ever met in Italy, Shelby was not in the least interested. Next!

Tall, dark, and rather handsome. A gentleman at the bar seemed to take quite a bit of interest in the ladies. His admiring gaze moved from one to the other, as if he weren't quite sure which woman he wanted. Soon, he made his move, approaching Nicola with a lecherous glint in his eye. Within seconds, tempers flared and rather heated words were exchanged. As best as the ladies could ascertain, here's what happened.

Turned out, the man was a *carabiniere*. In Italy, there are many types of policemen, each with their own elaborate and equally pompous uniform. However, for any woman who's interested, Dena and Shelby luckily managed to ascertain that carabinieri are rather high up on the food chain of Italian police, and the job is considered prestigious.

Nevertheless, Nicola wasn't impressed with the flatfoot's credentials, taking exception with the man thinking he could use his position to poach other men's preserves. Quickly, his cousin moved in to put out the flames. But Nicola the First was not to be appeased.

Eyes blazing, his body was rigid, seething with an uncontrollable rage. Stalking back to Dena, he took her hand in a death grip. "Come, we go," he ordered, practically dragging her to the door.

Thinking he just wanted a bit of fresh air and to let off some steam, she followed happily. But when he slung one lean leg over his motorino, Dena realized Nicola intended leaving the club altogether.

"I can't leave Shelby," she protested adamantly. What did he take her for? What kind of person left a best friend stranded with men she'd never met?

"Eez okay. My cousin take her home."

Oh, well then, that was okay. Sure, Dena had only known Nicola for a little over seventy-two hours. Yes, she'd never set eyes on *Due* before tonight. But Shelby was always harping about practically being Italian. Here was her chance to prove it.

And with that, Dena deftly hiked her leg over the seat of the motorino with nary a backward glance, and smiled gleefully as they sped off toward Nicola's apartment.

Back at the club, *Due* was nattering in Shelby's ear about the wonderful world of waitering, eagerly beseeching her to come to his restaurant. She was barely listening. Every few minutes, Shelby looked around the club, her eyes clouded with worry.

What the devil had Dena gotten up to? Maybe upstairs in the disco. As Shelby rose to investigate, *Due* stopped her, explaining Dena's departure.

"Gone?" Shelby crowed loudly. Impossible. The man must be daft. Dena couldn't have left her. Only a bitch would leave a friend alone with strange men in a foreign country. And I'm supposed to be the bitch in this friendship, Shelby fumed.

"Don't worry, I take you home," *Due* assured her. Shocked at her desertion, Shelby agreed, allowing herself to be led from the club.

Out on the quiet streets of Florence, *Due*'s motorino sped up one street, then down another, in one alley and around another corner. As what should have been a five-minute ride back to the Hotel Boston turned into an odyssey, Shelby's suspicions grew. Finally, when they pulled up in front of an elegant old palazzo, she knew those suspicions were warranted. The Hotel Boston could only wish to be housed in this stately building.

Shelby cursed herself for being in this situation. She should have known better than to accept the ride. Accordingly, she turned that anger on *Due*. "This isn't my hotel!" she accused hotly, indignation spewing from her.

"No, *è casa mia*," *Due* admitted with a sheepish grin. My house.

What kind of woman did he think she was? She'd never gone to the apartment of a man she'd just met. Well, that was if you didn't count Giancarlo. And, oh yes, there was her ex-husband Junior. And college...who knew? Those days were all a blur now. But it didn't matter. She had no intention of ending up in *Due*'s apartment tonight. Shelby jumped off the motorino in a temper and stormed down the street on foot.

"*Dove vai?*" *Due* called after her. Where are you going?

"I can get a taxi," she called over her shoulder.

"No, no, I take you back," he said.

Shelby stopped in mid-stride, and turned, casting him a suspicious glare.

"I promise," he added.

The embarrassed twinkle in his eyes and his contrite smile convinced her. Shelby retraced her steps and climbed back on the bike, her actions telling him she'd let him take her home.

And so *Due* did, but not without a glint of appreciation for this woman warming his heart.

On their last day in Florence, the ladies decided to ignore their lack of sleep and a lingering alcoholic buzz. They would mark their departure by going out and purchasing gifts for themselves.

"Oh, no you don't," India piped up once again. "Something's missing here."

"What? What?" the ladies asked simultaneously.

Their interrogator zeroed in on Dena. "You really left her in a bar with a bunch of strange men?"

"Yeah," Dena mumbled. A hangdog smile curved her lips.

"Friends don't do that to friends for no good reason. So, why don't you bloody well tell me what happened with you and Nicola that night?"

Shelby looked like a cat that had just lapped up a bowl of cream. One could almost see a milky white moustache above her lip as she echoed the Englishwoman. "Yeah, Deenie, what happened that night?"

"Is nothing sacred?" Dena squirmed.

"Well, some things are," India began. "But somehow I doubt the Pope would sanctify what you and Nicola were up to."

Dena nodded her head, forced to acknowledge the truth of this.

His apartment had a view of the Arno River. Gazing out the window, she admired the city lights dancing on the dark water. Nicola came up behind her, offering a glass of *Limoncello*, a lemony liqueur. Dena didn't know how, but she was dead sober, nervous with excitement. She brought the glass to her lips, draining it in seconds.

His arms curled around her waist. "*Ho paura?*"

"*Scusi?*" she asked.

Turning her in his arms he repeated in English. "You scared?"

"*Si, si, un po,*" she whispered back in Italian. A little.

Fingers, soft but sure, caressed her cheek. He tilted her chin upward, and brought his face closer, blotting out everything but the teasing promise of his lips. She gasped as he caught her bottom lip between his teeth and tortured its softness with a playful bite. But Dena, wanting more, moved her moist lips across the tempting curve of his neck. His groan was low and primal. Long fingers reached for the buttons of her blouse, and released them one by one.

Eager mocha eyes feasted on her lush, lace-covered breasts. "*Che bella!*"

"Please, that's enough! You're turning my stomach," Shelby squealed. "Che bella, my ass. And lush breasts. Now, that's a joke!"

Her friend's interruption jolted Dena to the present. "Oh, you're just jealous, Shelby."

Turning to India, she continued. "But you get the picture, I'm sure."

"Yeah, we all get the picture," Shelby grumbled. "Let's get on with the rest of the story."

Chapter 7

Once again...the next day found the ladies tired, with very little sleep, and a lingering alcoholic buzz. "Our last day in Florence," Dena said nostalgically. "What do you wanna do?"

"Shopping?" Shelby suggested.

Dena readily agreed, instantly warming to the idea of purchasing a little something for herself. After all, no one else seemed inclined to do so, she lamented silently.

Florence boasts quite a few year-round, open-air markets, but the granddaddy of them all is *Mercato di San Lorenzo*, near the Church of San Lorenzo in centro, the city's downtown area. Each morning, vendors file into the eponymously named piazza, pushing great wooden carts on wheels. Once in place, the carts are opened and voila. They morph into amazing, portable shops laden with veritable treasure troves.

All day long, shoppers flock to the piazza, tempted by Italian leather handbags and wallets, boots, coats, and jackets, as well as a staggering assortment of souvenirs ranging from calendars to t-shirts. At sunset, with their day complete and their coffers full, the vendors pack up their carts and trundle away, only to return in the wee hours of the next morning. For foodies, an old-style food hall located in the piazza is chock-full of Italian specialty foods.

Throughout the friends' weeklong vacation, the weather had been particularly cool. Definitely not the lazy, sun-drenched days that Dena and Shelby had hoped for. This final day was biting cold, and Shelby's lightweight raincoat was no match for the gusty wintry winds whipping through the streets of Florence, ferociously tossing the ladies to and fro. Sumptuous leather coats hanging everywhere in the piazza beckoned to her. But Shelby's practical side recoiled at the thought of spending more money.

"I don't need a new coat to keep me warm for one day. I can make it till tomorrow," she said, trying to walk away. Nevertheless, a beautiful black calfskin coat with a white kidskin collar and cuffs had caught her eye. It held her in its grip, practically talking to her. Her feet felt leaden as she took a step away.

"*Mi vuoi molto,*" it teased. You want me. Was this a man or a coat? Either way, Shelby turned back, unable to resist. Once she sank herself in its buttery soft folds, she was a goner.

"*Quanto costa?*" How much?

When the vendor quoted a price much lower than she expected, Shelby bit like a piranha on human remains. Like a good American without a clue, she promptly paid full price, no questions asked.

While her friend settled her bill, Dena found herself being accosted by a deep chocolate brown, full-length shearling. She too wavered a bit. After all, if she didn't have a man to keep her warm next winter, then this coat would be the next best thing.

"Shel, look at this. It's beautiful," she beckoned the other woman.

Shelby looked up and let out a scream. Someone had killed and skinned the abominable snowman, dyed it brown, and left its furry remains on a hanger. "It's hideous," she declared.

"No, no," the salesman contradicted. "Eez beautiful coat." In the blink of an eye, he liberated Smokey the Bear from its high perch, and Dena was prancing around in it. She seemed as enthralled with it as she was with Nicola.

At least this Italian flesh could go home with her. Okay, so it couldn't talk, couldn't walk, would never whisper sweet Italian nothings in her ear, and certainly would never be an adequate dance partner. Sure, she knew it was dead, but this coat could provide other compensations. It could accompany her to dinner, to the theater, on moonlit strolls along the Hudson. It just might prove to be the perfect companion. It would shop with her, go to church with her, see any chick flick she fancied, and go to any cultural event of her choosing. All without the slightest complaint. And best of all, if Dena chose, she could take it to bed to keep her warm and snugly. And when she tired of it, she could simply banish it to the closet. Hell, if it had money, it would be better than a husband.

Now Dena, aiming to save some of that grocery money she had filched over the past few months, decided to try her hand at haggling even though the asking price was almost a steal. Stubbornly, the salesman shook his head with vigor, refusing to negotiate. It was a good price, he assured her.

Still, Dena was determined. She wasn't just some country bumpkin from upstate New York who'd never been anywhere. Well, actually she was, but she'd seen people haggle in the movies.

"Well, it may be a good price, but it's still too much. You can do better," she insisted. Now she would make a strategic retreat, certain he'd cave like a house of cards.

There was just one problem. Apparently, those movies Dena had watched had omitted one vital piece of information. When negotiating the purchase price of an item, one should neither fondle, caress, moan longingly, nor exclaim tearfully over the coveted merchandise.

The salesman had bested her, and he knew it. But being Italian, it was in his genes to be smooth and charming, so he decided to throw a bone to soothe the poor girl's battered pride. Massimo, the Merchant of Florence, and friend to all would-be shoppers, flashed a sly smile. "I give you two receipts," he offered.

Dena arched one eyebrow doubtfully. "What good is that?" she quizzed. "I'm still paying the full price."

"Si, but you not pay too much tax."

The ladies eyed him with a blank look of confusion. He continued. Massimo would issue them two receipts, one of which would reflect the actual purchase price and another, which would show a much lower price. The second receipt could be used when declaring purchases to the United States, thereby reducing the customs duty bite.

How magnanimous of the Merchant of Florence! He'd given the ladies a choice that didn't take a single Italian cent out of his slimy pockets, but could land the shopping-crazed chums in the pokey.

"Can you believe our luck?" Shelby began. "Our last day and thousands of dollars later in Italy, and now we're learning the fine art of avoiding customs duty and the Value Added Tax."

"Yes, but it seems terribly dishonest," Dena added. Her brow knitted in confusion, torn between right and wrong. "What do you think we should do?" Ding, ding, ding! DIQ Test question time!

What choice do you think the penny-pinching pair made?
A) Reported Massimo the Merchant of Florence to the *Guardiadi Finanza*, aka the tax police, and refused his offer,
B) Soundly lectured Massimo on the importance of being a law-abiding citizen and taxpayer, and refused his offer,
C) Completely horrified by the proposal, walked out without making any purchases, or
D) Took both receipts and, without batting one pretty eyelash, proceeded to perpetrate a tax fraud on their government.

"So, what did the two of you decide? Which receipt did you use?" the Englishwoman probed.

I thought the British were reserved and circumspect, Shelby reflected testily. The woman is like a bull in a China shop with her impertinent questions.

Meanwhile, Dena could practically feel the hairs on her neck curling as if her tax attorney husband were breathing down it. *No words were necessary between the friends, their brains working as if one. Okay, maybe there only was one.*

"No need to become mired in the details of this little test question," Dena said with uncharacteristic shrewdness. "It's really not important what choice we made, India."

Shelby gave Dena a smile that signaled her wholehearted agreement. Then she trained her eyes on the inquisitive Brit. "Yes, India, what is important is what you would do in such a situation. I say let your conscience, or your pocketbook, be your guide."

Shelby indulged in a private fantasy. Snippets of the tightfisted Brit being detained by British customs panned through her mind. Being led away to the interrogation room, having lights shone in her eyes, being strip-searched. With precipitous speed, the amusing fantasy ended. *Impossible,* Shelby cackled to herself. *Hell, only a blind person could stand strip searching this old bag.*

She had no idea what was truly behind the funny look on her friend's face, but Dena met the amused grin with one of her own. "Well then, enough said. Moving on."

The Englishwoman drew her eyes from first one woman to the other. The glacial look on both faces spoke volumes. Dishing the dirt on each other's love lives...fair game. Dishing the dirt on anything really important in each other's lives? They seemed to be saying, kiss our asses.

Grudgingly, India had to admire that. And, if she were totally honest with herself, she was a touch jealous. *Annabel and I used to be like that,* she thought sadly.

After a few more purchases, Dena and Shelby made their shopping bag burdened way back to the Hotel Boston. Dena nearly kissed the little gnome masquerading as the concierge when he handed her a message from Nicola. He had called at five o'clock to say he'd taken the night off from work to spend with her. Please call, he'd said.

Ooooh! Another night with Nicola. Her skin began to tingle, the hairs on the back of her neck stood up. In fact, hair everywhere...yes, everywhere...straightened up and stood at attention. She dialed his cell phone floating on air.

Within seconds, her heady anticipation of the night to come was supplanted by abject disappointment. *"Lavori?"* she shrieked. What did he mean working? "But your message said you took the night off?"

"Aahh, but Dena. I call five o'clock. Eez six o'clock now."

Of course, how silly of her. What could she be thinking, expecting him to wait for her return call for more than five minutes before making alternate plans?

"I work until one o'clock. I come then," he offered.

She hung up the phone, her humiliation complete. Remember the stellar accommodations of the Hotel Boston and its lack of outgoing phone service? Dena had been forced to avail herself of the hotel lobby phone. How lucky for her to be stood up in front of Shelby, the little hotel gnome, and a newly-arrived contingent of Japanese tourists just checking into the Hotel Boston's lavish accommodations.

Her sole comfort was her friend's rare, but solicitous, reassurance. Shelby gave Dena a quick hug.

"Don't worry, Deenie. The little gnome barely counts, even if he did look slightly disapproving. And, as for those Japanese tourists," she said, giving a little snort at her thought before continuing. "Well, they have to follow a tour guide holding up an umbrella just to get to their rooms. They probably can't understand a word of Italian or English."

And on that note, the ladies ascended the stairs to their rooms. Of course, had they bucked the egocentric American tradition of failing to learn any language other than their own, one of them might have been proficient in Japanese. Should that have been the case, they would have been privy to the whisperings of those tourists.

"Poor girl, she's just been dumped...by an Italian waiter."

"So, what else is new? Isn't that what happens to American women who come to Italy?"

If Dena had known that their tittering laughter was all for her, she might have committed hara-kiri. Not only had the tourists probably understood completely, they were likely amused by our clueless heroines and no doubt privately wondered how two such foolish women could possibly make their way in this world. And without an umbrella no less!

At a loss about where to go for dinner that evening, the ladies consulted the little gnome, who quite kindly suggested a nearby restaurant.

Upon their arrival, they were warmly greeted by the hostess, who told them to have a seat while their table was prepared. As they sat waiting, a light bulb went off in Shelby's head. True, it didn't happen often, but when it did, it was usually worth all her cognitive dry spells.

"I know where we should have gone," she revealed excitedly.

"Where's that?" Dena asked lethargically. She couldn't shake her despondence. Truthfully, she had no interest in food whatsoever. It simply wasn't the Italian that she was hungering for.

"Harry's. We should have gone to Harry's. It's quite renowned and worth the splurge for our last evening."[15]

"Where is it?" Dena asked, trying to feign interest. But when she heard the word Arno, her heart quickened. "The Arno! Let's go."

Nicola's apartment was near the River Arno. She could be close to him in spirit if not in body. Maybe he'd race by on his motorino. He'd stop, scoop her up, and they'd ride into the Tuscan sunset.

Yes, the environmentally hazardous cloud of smoke puffing from the bike would leave Shelby gasping for breath, along with the unpleasant task of telling Dena's family that she wouldn't be returning stateside for the foreseeable future. Nevertheless, she'd be sure to send Christmas and birthday presents and could be reached via the Buca, where she could be notified of any impending graduations, marriages, births, and deaths.

But before any of these ravings could possibly come true, the ladies had to get out of this pleasant restaurant with as much grace as possible. What to do?

"*Abbiamo dimenticato qualcosa. Torniamo subito.*" We forgot something; we'll be right back. Does this sound familiar? No? Here's a subtle clue --- Mario the Hairdresser. He and his octogenarian hairdressers were still waiting for the ladies to return. And now, Dena and Shelby were adding the good proprietors of this nice restaurant to their list of misdeeds, which leads to another traveling tidbit.

Traveling Tidbit for the Cornered Traveler: It pays to learn a few strategic phrases to get through any awkward moments. The ladies' favorites are:
1. Non ho capito - I don't understand.
2. Non parlo Italiano - I don't speak Italian.

[15]Harry's Bar and Grill, Lungarno Vespucci 22r, 055/2396700

3. Non ho soldi - I don't have any money.
4. Torno subito - I'll be right back.
and when all else fails,
5. Ho una malattia – I have a disease.

Shelby had been told that Harry's Bar in Florence was part of the famed Cipriani family of hotels and restaurants. Later, she heard that this was not true. While some might have researched this discrepancy, Shelby didn't really care one way or the other. What was important was that it was just the place to go to be spoiled.

Guests may dine near the bar in a more relaxed setting of wooden tables, or for more formal dining, may sit in the dining room at tables topped with pink linens. Diners will not feel out of place whether dressed to the nines or casually. The staff is quite attentive and absolutely bilingual. No matter what you order, you will no doubt be pleased.

The ladies scanned their menus. "I think I'll have the hamburger," Shelby announced.

"Yeah, might as well get used to the idea of going home," Dena said. Her eyes were limpid and her voice despondent.

When the waiter placed the burger in front of her, Shelby tucked into it with gusto. In contrast, Dena barely touched her plate. She had been surviving on her raw attraction to Nicola since she'd met him. Shelby easily understood since she had only recently recovered from her bout of starving for love. But Giancarlo wasn't in Florence, and so, food and wine had become her closest companions.

"Dena, you should ask for a doggy bag. You may be hungry later," she suggested with concern.

"Oh, yes. That's a great idea." Dena answered with more enthusiasm than she'd had all evening. The remains would be perfect for a romantic, candlelit repast.

Back at the Hotel Boston, Dena packed for the trip home, all the while daydreaming of her upcoming date with Nicola. Again, date may be a stretch, since he wasn't going to show up until after one in the morning. But why quibble?

Time dragged. One o'clock, one fifteen, one thirty, one forty-five. Still, Dena kept her lonely vigil, peaking out her window every few minutes. By two-thirty in the morning, even this lovesick fool was finally forced to wake up and smell the espresso. Something untoward had obviously befallen Nicola.

Not able to stand it any longer, she marched across the hall and pounded on Shelby's door. "Wh..what!" came her friend's groggy reply.

"Are you asleep?" she asked, when Shelby finally stumbled to the door.

"No, I was contemplating Einstein's theory of relativity," Shelby snapped, unable to stifle a yawn. "What the hell do you think I was doing?"

"I'm so worried. Nicola never came. He's probably lying in a hospital somewhere."

I need a flashlight, Shelby thought. I'm sure if I shine it in her eyes, there'll be nothing behind them. Still, she controlled herself. "Don't worry. Of course, he's fine. Maybe the Buca ran an all night special and needed him to work late," she said, trying to console.

"But he didn't call." Dena's voice quivered with uncertainty.

"His cell phone probably died," Shelby offered.

"What about the restaurant phone?" Dena countered.

"Out of order, maybe?" Shelby postulated. Hope that was her last one because I'm plumb out of excuses.

"You know as well as I do that's not likely," Dena accused. "Maybe he's been mugged!"

"And they stole his cell phone?" Shelby repeated.

"I just know something dreadful has happened."

"And his cell phone's dead?"

"It's just so awful," Dena moaned.

Shelby laced her arm around Dena's shoulders and walked her back to her room. "I know it's hard, dear. You two are young and in love." Well, at least, one of them was young, and one was in love. "Go to sleep. I'm sure you'll hear from him in the morning."

Like a robot, Dena followed her friend's advice. But sleep would not come as she lay in bed for hours staring at the ceiling. Finally, a fitful dozing claimed her, but not before she whispered a swift prayer for Nicola's safe return to her arms.

Both ladies halted their tale and looked at India expectantly.

"What?" the Englishwoman asked defensively.

"Surely, you're bursting with questions by now?" Dena said.

"Just one little one," the Englishwoman admitted, too curious to let embarrassment rule her. "Did you hear from him the next morning?"

"Well, as a matter of fact, I did," Dena answered, triumph punctuating each word.

Astonishment lit up India's eyes. And, is that a bit of jealousy I see, Dena mused.

"Just before we boarded the plane, I spotted him racing through the terminal," she elaborated.

Shelby smiled at Dena. An imperceptible nod between the friends signaled their synchronous thoughts. "Yes, he was in a frantic search," Shelby joined the conspiracy.

"I called out to him. He ran to me, gathered me up in his arms, showering my face with sweet kisses," Dena said smugly. "He kept saying how sorry he was, but that he'd had a family emergency."

"It was all so romantic," Shelby's eyes clouded over dreamily.

"Really? He really came?" pressed the Englishwoman. Now, her jealousy and disappointment were evident.

Again, the two friends shared a secret smile.

"No, not really," Dena reluctantly admitted. "But we had you going for a minute, didn't we?"

"Maybe so," India conceded. "So you were back in the States. Anyone with even a tenuous grasp on reality would have shaken Italy off like a bad cold and settled into normal life."

Dena and Shelby both blushed with embarrassment. "Yeah, and...?" Shelby blustered.

"And that leads me to another question." India's eyes were sharp and shrewd. "What happened when you got home that could possibly have made you want to return for another go round?"

In this verbal game of chess, India had made her move. Check!

"Well, that was great fodder for another DIQ Test Question. Here, read," Shelby encouraged, shoving the purple book across the table.

Chapter 8

*A*nd read India did, hungry for an answer.

What do you think the dumped duo did when they returned home?
A) Dena put the trip and Nicola into proper perspective and returned to her pre-Italy life,
B) Dena realistically discouraged Shelby from adding her and Giancarlo's names to Tiffany's bridal registry,
C) Shelby tried to convince Dena that following her erect nipples back to Italy would be a huge mistake, or
D) The ladies convinced themselves and each other that they had unanswered questions and unfinished business with Giancarlo and Nicola and should return to Italy.

Has anything Dena's done so far indicated that she's savvy or even one step above a dullard in her dealings with Nicola? Yes, most people would have tossed any hope of a future with him in the trash with that very aptly named doggy bag. But not Dena. Ergo, toss Answer A.

As for Answer B, should Shelby have had even half a clue, she wouldn't have been able to convince herself Giancarlo was just having a tiny problem expressing himself in English when he said weddings with an S.

Likewise, when it comes to Answer C, take a minute to remember Dena's tender concern for Shelby as she bawled her eyes out in Giancarlo's arms. And Shelby's compassion for her friend's distress over Nicola's no-show. Doesn't ring a bell? No kidding. Shelby had no time to worry about Dena or her nipples. She had her own erect nipple problems. They were pointing across the Atlantic.

You got it. Both Shelby and Dena were so far gone that Answer D is the only plausible choice. That's D for Delusion. "A fixed, dominating, or persistent false mental conception, resistant to reason with regard to actual things or matters of fact."[16]

---

[16] *Webster's Encyclopedic Unabridged Dictionary of the English Language*, 1989

India returned the book to Shelby. "Okay, so it's clear one half of your transformation was complete. You were definitely delusional," she began and shook her head in puzzlement. "But I just don't understand."

"Understand what?" Shelby asked accommodatingly.

"I just don't understand how either of you could have possibly thought that these transatlantic relationships with men who'd treated you so shabbily could ever work? What made you so delusional?"

"I can only speak for myself," Shelby explained. "Being with Giancarlo was the only time in my life I remembered being truly happy and fully alive. I wanted that feeling again."

"And you thought returning to the scene of the crime would do that for you?" India probed.

"I guess so. So sue me!" Shelby admitted with eyes fiery with defiance.

"And what about you?" India trained her gaze on Dena.

"It might not make sense to anyone. But I make no apologies. I'd felt unattractive for years. Nicola literally brought me back to life in that regard. Made me feel things I thought I'd die without ever feeling again." Tears formed in Dena's eyes, but she pressed on. "I felt sexy and alive again, and nothing and no one was going to turn back the clock on that."

"Have you ever heard the term midlife crisis?" Shelby chided their companion. "Chalk it up to that."

India had no choice but to accept the explanation. "Okay, even if I give you that, you mean to tell me no one tried to talk sense into the two of you?"

"Please, please!" Shelby said with open irritation. "How stupid do you really think we are?"

Don't make me answer that, India thought. But she remained quiet.

"We had more sense than to tell anyone our real plans," Dena revealed. "We barely admitted the truth to each other."

"What do you mean?" asked India.

Yes, they were home. They were miserable. And, most of all, they were desperate. Desperate to return to Italy and the men they had left behind.

Within a few weeks, Dena had hopped a train down to the city to visit her friend. She suggested eating Italian.

"Didn't get enough in Italy," Shelby shot back sarcastically.

"That was just an appetizer," Dena winked. "I need to go back for the main course."

"Go back? Where?"

"Italy, naturally. And *you're* going to help me." Dena reached in her purse and plucked out a dog-eared piece of paper. She handed it to her friend.

Shelby put on her reading glasses. With each word, her eyes ballooned further, and her mouth opened wider. When she finished, she fixed her gaze on Dena, who was sitting there with a gleam in her eye.

"You're writing to Nicola? About buying an apartment in Italy?" Suspicion lurked in Shelby's questions. "What are you up to?"

"Nothing," Dena denied with ease. "I love Italy, and just thought I'd get a little piece of property."

Shelby couldn't believe her ears. What did Dena take her for? The girl wanted a piece all right. But it wasn't of terra firma, just firma, and Shelby said as much to her friend.

"Believe what you like," Dena shot back. "But can you look me straight in the eye, and tell me the thought of returning hasn't occurred to you?"

Shelby took a sip of her Chianti, refusing to respond to the accusation. Instead, she changed the subject, smugly pointing out that Dena didn't know Nicola's last name or his address. But, if Shelby thought these facts would put paid to her friend's latest scheme, she was wrong. Dena had it all figured out.

"Don't you worry about that. I'll send it to the Buca," she announced. "The only thing I need from you is translating services."

"That's all?" Shelby asked with distrust.

"Well, yeah, and...oh, okay," she admitted with a heavy breath. "And for you to go back to Italy with me."

The flinty glare in Shelby's dark brown eyes and the resolute shake of her head told Dena this was going to be a hard sell. Time to pull out all the stops. Motioning to their waiter, she ordered a second glass of wine for both of them. "On second thought, make it a bottle," she told the waiter. That would loosen her up.

Then, Dena launched her campaign, reminding Shelby of how much she loved the country and her dreams about a life with Giancarlo. At the mention of Giancarlo, Shelby seemed to soften a bit. Her eyes lost their hardness and suspicion, and her shoulders shed their tenseness.

"But we'll look like two fools," she hesitated.

"Not if we actually *are* going to look at property," Dena countered. The ladies shared a sly smile. And the conspiracy was born.

Over the next few days, Dena and Shelby's fertile brains kicked into overdrive. How to return to Italy and maintain a modicum of dignity, not only in the eyes of the world at large, but in each other's? Not a problem.

On one of their endless phone calls, Dena proudly suggested they purchase an apartment in Florence big enough for them, Dena's kids, and their mothers for vacation. It was the perfect solution, an investment property they could rent out. "It'll pay for itself," she declared.

How expensive could an apartment in Florence be? It wasn't New York, after all. Ah, the simpleminded egotism of these two American women. Suffice it to say, after roughly two minutes consulting their real estate agent, also Mr. Web, the would-be realty moguls were forced to accept a disappointing reality. Someone had discovered Florence before them. The ladies couldn't afford a manhole cover in the city, never mind an apartment. On to Plan B.

"How about import-export?" Dena suggested. But of what?

Shelby remembered the cookie jars she had purchased in Capri, whose arrival she'd been eagerly awaiting. They were only reproductions, but originals were rare, and their prices were going through the roof. As soon as the cookie jars arrived from Capri, they would contact the manufacturer.

A few weeks later, Shelby was nearly beside herself with anticipation when the UPS man knocked on her door. After he handed her the box, she grew a tad concerned when she heard the contents moving around.

"Like cereal," the delivery man explained. "The contents are settling."

Somewhat mollified, Shelby signed for the package and sent the man on his way. Grabbing a box cutter, her hands trembled with excitement as she tore through the heavy-duty packing tape. She pulled out the first bubble-wrapped piece. Something wasn't right. Even through the wrapping she felt jagged edges. Tape undone, tiny shards of shiny, multicolored ceramic spilled onto the floor.

She grabbed the next piece, hoping Mammy had fared better than the Chef, as she opened it with shaking hands. She tried, but couldn't stop the tears for the once beautiful jars. The damned UPS man was right. They had definitely settled, but not before they'd fought to the death. This Mammy and Chef had fried their last pork chop and had baked their last sweet potato pie and melt-in-your-mouth flaky light biscuit.

Shelby decided to wait until Dena came to the city for a weekend visit to break the sad news. She was hoping an Italian restaurant and a glass...or two..of Chianti would soften the blow.

"Forget importing cookie jars," she began.

"Why, what happened?" Dena whined with dismay.

"They arrived in pieces smaller than the Oreo cookie bits they were meant to hold. It's a sign," Shelby hissed, her eyes saucer wide with fear.

Dena rolled golden brown eyes in exasperation. Here we go again. Some of her airy fairy mumbo jumbo.

"We're not supposed to go back to Italy," Shelby decreed predictably.

I knew it. Some perfectly normal occurrence, and she's convinced it's some crazy sign from on high. Bammo...and just like that, the trip's off. Over my dead body.

"Everything will end up in broken pieces, just like my jars. Count me out," Shelby concluded.

"Broken pieces? What are you babbling on about?" Dena screeched.

Shelby didn't care what Dena thought. Lightening wasn't going to strike her twice if she could help it. "Look, my life ended up shot to hell once because of Giancarlo. I'm not interested in it happening again. And if you know what's good for you, you won't let your little teenage fascination with Nicola blow your life to pieces."

"Pieces? Pieces?" Dena eyes bulged. Her mouth contorted in shock and anger. She was practically shaking.

"Calm yourself, have a sip of wine," Shelby said.

"I don't need any damn wine," Dena shot back in disgust. Nonetheless, she took a healthy gulp before continuing. "The only thing getting blown to pieces is my plan, and Nicola has nothing to do with that. My supposed best friend is taking care of that rather nicely."

A silence grew between the women. Against her will, an avalanche of conflicting feelings descended on Dena. Unwelcome visions of her children's hurt and angry faces overtook her, burying the blissful images of her time with Nicola. "Maybe it's for the best," she finally admitted with resignation.

That was easy, almost too easy, Shelby thought. What's the strumpet up to? Sneaking off to Italy without me? "For the best?" she repeated disbelievingly.

Dena didn't answer, instead allowing bits and pieces of her home life to run like a movie reel through her mind. Finally, she began confiding in her friend.

"Adie, call your father for lunch," Dena bade her youngest.

"Where is he?" Adie asked her mother.

"Where he always is these days," Dena muttered to herself. Outside in the yard, adding yet another stone to the Eighth Wonder of the World, the Great Wall of Millbrook.

As the family was gathered on the deck for their traditional Sunday afternoon meal, Maurice wondered aloud what this Sunday's family game would be...volleyball or bocce ball.

"Playin' mom?" Giselle turned to her mother. Silence greeted the hopeful question. "Mom!"

"Hmm?" Dena mumbled by way of an answer, her eyes never leaving the newspaper.

"Mom! Are you listening to me?" barked Giselle. "Ohhhhhh, but if I were Shelby, you'd answer me."

"Yeah, she's the only one you have time for these days," Maurice cut in.

"MOM!" Giselle poked her mother in the arm angrily.

"Si, si," Dena answered distractedly. Still, she never looked up from the newsprint.

"See Poppa, did you hear her? Si, si. She did that to us in the store. She says it everywhere. People think she's lost it," Maurice accused. Turning back to his mother, he erupted, his face contorted with anger. "The word is YES. We're in the United States. We speak English. The word is Yes, Y-E-S. Got it?"

Not to be outdone, little Adelaide joined in. "Yeah Poppa, you should've heard her trying to talk Italian with Mr. Lucca the other day. He was laughing at her." Dena's youngest shook her head in disgust. "It was sad."

"It's nice to learn another language," Dena defended herself.

But it was too late. The floodgate had been opened and a torrent of angry, pent-up emotion followed in its wake. With rapid fire precision, the children shot off their laundry list of gripes. We eat pasta every night. Every shoe, hat, skirt or dress she buys has to be Italian. She can't pass an Italian restaurant without wanting to stop in. No more French wine for Mom, no, it's got to be Italian. And guess what, Poppa, she was on the Internet looking for Italian cars...Fiats, Lancias, Lamborghinis, Ferraris, and Maserati.

"And that stupid newspaper she's always reading," Giselle concluded the tirade, "Oggi America. It's Italian."

"You know what's she looking for in it, don't you, Poppa? A house or an apartment."

"Or a willow!" little Adie chirped up.

"No, you dope," Maurice sneered at his sister. "A villa, not a willow. In Italy. She wants to leave!" he screamed with accusing eyes shooting at his mother. With that, her son threw his napkin on his plate, knocked his chair backwards, and stormed to his room. The next sound within earshot was the angry slamming of doors.

Dena looked at her husband and daughters. It seemed as if the eyes of the world were on her. In any event, the eyes of her world were. Tears of anger and hurt spilled down Adie's and Giselle's faces. Again, Dena brought her gaze to Luke. There she saw hurt, anger, and blame staring back at her.

"You'd better go talk to him," he said quietly.

Just as Dena finished reliving her family woes, the waiter arrived with the ladies' lunches.

"So, let me get this straight," Shelby began. "You want me to go back with you so your kids can resent me even more than they already do? What did you say to Maurice?"

"Oh, they do not hate you," Dena pooh-poohed.

It was worse than Shelby had feared. She'd never said the word hate. She could see it all clearly. She'd visit for one of their birthdays. They'd celebrate with a glass of one of Dena's fine Chiantis...that those three little angels had secretly laced with arsenic. She'd gasp for breath as they laughed in her face. Oh no, they didn't hate her.

Taking note of the mistrusting look on her friend's face, Dena continued. "Really, don't worry. I've taken care of the situation. I talked with Maurice, and the girls, too."

"Really?" Shelby asked, her voice doubtful. Did Dena really think she was fooling her? "Situations like that don't get re-solved that easily."

"Okay, Shelby, want the pure unvarnished truth? Here it is," Dena's voice quivered with raw emotion.

Slowly at first, then gathering the speed of tumbleweed in a southwest wind storm, the words came overflowing. Yes, her kids were upset about her relationship, or lack thereof, with their father. Yes, they were resentful of Italy and everything to do with Italy, including Shelby. Yes, Dena's desire to live in Italy frightened them. And yes, everything Dena was doing threatened to shatter not only her own life, but her entire family's into tiny bits, just like those poor cookie jars.

Shelby listened as her friend catalogued what she already knew must be true. "Then what the hell are you thinking?" she asked, her voice not without compassion.

Dena raised her hands in sad defeat. "It's no use denying my feelings," she began and stopped, not sure what to say next.

How did she explain to anyone, including her best friend, what she was feeling? That much as she loved her kids, as important as they were to her, it wasn't enough. She looked at Shelby, her eyes almost pleading for understanding, and gave it a stab.

"I cannot go back to simply being someone's mother. I need to be more than that. I *am* more than that. I know it's hurting them, but if I don't have a life I think is worth living, how do I teach my children to have one? And, won't that hurt them more in the long run?"

Shelby nodded her head in an agreement she really didn't feel. Dear Dena, she thought to herself, that heart wrenching little speech may all be so terribly true, but I know something else that's just as true. Nicola, and more importantly, little Nicola are the life you're looking for.

Still, who am I to criticize, Shelby argued with herself. She may not have had children, but six years ago, she'd had a mother whose heart she'd broken every time she talked about moving to Italy for Giancarlo. And don't forget those Hershey bars. But she couldn't live her life for Junior any more than she could live it for her mother. And, Dena couldn't live hers solely for her kids.

"All right! I guess the trip's back on," Shelby relented. "But what about my signs from the universe?"

Dena beamed at her triumph. She could count on one finger the times she'd won an argument with Shelby. This one was it. Regardless, Dena was very careful not to gloat for fear her vanquished friend would do an about face. "Don't worry. That's only a sign it's time for Plan C," she soothed.

It didn't take long for the co-conspirators to hatch another scheme. Shelby had a passion for browsing through thrift shops. Actually, her real passion was getting something dirt cheap. Like mother, like daughter. In all her travels to Italy, she'd never come across such a place. Maybe it was time to introduce Italy to the joys of secondhand shopping.

It sounded like a good idea, so Dena dusted off her international business textbook. She spent so much time searching on the computer that it's believed she's one of the few persons who has actually reached the end of the Internet. She was giddy with excitement as she researched for their business plan.

Then, after a rather disheartening conversation with an Italian citizen, Shelby had to place a call that would burst her friend's bubble. She was afraid her news might break Dena in two, but it had to be done.

"Listen, I spoke to somebody who's Italian," she began cautiously. "He howled at our idea. Seems Italians would rather stroll through the piazza naked than be caught shopping for, or wearing, used clothes. I'm telling you, it's another sign."

"You and these damned signs!" Dena swore. She was about to say more, but got no further.

"Hold on a minute," Shelby whispered quickly. She had called Dena from the law library, and just then, a judge was looking down at her demanding assistance.

With saccharine politeness, Shelby focused her attention on his needs. Instantly, she tossed a book to him, not unlike throwing raw meat at a pack of hungry wolves. It was enough to send the half-dead octogenarian jurist on his way.

"I'm back," she said to her friend, returning to the phone. "I swear I'm going to shoot myself. They really don't pay me enough for all this aggravation!"

"You? Try not getting paid at all," Dena countered.

And the friends were off and running, trading complaints, running neck and neck for the Triple Crown of Misery. Back and forth they shot their poison arrows.

Try dealing with an irrational boss....How about an irrational husband...Being a personal slave to library patrons constantly asking for something...My little slave drivers are named Giselle, Maurice, and Adelaide...Patrons who don't re-shelve their books...Kids who don't pick up their toys...Getting up at 6:30am to get to work...Getting up at 6:00am to get the kids to school.

Shelby had run out of ammunition. So, with strategic precision, Dena moved in for the kill. "Do you think any of these may be signs, too? Signs that we need to get the hell out of here?"

"I hear you," Shelby conceded. "Bring on Plan C(1)."

The surrounding Tuscan countryside was quite beautiful. Maybe they should consider it. Yes, there was the minor inconvenience of transportation into Florence for the nightlife, but they'd cross that bridge when they got to it. They were flexible. They could adapt, which was a good thing. Because these modern day explorers...well, let's just say they quickly found out that someone had caught on to the Tuscan countryside before them, too.

And so, the wannabee real property tycoons moved on to Plan C(2). If they couldn't afford anything on the leg of the Italian boot, perhaps they should move down to its heel to the warm, sunny, and utterly magical region of Calabria. It wasn't long before Dena found a villa in the town of Cosenza. Fortuitously, the owner was in the States for a visit, and a few phone calls later, Maria had agreed to mail pictures of her property.

Dena could barely contain herself. The price was doable, it was big enough, and it was a villa blessed with Italian marble throughout. And the pièce de résistance? Only ten minutes from the sea. Twice a day, Dena skipped off to the post office praying for a first glimpse at her new home and dream life. Shelby, while not quite as enthusiastic, had to acknowledge that the price was right. However, while Dena was convinced that everything was coming up roses, Shelby wasn't so sure.

"Those roses you smell? Probably more like skunk cabbage," she said, trying to bring Dena back into the earth's atmosphere. Besides, wasn't the south a bit dangerous? Bandits on the road? The Mafia? Kidnappings? Another thing, wasn't goat a popular dish down there? And if it was such a tourist area, why hadn't Messrs. Frommer and Fodor mentioned it?

Finally, the pictures arrived. Dena was ready to book their tickets immediately. Never mind that her children guffawed like hyenas when they got a gander at the "villa." Even Maurice, budding entrepreneur and Dena's staunchest supporter of late, couldn't imagine anyone making a thin dime off the place.

And husband Luke? Well, he just shook his head with pity in his eyes. She could almost hear the wheels turning in his head, could almost divine his thoughts. Maybe my friends are right. Perhaps, it is time to consider committing her. Should I call the man with the white coat and net tonight, or should I give her one last evening with the kids?

Still, Dena refused to let these nay-sayers dampen her enthusiasm. Just wait until Shelby sees it, she thought, as she scanned and emailed her friend the pictures before calling her.

"Now, Shelby, keep an open mind when you see our villa. Use your imagination, and remember a can of paint can work wonders."

How can one accurately describe Shelby's reaction? If her husband asks, my vote would be for the men in white coats to come tonight. Poor Luke and the little ones. Perhaps, I should catch the next train upstate. They'll need me when they take my dear, delusional friend away. A can of paint! If they're called in for a consult, Bob Vila and the entire crew of *This Old House* will quite possibly face their first failure.

On to Plan C (3). A lovely hotel in Santa Fiora, a mere eighty miles south of Florence. They'd be real estate magnates. Hoteliers – the Leona Helmsleys of Tuscany. Okay, perhaps not quite Leonas. After all, the hotel only had twenty-four rooms, most with shared bathrooms and probably all with bedbugs. But all that really mattered was that there were two rooms with private bath, one for Dena and one for Shelby. The paying guests would have to make do with more meager accommodations.

A few emails back and forth across the Atlantic, and the pictures arrived of a quite lovely hotel. Finally, Dena and Shelby had something they could agree on. This was worth pursuing, and they began lining up investors.

Meanwhile, Luke was busy with some lining up of his own. The friends and family of both women for an intervention. They were like addicts. Luke had never spoken to Shelby's ex Junior before. But maybe it was time. Luke liked Shelby, had always thought she had a pretty good head on her shoulders. Maybe she still did. Just one problem. It was empty. And as for Dena, well, she was the mother of his children. For their sake, he had to try to reel his wife back to reality.

But Dena and Shelby were too far gone. Soon the ladies had dupes set up from Millbrook all the way down the Hudson River to the Big Apple. Friends and family had agreed to invest and share in their delusion. It was full steam ahead.

"We're buying a hotel!" Dena screeched with elation.

So, how does one prepare for an overseas real estate transaction? Find an international attorney? Make an appointment with realtors and the local Board of Tourism? Gather statistical data? Develop a business plan? Yes, these are all essential fundamentals taught in Real Estate Investment 101. Did the ladies do any of these things?

"Did Luke know the names of any real estate attorneys that deal in Italian properties?" Shelby asked her friend one evening.

"I forgot to ask him about that. How much info did you turn up about running hotels?" came Dena's answer.

"I've been so busy, I never got around to searching."

When Dena probed further, Shelby blamed her To Do List. "It's a mile long," she complained.

"What's on it?" Dena asked.

"Well, buy new underwear, get a new bathing suit..."

"Don't forget a sun hat. I hear the summers in Florence are brutal," Dena added.

"Yeah, and I need to find a hairdresser to give me a fab new 'do."

"Oh, yes, we'll be DIVAS! They'll be putty in our hands."

"Who? The real estate agents?" Shelby asked.

"Of course, who else?

Chapter 9

*T*he next three months were a whirlwind of activity for the manic travelers. They needed manicures, pedicures, depilatories, precious oils, and haircuts and color.

Briefly, Dena contemplated a bit of plastic surgery. After all, Nicola was a young thing, a tadpole, and she was hoping to be his young thing. Or, at the very least, appear to be. "My doctor's having a sale," she told Shelby.

"Sale? On plastic surgery?" Shelby had never heard of such a thing.

"Yes, it's a buy one, get one half price," Dena explained. "What should we have done?"

Shelby had no intention of letting anybody touch her body, especially someone offering tummy tucks and face lifts like a McDonald's special. Besides, she didn't need it. She had the genes of her African ancestors coursing through her. Her eighty-something-year-old grandmother looked twenty years younger. Everybody knew black didn't crack. And if Dena knew what was good for her, she'd pass on this all-beef patty with special sauce. The man was probably a charlatan.

"I can see it now," Shelby told her friend. "Your little nip and tuck doesn't heal right. One gander at your Frankenstein stitches, and Nicola will head for the Pyrenees."

Horrified at the prospect, Dena nixed that idea and settled for a day at a beauty spa. Polished and buffed, they were on to Stage Two. Shopping. Shopping for what? Business suits? Briefcases? Legal pads? Only if those items could be purchased in Victoria's Secret, Saks, Marshall's, Sephora, or any shoe store in their path. Make that war path.

The emerging divas were engaged in warfare. This called for battle dress and war paint. But this was no ordinary war. No, this was a war of love and lust, necessitating strategic planning and state-of-the-art weaponry. Their battle fatigues would be matching bras and panties. Fire power more lethal than hand grenades would be provided by skin-caressing dresses, daring teddies, and string bikinis. Clinique, Revlon, and Lancome were hired mercenaries drafted to provide the ladies' war paint. They vowed to die with their combat boots on. In this case, those boots would be strappy sandals, hopefully pointed straight in the air at the moment the enemy unconditionally surrendered.

With military precision, our Barbie Doll combatants (correction, Barbie's mother) plotted their course and picked their targets. From Poughkeepsie to Manhattan, with a detour through Danbury, Connecticut, no mall was safe as the ladies laid siege, store by store, department by department, sales counter by sales counter.

At one point, Shelby had to make a strategic retreat and call for reinforcements. Her credit card had suffered a meltdown from being swiped one too many times. In a frantic call to customer service, she explained that to crush the enemy and bring him to his knees, she needed not only a new card, but an increase in her spending limit. Her demands were met, and with new weapon in hand, she continued her advance.

One would think that with all this shopping, the ladies' armaments would be complete. Not. Two provisions remained necessary to supplement their war gear and render them battle ready.

First, helmets. But not metal helmets for these comrades in arms. Their headgear would consist of straw, lace, linen, and feathers. Millinery of the finest quality. But how to transport it?

On one of her shopping sprees, Dena found the perfect answer. She bought two, one for each of them. Then, she called her friend with the surprise.

"Hatboxes? Have you lost your mind? Don't we have enough to carry?" Shelby said ungratefully.

"But what could be more diva-like than a hatbox?" Dena countered. Shelby couldn't come up with an answer. And with that, surely their shopping was complete.

Again, Dena had other ideas, and on her next trip down to the city, she reminded Shelby they had one more important stop to make to the drug store.

Shelby was puzzled. What had Dena forgotten? Aspirin, sunscreen, Gas-X, facial wax?

"No, no. We need protection. You know, little raincoats," Dena elucidated.

"You're going to the pharmacy for a raincoat?" asked Shelby, more confused than ever.

"Let's just say there are heads other than ours that need helmets," Dena said with a sly grin.

Finally, Shelby's eyes lit up with comprehension. Practicing safe sex was their mantra. The ladies' battle shields would not be molded iron, crest-emblazoned works of art as carried by the knights of old. Theirs would be crafted of the sturdiest latex available. So, at the very pinnacle of their delusional state, both ladies purchased massive quantities of industrial strength condoms. With that, the transformation was complete, and it wasn't going unnoticed.

"Luke and the kids think I've lost my mind," Dena told her friend over the phone one hot July day.

"*Noooo*," Shelby denied. She wondered what had taken them so long.

"Just because I'm wearing fishnets and heels. What's wrong with that?" Dena continued.

"Ohhh, I bet you look ab fab. Where are you off to?"

"Off to? Nowhere. I'm grilling hotdogs on the deck," Dena said.

Okay, how can I let the poor thing down easy? "Well, maybe they have a point, dear," Shelby answered. "Perhaps you should save the fishnets and heels for filet mignon or lobster night. But I really can't talk about this now. Gotta go."

"Why, does a judge need something?"

Shelby peered out from under the cocked rim of her red straw hat. It matched her outfit perfectly.

"No, the library's pretty quiet. Thank God, they're leaving me alone today. It's just my hat's off kilter from talking on the phone. I need to straighten it."

No wonder they were leaving her alone. The hat is not the only thing a little off kilter, Dena mused. "You've got a hat on in the library?" she asked with disbelief

"Yes, and heels. What else would a diva wear?"

Finally, they were THE DIVAS, legends in their own minds. These soldiers were ready to bear arms. And here comes a Diva Do/n't.

Diva Do/n't

Divas don't really bear arms, but do bare anything else to reveal their charms.

The military objective? To march on Italy and emerge victorious. But Dena's and Shelby's was no ordinary march. The Diva March had been born on the catwalks of Milan, Paris and New York. Day after day, the ladies practiced strutting and swinging their hips, one foot in front of the other like a supermodel, all the while trying not to trip over their feet. This took some doing, and Shelby still bears (not bares) a trick hip from tripping over her feet one too many times.

Readiness is a relative term, and actually, there were a few things left to attend to, one of which defied the law of physics. Combat readiness requires all good soldiers be able to carry their own mobility bags on their backs and move out on a moment's notice of deployment. The ladies were in trouble. They had started packing their bags five days before departure, and Dena was about to issue an insubordination citation to three rogue pairs of shoes which refused take their proper place in her suitcase. The resourcefulness of a diva should never be underestimated. She gets what she wants, and Dena wanted these shoes. Giving new meaning to keeping something under her hat, she tucked her stray shoes in her hatbox.

"And, Bob's your uncle, you ladies are finally ready to find your place under the Tuscan sun," India concluded.

"Exactly," Dena concurred.

"Or more accurately, to find your places under someone's Tuscan son...s-o-n," snickered India.

This one was probably here trying to soak up some sun and son herself, Shelby thought. But with that pasty complexion, no doubt she struck out on both counts.

"So now I see how this diva thing was born, but mind if I ask a question?" India summed up.

Would it matter if we did, you nosy Brit? Almost three hundred years gone by, and you're still meddling in American affairs. Dena smothered a threatening giggle at her double entendre. "We're all friends here," she lied. "Fire away."

The Englishwoman opened her mouth to start, and then, closed it. Again, she made another attempt. A second time, her mouth closed without a sound. It was easy to see she was struggling for the right words yet again. Finally, she seemed to have found them.

"Well, to use your own words, you practically overdosed on sexy underwear, hats, shoes, dresses, mani-pedis, new hairstyles, makeovers, waxing every body part known to man ..."

"I think we get the picture," Shelby interrupted. "Your point?" She didn't know the English could get themselves this worked up. It didn't look good on old pasty face, but could be quite attractive in a man. Maybe Dena's and her next trip should be to London.

"My point is this diva thing seems rather superficial." India hesitated a bit to gauge the ladies' reaction. Perhaps, she'd gone too far. But when neither Dena nor Shelby seemed in the least

uncomfortable, she forged ahead. "It's like you believe the only way to get a man is by trading on sexual currency."

The ladies remained silent, but their minds were abuzz. Well, at least we have some to spend, Shelby thought snidely. By the looks of it, you're stone broke in that department. Dena was bit kinder in her ruminations. Poor India, she's just a bit envious. But a little makeup and a good haircut, and she could be presentable. Maybe.

The silence that greeted her didn't deter the British woman. She'd gone this far and was determined to proceed. "So, why did you choose this way? As if what you were wasn't good enough. Don't you think that some women may find all of this a bit insulting?"

"Maybe I didn't think I was good enough," admitted Shelby. "I had never felt sexy or seductive. That's not a thing my family ever put a premium on. School and achieving. That's what was important."

"So what changed?" India probed.

"Giancarlo dumping me. That's what changed. My God, he chose a woman with the brain of a peanut, who was literally an obsessive compulsive and a slob, all of which he readily admitted," Shelby burst out. "But by God, she'd been a model! And I guess that's what mattered to him...her looks."

Part of India was sorry she'd asked, sorry she'd touched a raw nerve, but not sorry enough. She turned to Dena. "And you? You never felt sexy either?"

Could you get those spotlights out of my eyes, Inspector Gadget, Dena thought to herself. "Oh no, I had always thought that I was sexy and desirable. Unfortunately, that's the only thing I ever felt confident about."

Bully for you, thought the Englishwoman jealously. "So you didn't need to become a diva...you already were one," India postulated.

"Hell, no! I needed it alright," Dena contradicted Scotland Yard's newest recruit. "Years of scooping up baby poop, cat poop, chicken poop, and hamster poop, took care of any confidence I did have."

"But plenty of women do those things and still feel sexy," countered India.

I suppose they do, Dena thought. But let them try maintaining it living in the boondocks. Not having much life outside of the home. Marriage going down the tubes and an unsympathetic husband as their only mirror...doesn't make for a pretty reflection staring back at you. She didn't say any of this aloud. Suddenly, Dena was tired of explaining herself.

Shelby didn't need an explanation, practically able to read her friend's mind. She knew how depressed and lonely Dena had been for years. She crossed her legs and leaned forward, ready to do battle, to defend her best friend.

"Well, India, perhaps it is insulting to other women. Okay, and even to ourselves at times," she admitted. Then, she paused and gave the matter a bit of thought. "But the femme fatale delusion got us out of our rut. And eventually, it carried over into other areas of our lives. So, why should we apologize for it?"

India would have liked to argue the point, and searched her mind for an answer, but for once, the Englishwoman was stumped. She let the ladies continue their tale.

One o'clock in the afternoon, and Shelby left the law library floating on air. She was on her way to Italy and Giancarlo again. Promising to send postcards, she bid her co-workers a teary-eyed arrivederci, telling one and all that she would miss them terribly. Two steps out the library door, her determined eyes dried faster than a New York second. For the next two weeks, she would not spare a moment's thought for her job or her co-workers. She was a Diva, after all. It was all about her. Should one need a Diva Do/n't to remind them of this, here it is:

A diva does not miss a soul; being missed by others should be her goal.

Certainly, Shelby had more important things on her mind than her co-workers and the postcards she'd promised but had no earthly intention of wasting time writing or mailing. As her subway train made its way uptown, she daydreamed about the beautiful clothes packed in her suitcases and the glittering events to which she'd wear them. Would Giancarlo take her to a movie premiere? Or better yet, she wondered if it was Fashion Week in Milan. A quick trip to see Prada, Pucci, Versace. And in the evening, the opera at La Scala would be divine.

But she was getting ahead of herself. There was still this evening, and the romantic dinner planned with the love of her life. Well, at least the one on this side of the Atlantic.

With much effort, Shelby had managed to put her relationship with Rick in perspective. She'd concluded long ago that a friend who genuinely cared was hard to come by, and Rick had proven to be just that over the years.

Still, although she'd chosen to fly in the face of conventional wisdom and accept poor Rick's one weakness, his marriage, her largesse was not boundless. Rick must pay a price for his faults. Hark! Can there be another Diva Do/n't so soon?

Diva Do/n't

When the duties of his office one man cannot fulfill, do enlist runners-up to fill the bill.

Shelby and Rick met for dinner that evening. He wanted to see her before she took off for Italy and Giancarlo, whom he knew about all too well. He'd chosen one of their favorite Indian restaurants. Their corner table, together with the soft, low candlelight, lent just the romantic touch Richard had wanted.

When he'd picked her up, Rick had been smiling and in a good mood, but even in candlelight, Shelby could see the tension just beneath the surface. It didn't take long before he broached the thorny issue.

"Giancarlo? I'm not going to see Giancarlo. I keep telling you we're going to look at a hotel," she reiterated for the umpteenth time.

"Right," he fired back. The sarcasm in his voice matched the disbelieving smile on his face. "And if you buy it, you'll be moving to Italy. Where does that leave me?"

Shelby couldn't believe what she was hearing. She leaned across the table and spoke in a low, deliberate voice. "Let me see...with your beautiful wife and children, where you've always been?" she returned smoothly. "Not exactly as out in the cold as I've been."

They decided to call a truce and enjoy the time they had together. Rick took her home and saw her to her door. Shelby turned to him, brushing her lips across his cheek and stroking his neck with her hand. When Rick tried to draw her closer, she put up a token resistance. Then, his arms became more insistent, and she rubbed her body against him.

"I can feel Little Rick wants to come out and play," she teased.

"Mmmmm," he groaned seductively. "Let's go in."

Shelby squirmed out of his grasp. "I don't know...." she hesitated.

D-day, as in Diva Day, dawned bright and sunny. The only tomorrow that mattered had finally arrived. The ladies were leaving for Florence.

"Arse!" the Englishwoman let fly. "Damned if you're not doing it again."

What a Peeping Tom the woman is. Shelby had to laugh to herself, but her face was all innocence. "Doing what?" she asked.

"Leaving me hanging!" answered the Englishwoman.

"I really don't think I should say anymore," Shelby prevaricated.

The Englishwoman looked over at Dena. "Give me that journal," she demanded. "There must be a DIQ Test Question that'll help me."

Dena shook her head, indicating India was mistaken. But seeing the Englishwoman did not believe her, she handed her the book. Soon, India realized that Dena was telling the truth. No illuminating test question. Nevertheless, Dena hadn't left her high and dry, having opened the book to the perfect Diva Do/n't for just this situation.

Diva Do/n't

Unless her bank account would swell, a diva doesn't kiss and tell.

A flash of grudging admiration played across India's face. "I'll say one thing for you two," she hesitated, as if trying to find the right words. "With all your ribbing each other, you certainly do stick together."

Then, in the blink of an eye, India's look of admiration slipped into one of profound sadness and loss. "Annabel and I used to be like that."

Shelby would have been content to let the moment pass, not prying into her pain, but not Dena. Hell, here we are spilling our guts. What's her story, she wondered. "India," Dena said, pulling the Brit from her silent musing. "This isn't the first time you've mentioned your friend Annabel. What happened with you two?"

The fear in her face made Shelby and Dena feel like KGB operatives. India's eyes darted quickly in either direction, as if searching for a means of escape. Then came a look of resignation. She had to talk about this with someone. Who better than two dopes she'd never see again?

"She told me my husband Malcolm was cheating on me!" India blurted out. Unwelcome tears welled up.

"Oh!" both her companions gasped in unison.

India swiped the tears from her eyes, and sat up a little straighter. With great effort, she gathered herself together. "Of course, she was lying through her teeth," she said with pent-up anger.

Dena and Shelby looked on in amazement as the tirade from this characteristically reserved Briton burst forth like the released waters of a dam.

"Had the nerve to tell me that she thought the man I have been married to for over twenty years, the father of my two children and my soulmate was having an affair with a co-worker. Claimed she saw them at a restaurant holding hands."

India's words erupted like the lava of a volcano, too long held within the deep cavern of her mind, and now escaping with a red hot fury. The two ladies stared in amazement as she continued, barely taking a breath.

How does she do it, Shelby wondered. I need a hit of my inhaler just listening to her. A quick glance in her friend's direction, revealed a similar reaction. Dena's chest was noticeably rising and falling, taking in deep breaths, almost as if trying to breathe for India.

"Naturally, I marched right home to confront Malcolm," India's words shot out with rapid fire precision. "And he immediately explained that he had only been consoling the poor woman over her terminally-ill mother. It's easy to understand Annabel's

misinterpretation, but when I told her dear Malcolm's side of things... Well, then she went too far."

Throughout her tale, the Englishwoman seemed to become increasing agitated. Absentmindedly, she fidgeted with her wedding ring, twirling it round and round.

Fear of setting off India again warred with blatant curiosity inside Shelby. Curiosity won. "Too far how?" she asked.

"The tart had the audacity to tell me that my Malcolm had propositioned her. As if he'd ever do that with anyone, never mind my best friend!" India's eyes filled with hurt and anger.

"But didn't you say you'd been friends for thirty-five years?" asked Shelby.

Dena picked up on the train of thought. "What would possess a trusted friend to tell you something like that?"

Both women looked at the Englishwoman skeptically.

"Oh, that's easy. Her marriage had ended a few years earlier. Malcolm theorizes she is lonely and jealous. There's a lot of truth in that old adage that misery loves company," India said with supreme confidence.

Another doubtful look passed between the friends. Obviously, they weren't the only two with a touch of the delusional.

"So, you and Annabel?" Dena urged.

"Annabel and I haven't spoken in three years."

Dena's eyes widened in shock. "I don't know how I'd make it without speaking to Shelby for that long. She keeps me sane."

Shelby nodded in agreement. "And Dena me. It's a shame about you and Annabel."

India batted her hand at the air, as if the state of affairs was completely inconsequential. "Hardly," she contradicted. "A friend like that is no friend at all. But enough about Annabel. Let's get back to you two and Diva Day."

D-day, as in Diva Day, dawned bright and sunny. But Dena and Shelby, who believed that they'd alchemized themselves into femme fatales and were about to conquer what was left of the Roman Empire, really didn't care. Hail the size of golf balls falling from the sky, or a twister relocating people's homes to the next state, would have been just as fine, as long as the skies cleared in time for their plane to taxi down the runway and take off. The ladies were leaving for Florence, and all was right with their world.

While divas are by definition independent and resourceful women, they are also the first to recognize the usefulness of having a good man in their lives to smooth life's sometimes rocky path. The role this man plays in the diva's life can be varied.

Contrary to how she felt in her bad moments, Dena had to admit that her good man happened to still be Luke. Years ago, he and she had begun to lead separate lives. So, he was not about to drive his beloved wife to the airport. However, Luke did arrange for a driver to get her there. But his more important and vital contribution was enabling Dena to finance her vacation. No, Luke didn't arrive home one night and present her with the cash tied in a ribbon, but it didn't matter. The grocery money she'd been pinching from her husband's rather deep pockets had turned into a nice little nest egg. "Enough to let me go to Italy to buy my veggies!" Dena announced.

"Has all the earmarks of embezzlement to me," Shelby had accused.

"It's hardly embezzlement when it's your husband," she justified. "And besides, who's the one who told me to keep a secret bank account years ago. At least, I never did that." And with that, the subject had been quickly dropped.

Sadly, the ladies had learned long ago that the usefulness of a man goes only so far. In the present instance, that usefulness got Dena only as far as curbside at JFK Airport. From there, she was on her own, forced into the very un-divalike position of having to drag, tug, lug, push, and pull her suitcase, carry-on, and hatbox under her own steam. Arriving at the airport, she was extremely appreciative of the skycap, graciously giving the man a few dollars for his troubles on her behalf.

Looking first one way and then the other, she scouted around for her friend, who was nowhere to be found. She would just have to wait. The word "wait" is also a very important one for a diva. They expect to be waited for by others. They love to be waited on by others. But only under very rare and extreme circumstances, do they choose to wait on or for anyone else, even another diva. That being said, Dena tried to calm herself. Don't worry. She'll be here soon.

She maintained this sanguinity for an entire five minutes. Then, she blew. Where the hell is she? She lives in the city, for gods sakes. Is she coming by donkey cart? Let's face it...the girl may not make it in time. Damned if she'll make me miss the plane. I may have needed her in April, and maybe, I thought I needed her this time around. But I'm a diva now. This is a new day. Dear Nicola is awaiting my arrival. He'll most likely be at the airport with flowers in hand.

Yes, one wonders if fresh air was scarce in the airport, and if Dena was suffering from a lack of oxygen. Nevertheless, this does segue quite nicely into another very important Diva Do/n't.

Diva Do/n't

One diva don't stop no show! If she can't keep up, you gotta go.

And given that, Dena decided to check in without her friend. Promptness has its benefits, and she was rewarded for hers. She had no line at check-in, and much to her delight, she was serviced....oops, make that waited on...by a very attractive ground crew employee.

As she stood at the check-in counter, she had only one concern. She wasn't worried whether or not the plane was in good working order, or whether the pilot had been drinking the night before. She didn't care what was being served for dinner. What had kept her awake at night and in a dither was whether her luggage, or more important to her health, whether Shelby's luggage would make it to Pisa. Why in the devil had Dena offered to make the reservations? She knew if Shelby's luggage didn't touch down in Italy, she herself would be touching off for Jupiter free of charge and courtesy of Shelby.

Ah, the benefits and the pitfalls of purchasing airline tickets through Mr. Web. Dena had searched the Internet day and night looking for the best bargain. With summer ticket prices going through the roof, she'd been ecstatic to find tickets for hundreds less on British Airways through Travelocity.com.

"But it's into Pisa. Means we'll have to make our way to Florence," Dena consulted Shelby over the phone.

Agreeing a short train ride was a small price to pay for such a good deal, Dena clicked on purchase. She floated on air, daydreaming about seeing Nicola again, until a few days later when the tickets arrived. As she inspected them, Dena could literally feel the blood leaving her face. Shelby was going to murder her. Careful examination, something Dena should have done before clicking BUY, revealed that their flight landed at London's Heathrow Airport, but it was the connecting flight to

Pisa that had Dena wigged out. That flight left out of London's Gatwick Airport.

> **Traveling Tidbit for the Too-Quick-to-Click Online Ticket Purchasing Traveler:** When traveling via British Airways from the U.S., a change of airports may be necessary if venturing to other European destinations.

Maybe it's not so bad, Dena prayed. She scrambled to the computer, desperate to see the distance between the airports. She let out a frustrated groan at what she saw. They were forty-five miles apart.

Panic set in as the gory possibilities raced through her mind. How could they call this a connecting flight? How were she and Shelby supposed to get from one airport to another? And what about their luggage...Shelby's luggage? She'd die of an asthma attack trying to lug it all.

Yup, Dena thought, I don't know how, but she'll murder me. Slip a pill in my wine, slit my wrists for me, whack me over the head with a beaded purse...filled with rocks. No, that's ridiculous, she laughed to herself. Shelby wouldn't do that. She wouldn't dirty her own hands. She'll probably hire a hit man. Regardless, the details don't matter. However, it happens, Shelby is definitely going to murder me unless I make this disaster go away.

The friendly British Airways travel agent undoubtedly held the phone in midair, trying to escape the offending screech as Dena pounced on her. Finally, the agent was able to get a word in. With reluctance, she revealed the existence of vouchers entitling holders to a free bus trip between airports.

"It took her a while," Dena recounted to Shelby later that evening. "You would have thought the money was being debited straight from the woman's paycheck, but she finally told me we can just pick up vouchers at the British Airways counter at Heathrow." Dena let out a sigh of relief before continuing. "But still, what would've happened if I hadn't called?"

"We'd be paying a mint for a taxi," Shelby answered. And I'd be traveling solo, because you'd be dead or at least slightly maimed, she thought. Keeping mum about this, Shelby moved on to the luggage.

"They say it'll be transferred between airports automatically," Dena reported.

"I don't know," Shelby said warily. "Do you trust it to happen?"

To which Dena lied quite easily. "Of course. What a thoroughly silly question."

"Well, that's helpful to know," India remarked. "Your readers will appreciate the heads up."

"They'd better," declared Shelby. "The disclosure will probably cost us a pretty penny."

"How so?" asked the Englishwoman.

Dena leaned in closer. "We were considering keeping this Traveling Tidbit under our beautiful straw hats," she whispered conspiratorially.

The Englishwoman was clearly confused. "How would that help your readers?"

"Oh, it wouldn't," Shelby admitted, "but if British Airways wanted to deposit a little something-something in an off-shore account for us to keep mum...well, that would be great!" Shelby let the implication hang in the air. With closed eyes, she savored the thought as though it were a rare perfume.

"You mean a kickback or a bribe?" India screeched incredulously.

"Certainly not," Dena denied hotly. "Shelby's a lawyer, and I'm married to one. We like to think of it as a gift...one not worth troubling the IRS about."

"Besides, all that pesky paperwork would cost the government more than it's worth," Shelby rationalized.

San Quentin, here come the Divas, thought India.[17]

"But as usual, we digress," Shelby continued.

Back to the luggage. In truth, Dena was quite concerned that her thongs, bikinis, lacy lingerie, and Imelda Marcos shoe collection might not be waiting for her in Pisa. Considering the

---

[17]Fortunately for their readers, the ladies have decided to forgo yet another opportunity for a British Airways kickback. Since their trip, British Airways no longer transfers luggage between airports. Passengers get the privilege of doing that themselves. Oh, and there's an added bonus these days. Those free vouchers for airport transfer? Discontinued. However, the National Express Bus service would be happy to ferry you and yours between airports for the bargain basement price of 17pounds...roughly$34...each way. Don't forget to add this to your ticket price when celebrating that great deal you got from BA!

gravity of the situation should her luggage be lost, and unable to resist a little flirtation, she decided to pick the brain of the lovely young man behind the airline ticket counter.

"Will my luggage actually make it from Heathrow to Gatwick and on to Pisa, or should I play it safe and transfer it myself?"

With twinkling blue eyes and the flash of a winning smile, the ticket agent assured Dena the luggage would arrive safely. It didn't take much to charm Dena, and she thanked him profusely, all the while wishing his service had included a little more...well, service.

Realizing she had received all she was going to, she gave the gentleman a farewell ta-ta and went on her merry way to await the arrival of her friend. She looked at her watch anxiously. It was getting late. Where the heck was Shelby?

Stuck in her own private hell, a traffic jam on the Brooklyn Belt Parkway with her own good man. Ex-husband Junior wore many hats in Shelby's life: cherished friend, confidante, and protector. Today, he was chauffeur and valet, and not doing a bang up job of it in Shelby's estimation. "You fool! I told you we should have left earlier."

"Don't worry. You'll make it," Junior tried to soothe his agitated ex, all the while wondering how he'd lived in the same house with the woman for ten years.

"We've moved ten feet in as many minutes. Unless you can make this car sprout wings, I'll still be sitting in it when the plane takes off," she shrieked, refusing to be mollified.

Junior spared a quick glance from the road in her direction. A blue vein was throbbing in her forehead. Her eyes were bulging and her mouth contorted in an ugly line. Any minute, her head might start spinning round on her scrawny neck. How far was the nearest church? How much did they charge for exorcisms these days, he mused.

"Oh no. Plane or no, you'll be out of here by then," he shot back.

He'd taken enough. His hand came dangerously close to activating the eject seat, which he'd devised specifically for Shelby during their marriage. It wasn't an elaborate device...quite inexpensive and easily installed. How does one get one of these? Reach over to the front passenger door. Open it. Give a forceful shove to whichever offending creature happens to be sitting there. Preferably while the car's doing upwards of seventy miles per hour. A dangerous smile spread across Junior's face as he fantasized.

Brakes screeching, Junior pulled up in front of the terminal. With lightening speed, he deposited Shelby and her luggage curbside. "She's all yours, my good man. Good luck!" he said as he tossed the skycap a tip and sprinted back to the car. With a wave of his hand, Junior muttered something over the squeal of burning rubber as he made his getaway.

Shelby couldn't quite catch his words. It was either "See you soon" or "She's a loon." No matter, as long as he was back there in two weeks to pick her up.

She'd made it to the airport in time for the flight, but her tardiness would cost her. She had to stand on a line. Obviously the others on line don't know who I am....a newly minted diva. Best to let them remain in their ignorance. No need causing a stir. They'd probably want my autograph...ask to take pictures with me.

While Dena continued obsessing over her luggage, Shelby had a more immediate concern. Their seating arrangements weren't quite up to snuff. She loved Dena dearly, but she didn't relish being sandwiched between her friend and a total stranger. So, she requested two adjacent aisle seats.

"No, sorry, nothing available," the same attractive gentleman who'd helped Dena informed her.

Time to go into Diva mode. Tilting her head and lowering her eyelashes seductively, Shelby delivered her thousand-watt Diva smile.

"Oh, there must be something you can do. Pretty please," she purred. Surely that would do the trick. How could anyone resist when she turned on the charm?

"Really, my hands are tied," snipped the attendant. He barely spared a second glance as he pronounced the dismissive verdict. "Inquire at the service desk just across the way. Perhaps they'll be able to help."

"That thousand-watt smile sounds more like a ten-watt Christmas tree bulb," India said with a little smirk. Her eyes gleamed with satisfaction, and her cheeks turned apple red.

Most color the woman's probably had in her whole life...kind of like the devil. Dena and Shelby shared an apprehensive glance. Here she goes again. Both women braced themselves for the dig they knew was inevitable.

"So, DIVA...the envy of every woman...the desire of every man," she reiterated gleefully. "Just not the desire of this man, I guess. Bet that smarted."

And there it was, right on cue, the jab of Lucifer's pitchfork.

"Oh, heavens no," Shelby retorted. "There was a perfectly good explanation."

"Dena, that man didn't give me the time of day," Shelby whined. "First try at this diva thing, and I strike out."

Dena patted her friend on the shoulder in comfort. "Shelby," she whispered confidentially, "Pamela Anderson would strike out with him."

When her friend gave her a quizzical look, Dena elucidated. "Obviously, the man's gay!"

A beatific smile spread across Shelby's face. The ladies spun on their heels and continued on to the next service desk with renewed optimism.

"Hello, sir. How are you today? We'd like to change our seating arrangem...,"

Shelby didn't get any further. "Sorry, can't help you here. But do try at the gate."

With smug satisfaction, the ladies turned to each other. "Gay!" they mouthed in unison. Surely, they'd have better luck at the gate...on through the security checkpoints.

Dena and her carry-ons passed through without incident. Shelby was proceeding quite swimmingly also, sailing through the metal detector. Her purse slid along the x-ray machine conveyor belt with no problem. Next came her hatbox.

"Everyone always complains about security checks," Shelby began. "I don't see what the big deal is. I've never had a problem."

As she was about to gather up her belongings, a strong hand clamped down on hers, preventing her from collecting the hatbox. "I need to inspect this," issued the security officer.

"Oh, by all means, sir," Shelby agreed with a toothy smile.

"Aarrhh!" Dena let out a strangled gasp.

"What, what?" Shelby asked. Her eyes followed the direction of Dena's dazed stare.

There, for all the world to see, nestled atop her hats, were two boxes of raincoats for the one-eyed monster. Now given her skin tone, the red flush of embarrassment doesn't come easily to Shelby. But the heat suffusing her cheeks rivaled that of a nuclear reactor. Surely, if she were to have looked in a mirror, she'd have been glowing.

"I'm sure I don't need to tell you ladies to have a good time," the security officer offered. The sparkle in his eyes and the slippery smile on his face were no surprise.

Shelby frantically slammed the box top over the offending objects, and threw a thank you back over her shoulder.

"And you packed them in the hatbox why?" Dena squawked, as they slinked away from the security checkpoint.

For the past month, Shelby had been holding Dena's condom stash as a precaution against the prying eyes of Luke or the kids. "Well, I thought they'd be easier to give to you," she explained lamely.

"And it never occurred to you that you'd be going through security with them? That someone might see them?" Dena was like a dog with a bone.

"Well, it seemed like a good idea at the time!"

"That's what worries me. Perhaps we need to rethink who's the brains of this operation."

Diva Do/n't

If you're carrying something you don't want discovered, do not pack it where it may be uncovered.

Hats askew, hatboxes weighing heavily from their additional cargo, the travelers limped to the gate. Dutifully following the instructions of the handsome young gentleman at the check-in counter, the mortified friends sidled up to the gate attendant. They were quite hopeful and confident of their charms when they found yet another handsome, young gentleman. Taking their boarding passes, he promised to do his best to accommodate the women's request.

It seemed like a long time, but finally they heard their names announced over the public address system. "Oh, they must have gotten our seats!" Shelby surmised gleefully. She ran. Sorry. Correction. Divas don't run. She glided quite quickly to receive their newly assigned seats.

"Let me guess. They bumped you up to first class?" India's voice dripped with sarcasm.

"Not quite," Shelby admitted.

"No?" The question in India's voice wasn't a question at all. "They put the Divas in business class?"

"Uh uh," Dena answered negatively.

"No kidding," India said. "Did they hand you oxygen masks, wind breakers, and strap you two to the wings of the plane?"

Shelby fumed. Jeezus, how I'd love to wipe that superior smile off her cadaverous face. She looked over at Dena and got a bit nervous when she saw her friend's clenched fist and bared teeth.

She's going to clock the hag any second now. Under the table, Shelby held Dena's hand down.

"You're close. Actually, yet another handsome young gentleman returned our original boarding passes," *Shelby revealed. Almost in a whisper, she admitted their seats were unchanged.*

"Your explanation this time, ladies? Another Nancy boy?" *India supplied.*

Shelby groaned. "Even we weren't that delusional, India. No, with that rather curt dismissal, I was catapulted to my childhood, almost hearing my father's voice. Shelby, they must not know who you are. Did you tell them?"

"Much as we hate to admit it," *especially to you, Dena thought as she spoke,* "not one person had seen us for the Divas we thought we'd become."

"So all that time, money, and effort...a complete waste," *India observed.*

"Hardly," *Dena countered.* "Our little tale's not over yet."

"Well, riveting as it is, ladies, I'm afraid I need to make a trip to the loo." *With that, India excused herself.*

"What a bitch," *Shelby declared, when she deemed the Brit out of earshot.*

Dena didn't answer immediately. As she took time to mull over her thoughts, she tapped her finger on the table. "Yeah, it's like she's angry at us," *she said with a question in her voice.*

But why? Bit by bit, the ladies catalogued what they knew about the Englishwoman so far. A cheating husband. That would make anyone a tad out of sorts. Still, it was no reason to be mad at them. It wasn't like either Dena or Shelby was living in a wedded wonderland.

Money couldn't be it either. The British woman was sporting a rock on her finger the size of Gibraltar. At least old Malcolm was good for something rock hard, they laughed mischievously.

"It's got to be our beauty," *Dena theorized.* "But that's awfully petty. She really is a bitch. And if that's the case, why are we telling this condescending harpy our story?"

"Oh, I don't know," *Shelby started,* "I kind of like her. She reminds me of someone, but I don't know whom exactly."

Mirror, mirror on the wall, Dena thought, but decided to remain quiet.

Shortly, India returned. There it was again...that bit of sadness in her eyes when the Englishwoman looked at them. It never occurred to either friend what India envied most. Yes, it was solid as a rock, but it wasn't a diamond or a man's appendage.

It was their friendship. Nonetheless, India would be damned before she'd let them see it, so she plastered a fake smile on her face. "Good news, ladies. I just saw our flight's been delayed again," she announced, with all the gaiety she could muster. "So on with the story."

Navigating to the back of the plane without hitting another passenger in the head proved to be a feat. For although, according to the traveling duo, they each had only one piece of carry-on luggage, they also had their purses and hatboxes. Hatboxes stowed above, carry-ons stowed below, Dena and Shelby settled themselves for the first leg of their journey, both excited by their anticipated rendezvous.

Needing to take her motion sickness medication quickly before lift-off, Dena was having trouble getting the attention of the flight attendant for some water. Then she remembered that she'd come prepared.

Shelby's eyes widened in wonderment as she watched her friend unearth a one-gallon silver camping thermos from her carry-on. "Oh, you brought your own spring water. How smart. I should've, too," said Shelby.

"Spring water? Yes, that would've been a good idea, but this is a fine Chianti. Much better than the screw cap bottles on this plane," Dena pronounced. She decided to let Shelby think that she was a connoisseur rather than to reveal the thermos' true purpose. Nicola would surely be impressed with her forethought as they toured the Tuscan countryside, stopping for romantic picnics along the way.

Within seconds, Dena was out like a light. But not for long. Soon carts were going up and down the aisles bringing passengers their dinners. On the heels of the Alitalia fish fiasco, the ladies had decided to pre-order vegetarian meals for this flight. They had visions of a meatless pasta, perhaps a vegetable stir-fry. And to round out the meal, some fresh fruit and rolls. When their meals arrived, the ladies were incredulous.

"What is this? Rabbit food?" Dena hissed. "Does the rabbit come with it?"

Or, perhaps, a bit of cheese? An egg? Tofu? Any form of protein would do. But alas, all they received were sprigs and twigs. As they struggled to console themselves with the fact that it wasn't fish, and Shelby would be alive to eat another meal, the final humiliation was but a few steps away.

Proudly, the flight attendant pranced down the aisle with a tray in her hand. As she handed the food laden tray to the passenger seated next to them, the ladies' noses caught a whiff. Bœuf Bourgogne with a hint of thyme, Dena calculated. And either a cabernet or a fine burgundy they've used in it, Shelby hypothesized. Whichever wine it was, the ladies watched with unabashed envy as their fellow passenger unwrapped a sumptuous beef dinner.

"I'll create a diversion," hissed Shelby. "You steal his plate and meet me in the bathroom. It'll be our version of the Mile-High Club."

Dena was with her until last statement. She shot her friend a befuddled look.

"Well, it is a piece of beef!" Shelby explained.

"Calm down, look at it this way, our meal will keep us regular. You know how we get when we travel," philosophized Dena with a smug smile on her face. She didn't see her friend's hands itching to wring her neck.

For the remainder of the dinner hour, the ladies were perched in their seats, noses in the air, catching whiffs of the tempting aromas wafting past. Even though they didn't get so much as a morsel, and acute hunger may have affected their judgment, they felt certain British Airways had the best meals of any airline they'd flown. And, another Diva Don't sprouted wings.

If you are a woman longing for a piece... of meat, do fly British Airways. It can't be beat.

"Won't that sound like a blatant plug in your book?" probed India suspiciously. "Sure you two aren't angling for a little monetary thank you from the airline?"

Shelby fidgeted with her hair, twirling a long, curly strand around her finger. "Heavens no. We'd never include a website for people to reach us."

Dena bobbed her head in avid agreement. "It'd be utterly tacky to write in the book that readers can send an unsolicited gratuity to www.DelusionalDivas.com. And, should that website be temporarily down, go to www.DelusionalDivas.net. Thank you in advance."

Again Shelby spoke up, trying to bolster their argument. "Besides, if we thought there was a snowball's chance in hell of BA making a small deposit in our off-shore account, we'd keep our next tidbit on the QT."

> **Traveling Tidbit for the Grazing Traveler among us (i.e., vegetarians):** When traveling on British Airways, carry-ons should consist of food and food alone. You don't need that heart medicine as much as you think you do.

Lack of food, or what homo sapiens consider food, left a gaping hole in the ladies' bellies. Dena's thermos of Chianti was just the trick. Swigging it down in record time, even for them, the women felt quite mellow and settled back to view the feature film. Little did they know that they would have their choice of several. And here comes another traveling tidbit, which the ladies hope might redeem them with the CEO of British Airways.

"No, India, not for a kickback," Shelby read the anemic woman's mind. "But he might be single and want to meet the ladies!"

"You mean his son may want to meet us, don't you, Shelby?" Dena contradicted.

> **Traveling Tidbit for the Movie Buff Traveler:** Not only does British Airways (and other foreign airlines) provide five or six continually running current feature films aired at your convenience, but passengers have a private screen on the seat in front. Do U.S. airlines offer this...not so much.

After touching down in London, there was a four-hour layover until their plane took off for Italy. Months earlier, Dena and Shelby had had visions of quick side trips to Harrod's, Big Ben, Westminster Abbey and onto Windsor Castle for a private audience with their dear friend Liz. Oh, many pardons, that's Her Majesty Queen Elizabeth to everyone else. They had been practicing their curtsy for quite some time, and their hats were almost as improbable as the monarch's. However, once they discovered the airport transfer snafu, they knew high tea at Buckingham Palace was a no go.

"We'll have to call Betsy and tell her we can't make it," Shelby laughed. "Maybe next time."

It wasn't quite the accommodation that the ladies had hoped for, but the bus did get them to Gatwick in time to board their connecting flight to Pisa. Down the airplane aisle they trudged, hatboxes in tow. Who would be their seat companion? How about a debonair English businessman on his way to Pisa? Or a sexy, smooth talking, Italian gentleman?

Oh, just great! Reaching their row, Shelby stared down at a ninety-year old, silver-haired, wrinkled crone. And crippled to boot. As she sucked in every possible inch, Shelby cursed her luck. Like scaling Mount Everest, she complained under her breath, climbing over the woman to reach her seat.

"Better not have any wine on this trip, or I'll have to pole vault over the old hag to go to the bathroom," she whispered to Dena.

"I won't have to worry about that," Dena complained. "It's hot as hell in here. I'll be dehydrated before we take off. I need air."

As the plane taxied to the runway, she fumbled frantically with the overhead controls in search of the air vent. Shelby was a bit worried for her friend. She'd never seen her this worked up unless it involved a man. Popped one too many Dramamine maybe? Perhaps all that Chianti hadn't been such a good idea after all. Dena looked positively green around the gills.

Just then, a deep, authoritative male voice bellowed from the back of the plane. "Stop! Stop that now!"

It never occurred to Dena the announcement was meant for her. She was just looking for a little air. Frantically, she continued fumbling with the buttons overhead. Oh, it must be this one. And she gave the knob a quick, firm twist.

Suddenly, a torrent of oxygen masks rained down on the passengers, hitting babies on the head, knocking dentures out of old men's mouths, and sideswiping the bifocals off the eyes of Shelby's crone. Pandemonium reigned as passengers screamed, jumping from their seats in fear.

"B...but, I just wanted air! You were hot, too, Shelby, weren't you?" Dena explained lamely.

As they taxied back to the gate, their departure delayed, Shelby turned to the woman beside her. "How stupid can one person be? Do you know her?"

Two hours, a few mechanics, and untold humiliation later, the plane took off. Since her friend was still not speaking to her, Dena decided to strike up a conversation with the only person on the plane who wasn't giving her the evil eye. Shelby's crone. She doesn't look so bad to me. In fact, she actually looks rather refined in her woolen winter white, even if it is the middle of July.

"Yes, we're going to Italy to buy a piece of property," Dena informed her.

"Oh, really, in what region?" asked the woman.

As Dena regaled her with their research of Rimini on the Adriatic coast, a look vaguely reminiscent of someone who'd caught a whiff of a sulfur experiment in chemistry class flashed across the elderly woman's face. "Ah, the Italian Jersey Shore. Good luck to you."

"What do you mean?" Dena inquired.

"Well, it's a typical beach town with many small, rather ordinary motels, loud and crowded nightclubs, and little shops hawking tacky Italian souvenirs. If you happen to like that sort of thing, you will be in heaven."

Dena's eyes glossed over as she dreamed about disco dancing with a hot, young Italian man. Then, she remembered that she was supposed to be a diva. "Oh yes, I know just what you mean. We'll cancel our reservations tout de suite," she replied, wrinkling her nose in feigned disgust.

Conversation at an end, the elderly lady excused herself and commandeered no less than three flight attendants to airlift her to the ladies room.

"Well, I never," hissed Dena. "Just who does she think she is?"

"Where is she going?" Shelby asked, deciding to relent and speak to Dena.

"I don't know. Some godforsaken place called Montecatini. Who ever heard of that?"

Shelby sat up in her seat and perked up rather quickly. Perhaps she'd judged her friend, not to mention the crone, altogether too harshly. Put together they might have the brainpower of a whole person and some smidgeon of usefulness.

"Do they have cable where you live, Dena? You know, the Travel Channel? Or is Europe still considered outer space in upstate New York?"

Dena looked at her friend in complete bewilderment.

"Montecatini happens to have a world-renowned health spa," Shelby informed her. "Who is this lady anyway?"

The word lady was quite prescient. For Dena had managed to find herself a true aristocrat...from Pennsylvania. How did the Divas discover this? While some might label it blatant snooping in the poorest of taste, Dena preferred to think of herself as an amateur detective. And so, when she noticed the mystery woman's Louis Vuitton carry-on (complete with name tags) right at her feet, she felt compelled to hone her investigative skills. What did they say? Lady Isadora.

"Finally, our social equal," Dena chirped, her voice bubbling gleefully. But Shelby was skeptical.

"Possible, possible," she began with a sly laugh, "or it's just as possible that her parents actually christened her Lady. You know, like people who name their kid Princess or Queen."

Dena would have contradicted her friend, but there wasn't time. Lady Isadora's retinue had jitneyed her back, and she was being lowered into her seat.

Undaunted by Shelby's cynicism, Dena continued to pick the brain of her new best friend, Her Highness, the Royal Lady Isadora. She discovered Izzy had been recently widowed and was off to Montecatini in commemoration of the trip she and her husband had taken annually. "Montecatini is not what it used to be, but we always loved it," she reminisced with a bittersweet joy.

As she couldn't help overhearing the story, a sadness fell over Shelby. Lady Isadora reminded her of her grandmother, who had passed away a few months earlier. God, I miss Mama, she thought to herself

Dena heard a sniffle escape from her friend. When she glanced over, there appeared to be a tear in Shelby's eye. Was she crying? Dena laughed at herself for such a silly thought. No way! Shelby probably hadn't cried when the obstetrician slapped her bottom at birth. More likely, she'd reached up and clocked the poor man. No, she was either suffering from an allergy attack or had poked herself in the eye.

Chapter 10

*B*y the time the delusional duo touched down in Pisa, they'd been awake for twenty-four hours. Try looking like a diva under those circumstances. Hunting for the restroom, the pooped pair stood before a wall-length mirror surveying the devastation. If the bags under both women's eyes had contained food, there was a distinct possibility that world hunger could have been eradicated that very day. Agreeing it would take too much time to hide the ravages of their flight, the ladies turned and left. Besides, they still had a train ride to Florence ahead of them. What was the use?

First, they had to see if their luggage had made it there as promised. As they waited, the two kept their fingers crossed and held their breath.

Before long, Dena's luggage, equaling the size of a small streamer trunk, was wending its way around the luggage carousel. One down, one to go, she thought happily. Down the conveyor belt came suitcase after suitcase...red, green, blue, black, black, black. There's mine, thought Shelby excitedly. It wasn't. Her foot started tapping an angry tattoo on the tile floor, becoming louder with each passing piece of luggage. Mine better have made it. That's all I need. Dena walking around like Astor's pet horse while I wear the same clothes every day for two weeks. Then she saw it, her distinctive Boyt luggage coming toward her. She ran to it like a mother to her newborn child. As she tried to lift it, she couldn't help but think her newborn should be carrying her.

"It's one thing to get the luggage to the train. All we need is a cab. But how are we going to lug it onto the train without a small army of helpers?" Shelby whined.

Dena patted Shelby on the shoulder and smiled with confidence. "Come on. We're the Divas. Men will be clamoring to help us."

"Divas!? Has anyone even recognized that we're breathing? I'd settle for that."

"They're just intimidated by our beauty and grace," Dena explained. "But don't worry. I've got a plan."

Dena and a plan. Shelby stood back, sure that thunder bolts would attack from the sky any second now. Her friend ignored her physical hyperbole and continued on. "No, no, this really will work. All it requires is a little precision timing."

"Okay, let's hear it," Shelby acquiesced.

The plan was really rather simple. Dena would stand on the train track and hand the luggage to Shelby one piece at a time from the platform. If all the luggage wasn't aboard before the train rolled out of the station, Dena would follow on the next train and meet Shelby in Florence. "See? It's foolproof," Dena beamed proudly.

Proof of a fool. And Shelby was going to make sure the fool wasn't her. "Sounds good. Just one teensy minor change," she replied.

Dena waited for the amendment, surprised at how easy it had been.

"You really do need to get to Florence ASAP. Nicola's expecting your call. Perhaps, you should be the one to board the train while I hand you the luggage." Shelby's voice oozed solicitous concern.

Dena was touched at the sweet gesture. There weren't many people lucky enough to have such a friend. And Shelby was right. If she was too late, Nicola might make other plans for the evening. She thanked her friend for her thoughtfulness.

"Oh, it's nothing. Believe me," Shelby replied, waving off Dena's gratitude. Well, that worked out splendidly, she congratulated herself. No way was she going to be the dupe ending up on a train by herself with sufficient luggage for a small tour group.

As it happened, the Pisa train station and airport were located in the same complex, making a cab unnecessary. While this was a stroke of good fortune for the two young...yes, young travelers, the ladies' luck died thereafter.

They huffed. They puffed. They pulled. They tugged. They hoisted. They lifted. Midway into their ordeal, a young Italian sauntered past. Dena halted her struggle, and gave him a pleading smile. She was heartened when he fixed a white-toothed smile in her direction. Without slowing his pace, the man made for the next car and hopped aboard. Diva, Diva, Diva, she reminded herself.

Meanwhile, throngs of Italian men walked by, with nary a one lifting so much as a pinky in assistance. "You know, I was reading the obits the other day. Guess who was in there?" Dena said as she continued her tugging.

Too out of breath to respond verbally, Shelby simply quirked her eyebrow questioningly.

"Chivalry!" answered Dena. The ladies shared a giggle. "Yeah, I don't think anyone knows who we are yet, Shelby."

Nodding in agreement, Shelby nearly caved as she hoisted up another suitcase, the weight of which was akin to that of a newborn baby whale. Bobbing to and fro, the sweat cascaded...correction, tiny pearls of perspiration beaded on the diva's upper lip. Her situation was becoming desperate, and Shelby had to make a choice. Possibly maiming her dear friend Dena's foot or falling ignobly to the pavement with a suitcase atop, sucking the life out of her.

Losing a foot's not so bad these days. They've made great strides in the authenticity of prostheses. And Giancarlo's waiting for me. Besides, maybe Dena's foot would only be crushed. Wouldn't any doctor she sees just recommend that she keep it elevated? In that event, everything will work out perfectly. Dena plans to spend the entire vacation on her back with her feet in the air anyway.

In the end, Shelby felt she really had no choice at all. If that behemoth fell on her, she might sustain a crushed pelvis. That would mar anyone's vacation plans. They'd have to send her back to the States. Lord knew, Italy was no place for cripples. Surely Dena would understand.

"What the fu... fu... fu are you doing?" Dena yelped in pain, when the suitcase landed on her foot with a crash.

"So sorry. It slipped without any warning at all. Are you okay?" Shelby apologized. "I promise the first thing we'll do when we get to Florence is get you a tetanus shot."

Then, Shelby practically flung the rest of the luggage at Dena. "Now quick, catch this, or we'll miss this train."

While it is quite obvious that the Divas aren't too particular about their own morals, there is a moral to be learned here.

Diva Do/n't

If you are traveling and don't have a mate, don't pack or lug more than one-third your weight.

"*Of course, this rule doesn't apply to everyone,*" Dena interrupted.

"*No?*" *queried India.*

Dena and Shelby shared a secret little smile. Should we, they both wondered. Dena gave a barely perceptible nod of encouragement. Let her rip, it seemed to say.

"Well, naturally, those of us over two hundred pounds," Shelby stopped and trained eagle eyes on India, *"are excluded from this mathematical formula."*

The ladies enjoyed seeing their companion's sallow complexion flush crimson red. Checkmate!

They let the implication hang in the air just a tad longer before Dena released the spider from the web they'd woven. "It goes without saying that the formula doesn't apply to the underweight either."

Getting their luggage off the train proved to be a much easier proposition. The ladies really can't explain it scientifically. Something about gravity, a man named Newton, and his Adam's Apple. No, no, just a regular apple.

"I don't know why he chose an apple," Dena remarked. "What good's an apple? Now a banana. A cucumber. Or maybe a good hard zucchini."

Shelby let out a frustrated sigh. The girl was a walking hormone. "Please, Dena, you're a diva. Have some grace and dignity!"

They found a cab and settled back for a ride to their hotel. A breath in, a breath out, and POOF, like magic, they were there. Much to their surprise, the Hotel Machiavelli Palace was less than a block from the train station.[18]

Their hotel choice...what to say about this wonderful establishment? Well, it is a hotel, it has beds, it has bathrooms, and it is old, like everything else in Florence. What? People need to know more? Okay, it is conveniently located in the heart of Florence. Perhaps heart is stretching it a bit. More like a valve in the heart of Florence. No matter, it's close enough for anybody. And for anyone on a budget, it's perfect.

Formerly a convent, the ninety-room hotel had been completely renovated. It is traditionally appointed with lovely old wood-carved ceilings, frescoed walls, antique furniture, and Oriental rugs. For the sightseeing weary tourist, it is a welcoming oasis from the hustle and bustle of the city. Internet access, air conditioning, satellite TV, and soundproof windows make it a far cry from what the good Catholic sisters were used to.

The ladies couldn't possibly recall the exact dimensions of their room. While they readily admit that size does matter and

---

[18]Hotel Machiavelli Palace, Via Nazionale 10, PH 055/216622

could recite the size of some things within a centimeter, they have no idea the measurements of their room. All they can say is that it was big, and as with other large things, this put a smile on their faces.

The bathroom was a small palace. Like their Capri hotel, it had a bathtub. More importantly, unlike the Hotel Aldini, guests could sit on the toilet without their knees making love to the wall.

As usual, none of this really mattered to Dena, her only concerns being whether Mamma Mia Bell had made it to the Hotel Machiavelli and that the phone worked better than those of the Hotel Aldini or the Hotel Boston. Because if they didn't, she was out of there pronto.

Did she long to hear the voices of her children? Did she want to let her husband know she'd arrived in one piece? Hardly. The voice she longed to hear was Nicola's, and the only piece that she was interested in...

"Dena, you in Firenze?" The welcoming enthusiasm suffusing Nicola's voice warmed the cock...cock...cockles of her heart. So sorry. The ladies really are going to have to practice not stumbling over that word.

"You come to Buca tonight?" he encouraged when she answered affirmatively.

Dena was reluctant, telling Nicola that she and Shelby were exhausted from traveling, and tomorrow would better. Besides, she and Nicola had two weeks to be together, she reminded herself.

"Please. You come tonight at 9:30." His voice was low and insistent, and its velvety tone proved to be more than Dena could resist. How could she disappoint the poor man? He was champing at the bit. He'd probably suffered more than she from their separation...lost weight, lost sleep, a mere shadow of his formal self. Wasn't true love wonderful?

"Si, si, si, we'll be there. Ciao, bello."

Although it is hard to believe that women as beautiful as they really need beauty rest, the truth is the tempting twosome needed the equivalent of a bear's hibernation. Within seconds, they'd stripped, crawled into bed, and fell out for hours.

So all the months of training, preparation, and strategic planning with military precision came down to this first face-to-face encounter with the enemy. The ladies decided that perhaps a summit, rather than a battle, should be their first plan of attack. Catch their enemy off guard. They needed dress whites instead of fatigues.

Dena chose a little hot pink linen number with sequined spaghetti straps and matching strappy sandals. They debated the merits of going braless. To bare or not to bare? Which one was more likely to gain the most concessions from their opponent? In the end, they both had to reluctantly admit the obvious.

"Do we really have an option?" Dena said, standing in front of a mirror.

"Damn that Newton!" Shelby agreed.

Was no place sacred from him, his apple, and his confounded law of gravity? Surely not the breasts of a woman of a certain age.

"Exactly," said Dena. A diva simply couldn't be tripping over her sagging bosom for an entire evening and hope to have any credibility as an adroit negotiator.

Recognizing that this was strictly Dena's battle, and she wasn't being called up to the front yet, Shelby was much less scrupulous about her attire. Naturally, no matter what the occasion, a diva dresses carefully, but Shelby didn't have to follow the rules of engagement tonight. Her choice of a chic, somewhat Indian-patterned dress in shades of turquoise, violet, and lime green accessorized with dainty violet silk sandals had been easy, but still, she stood in front of her lingerie draw in deep thought. She was torn between her white cotton bloomers and the diva garb of matching lacy bra and thong. Finally, she grabbed the granny panties and slipped into them. Sure, she was a Diva, but she'd be a comfortable that evening.

As Dena was putting the final touches on her war paint, Shelby surprised her with a small token of her affection, in appreciation of an enduring and sometimes torturous friendship. "Here, this is for you," she said almost silently, shoving the small package toward her friend.

Dena was touched by the uncharacteristically kind gesture, but she figured better safe than sorry. She surveyed the package with suspicious eyes. "Me? Are you sure? Is it booby trapped?"

"Don't be a fool, just open it," Shelby's eyes flashed with mock irritation.

Hallmark. When you care enough to send the very best. This time, the card publishers had outdone themselves. Two little girls, one black and one white, primping in front of a mirror. They were clad in boas and lace, and atop their heads were feather hats bigger than they. D.I.T.S...Divas-in-Training! Upon closer inspection, the similarity between the little divas and the delusional duo was uncanny.

The little Shelby Diva exuded a smug self-confidence. Perfectly pleased with herself, her eyes were closed and her lips pursed in a haughty smile of complete satisfaction. Meanwhile, in front of a mirror, the little Dena Diva was lustily adding yet another layer of lipstick. This little diva was certain the Duchess of Windsor had forgotten one small caveat. Sure, one could never be too rich or too thin, but according to the little Dena Diva and her adult counterpart, one could never be too made-up either.

"Oh, it's simply ab fab. You found a diva card just for this occasion. But why does it have two different dates with two different messages?" Dena asked.

"Read it," Shelby commanded.

July 16

Well, girl,

You can see from the other side that I never got the chance to give you the card on our 1st trip.

Now I know why. It wasn't time because we weren't DIVAS yet.

But now, like the little girls in the picture, we are THE DIVAS, hats and all!

I love you,
Shelby

March 31

I couldn't make up

a better friend

than you.

Dear Dena,

I've had this card for years & always knew it was for you; just didn't know when. Whenever I look at it, I am reminded of us.

Anticipating this trip & all the fun we'll have, it seemed time to let go of the card & share it with you.

Thank you so much for your love & friendship all these years.

love, Shelby

"It's perfect!" Dena exclaimed. "I've always known you were psychic. Now tell me, what does your crystal ball see for us this evening?"

"For you, hot sausage and meatballs. Italian style, of course. And for me, well it says better luck next time," Shelby laughed.

In the summer, the Buca serves dinner alfresco. The court-yard becomes a dining room under the stars. Twinkling fairy lights, the soft glow of a candle at each umbrellaed table, and the night's gentle breeze provide a warm and intimate atmos-phere. When the ladies arrived, the only thing missing was music man Vittorio and his electric piano. They would miss being serenaded over dinner. Entering through the massive wrought iron gates, Dena saw the eager welcome on Nicola's face. "I feel like Cinderella going to the ball," she whispered excitedly.

"You may be Cinderella, my dear, but your prince is a foot-man," Shelby replied with her trademark cynicism. She was not about to let her friend bask in glory.

"Tonight hopefully he'll be a foot man, a leg man, a breast man, and..."

Shelby held up her hands in surrender. "Okay, stop. I get the picture."

For their *primo piatto*, they chose *gamberetti con radicchio*, an appetizer consisting of fresh shrimp sautéed with radicchio and salt pork. Simply divine. Shelby's next course was *maiale con patate*, a sliced pork with potatoes in a rich cream sauce, which she enjoyed immensely.

The next day, poor Dena wouldn't have a clue what she'd eaten, as her brain had gone into power save mode. Hers was the food of love. Still, although she wasn't interested in eating solids, her appetite for wine hadn't waned one iota, and she consumed her fair share of the Chianti.

As the restaurant cleared, the men started to gather. Little pudgy Pasquale; Nicola, the object of Dena's affection (or some might say affliction); and Nicola (not Dena's Nicola, but Dena's Nicola's co-worker, Nicola).

India's head was spinning with too many Nicolas. "If your readers can follow that, they'll deserve a sizeable remuneration in their off-shore accounts. Why the devil don't you just use their surnames?"

"Please, please, please," Shelby said, disdain dripping with each word.

"You think that hasn't occurred to us," piped up Dena.

"*We've forgotten their last names,*" Shelby quickly jumped in before Dena said too much. "*You know, so many vowels. Too hard to remember.*"

A sanctimonious smile spread across the washed-out face of their companion. She didn't need to utter a word. Both women knew exactly what she was thinking. That they had no idea of the men's surnames.

Shelby was livid, deciding to answer the Englishwoman's silent accusation. "*For chrissakes, do you really think I spent two months with Giancarlo without getting the man's last name?*"

Dena's face suffused with a telltale bright redness. Then, her embarrassment turned to irritation. "*Do you want to hear the rest of the story or dwell on these pesky little details?*" she huffed.

First the owner, little pudgy Pasquale, joined the ladies at their table. "Ahhh, the lovely ladies from New York. You love Italy, no? Or you love the Italian men, yes?"

Shelby hurried to deny the accusation with a straight face. "No, no. We love Italy. We want to buy a house or apartment to rent to tourists."

"Oh, where?" Pasquale asked.

Just then, Nicola joined them. Not Dena's Nicola, and not Dena's Nicola's co-worker Nicola, but Dena's Nicola's cousin Nicola, aka Nicola *Due*. When she saw him, Shelby chuckled to herself as her mind traveled back to April and *Due*'s unsuccessful kidnapping of her on his motorino. His humiliation not yet complete, he had apparently come back for more. Poor *Due*, try as he might, he hadn't been a blip on Shelby's radar screen in April, and nothing had changed in July. However, he did seem to have an uncanny, almost freakish knowledge of Italian tourist areas. So, with uncharacteristic warmth, Shelby smiled at him.

"We're thinking of buying a small hotel in Santa Fiora. Do you know the area, Doo...uhh...Nicola?" she asked.

His smile spoke volumes. At last, he had something Shelby wanted, if only information. No, it wasn't much, but couldn't it eventually blossom into love?

He probably records the portable electronic guides for museums, Shelby thought as she listened in amazement to his encyclopedic knowledge of the area.

Santa Fiora in Grosseto province. A medieval town on Monte Amiata and a tourist area in the Maremma. Sixty kilometers from Siena, one hundred fifty kilometers from Firenze, and one hundred sixty kilometers from Roma. A visit to the Terme (thermal baths) in the area is a must. One can read about Santa Fiore in Dante's <u>Divine Comedy</u>.

"And where else would be good for us to look for property?" she asked when he finally stopped.

"Oh, Grosseto is near *il mare*... the sea. More *ovest*...west eez Grosseto. Are beaches there where many Italians go on vacation."

Who needed <u>Frommer's Guide To Italy</u>? They had *Due*!

Grosseto, what a coincidence. Certainly, Giancarlo will invite us there this trip. After all, I do need to see if it would be the proper setting for our nuptials. Would the dining room hold a party of one thousand or more? Was the ballroom big enough for an orchestra? Would the villa's gardens be sufficient to supply the flowers for the weddings. Damn...wedding, wedding, singular wedding! I have to check out the local caterers. And, I mustn't forget my trousseau.

As Shelby was experiencing yet another delusional episode, Nicola...that's Dena's Nicola...joined the party, seating himself next to her. He hadn't seen her in months, so what were his first intimate words to her?

India noticed Dena reaching for the purple journal, and couldn't stifle the sigh of impatience. "Not another one?" she practically pleaded.

"Yes, we do love a DIQ...uh, uh, I mean a DIQ Test Question. So try this one, India," Dena urged her to take the book.

Reluctantly, the Brit held out her hand. Her eyes rolled with exasperation. "If your readers have a fear of test taking, rest assured that by the end of this book, you'll have exacerbated the problem," she vowed. Nevertheless, India's curiosity won the battle, and she turned her attention downward.

What were Nicola's first words to his beloved Dena?
A) You are lovelier than ever, but are you well? You've lost weight,
B) Your eyes in the moonlight inspire a sonnet,
C) I've missed you so; will you marry me? I can't bear for you to leave, or
D) I like your shoes. Are they Jimmy Choo?

Now it was the Englishwoman's turn to quote Shelby's father. "Please, please, please!" she cried. "Does your footman even know what a sonnet is?"

"You're good," Dena *said in admiration.* *"Our sentiments exactly."* *She reached for the book, but India resisted, anxious to finish reading.*

> If you chose Answer A, it stands for what you are, an amoeba...a one-celled organism, and we don't mean brain cell. Let's face it, the only well that Nicola was interested in was the well...well, you know, her womanly well.
>
> If you chose Answer B, you could be a footman, too. You probably think the word sonnet means the youngest son.
>
> For those that chose Answer C, you are either on drugs or massive quantities of alcohol. Your best bet-- an extended stay at the Betty Ford Clinic. To date, Dena's contact with Nicola consisted of a brief encounter in an alleyway and one night in his apartment. Hardly the stuff of romantic elopements. So don't call to see if there are any vacancies at Betty's. Just show up at her doorstep with your bags.
>
> If you chose Answer D, you are correct. As he slipped off her dainty sandals and discreetly checked the label, Dena cooed while he massaged her feet and worked his way toward that well.

India laughed heartily as she read. She wondered aloud how readers would respond to being insulted in these test questions.

"Oh, it's all in good fun," Dena *dismissed the concern.*

"Besides, the book's going to be so funny, the story so riveting that agents and publishers will be vying for it," bragged Shelby.

Published? India struggled to remain impassive. Well, these two were due for a spot of good luck, weren't they? Unfortunately, nothing less than a miracle would get this book written, let alone published. "So, how did your first night back with Nicola go?" *India asked, forging ahead with the story.*

"What you will do tomorrow?" inquired Nicola.

Only tomorrow, Dena thought with dismay. She already had their itinerary for next two weeks planned. She and Nicola would rent a car, meander through the Tuscan countryside, have romantic picnics amidst fields of sunflowers, and make madly passionate love in the olive groves. Their nights would be spent in medieval villas. Of course, she'd meet his family, who would adore her. Finally, he would no longer be able to contain himself. He'd ask her to marry him.

Yes, there were a few annoying little details to attend to. First, it might be important for her to know his last name for the marriage license. Next, did she need to fly back to the States for her divorce or could she phone it in? And third, they'd have to remodel his studio apartment to accommodate her three children. Shelby would be delighted. They'd have a double wedding at Giancarlo's villa.

"Tomorrow? I hadn't really thought about it at all. Maybe to the beach?" Dena fished, hoping he'd want to join. Still, as she baited the hook, she battled to banish the errant hopefulness from her face and voice.

Her fish slipped off easily. "Viareggio is not far, just a one-hour train trip. It's a nice little town," Nicola advised.

"Oh, let's do that tomorrow!" Shelby interjected with enthusiasm.

But Dena hesitated for a moment, certain that Nicola would pipe up with his own rather more romantic plans for the just the two of them. Sadly, silence hung heavily in the air. Oh, I guess he wants to surprise me with his plans when we're alone.

"Maybe. We'll see," Dena answered Shelby noncommittally. Then, she quickly changed the subject. "Are we going dancing this evening?"

Immediately, Shelby perked up, suggesting they go to Full Up. She could reminisce about the night she met her intended, Giancarlo.

"Or Yab Yum, I just love to dance to Techno," Dena lied. It makes me look younger, doesn't it?

Pudgy Pasquale shook his head vigorously. "Discos are *chiusi*...closed for the summer. Too hot...no air-conditioning."

Traveling Tidbit for the Jitterbug Traveler: Avoid Florence and most Italian cities in July and August if you wish to keep your make-up on your face instead of sliding down your chin and onto your chest. The summer heat and humidity are relentless, and much to the Divas' dismay, many of the restaurants and clubs are closed for the entire month of August. If you are looking for Italian men, go to the beaches.

"So where do people go?" the ladies chirped in unison.

Pasquale mentioned two outdoor discos, Meccano[19] and Central Park,[20] which were known as popular summer venues. "But they not open tonight. Feel you the rain?" he asked, raising his palm upward. And indeed, out from under the protection of their dinner table's canvas umbrella, raindrops were christening Florence.

With no place to go, the little party disbanded, scattering like rats. Knowing that she was on her own, and glad that the hotel was only a few blocks away, Shelby rose to leave, but before she got far, Pasquale offered her a ride home. She accepted readily, not wanting to ruin her shoes, or given her tiny sandals, to break her neck on the rain-slicked, cobblestone streets. So, off she went with a queen's wave to a crestfallen *Due*.

When Pasquale led her to a sleek, black convertible sports car, she was delighted. She had not looked forward to straddling a motorino and arriving at the hotel looking like a wet dog. It was a short ride, and her shoes were worth the small price of having to spend a few minutes enduring the advances of Pasquale. However, as if on cue, the ride home was more circuitous than she'd expected.

"I take you to a wonderful place," he announced conspiratorially, shifting into fourth gear. And they were off. As the car wound its way upward, it didn't take long to intuit their intended destination was Piazzale Michelangelo.

Do Florentine men have only one brain among them? Are they totally lacking in imagination? Then, Shelby remembered something she'd heard long ago. M*ammini*, mamma's boys. Seemingly, no man under the age of forty-five manages to move out from Mamma's. Why would they when they can get their meals made and laundry done without the nagging of a wife? Shelby surmised that Piazzale Michelangelo had become the casa romantica of choice for Florentine mammini because Mamma certainly wasn't having them bring their lady friends home for sleepovers.

Resigned to her fate, she settled back for her umpteenth visit to the Florentine landmark. It was beautiful, and at least she could enjoy the view, if not the company.

Meanwhile, Dena's dreams were taking shape. "We no can go to my apartment," Nicola announced. "My parents, they stay with me. Eez wedding of *mio cugino.*" My cousin.

---

[19] Meccano, Via degli Olmi 1, PH 055/33-13-371
[20] Central Park, Via Fosse Macinante 2, PH 055/353505

Noting the crestfallen droop of Dena's smile, he attempted to soften the blow. "But no worry, Dena. I no work on Monday and Tuesday. We see each other and do things together."

"But what about tonight?" she pressed.

Nicola thought for a moment. A smile played on his lips. "Follow me," he said, taking her hand.

They ended up in a fifteenth-century historic landmark. True, it wasn't a villa, but it was dimly lit. Not by virtue of romantic candlelight or moonlight streaming through stained glass windows. No, it owed its darkness to its unique underground location. Nicola had a truly special evening planned for the Diva. In the restaurant's subterranean storage rooms.

Now, to the unsophisticated, this might be a basement or cellar. However, Nicola quickly informed Dena that they were in none other than a section of *Il Battistero*, the famous medieval Baptistry.

Oh my, Nicola certainly does go all out for me. Love must be in the air. Or is that the smell of mold and mildew? Perhaps, the rotting carcass of a small rodent?

Years before, Luke had taken Dena to New York's Waldorf Astoria for a romantic weekend, and obviously Nicola was not to be outdone by her husband. Sure, the Waldorf was above ground, but wasn't underground cozier? A Park Avenue view and a king-size bed with triple sheeting was highly overrated. She and Nicola had two bar stools and restaurant linens. Large boudoir with make-up and dressing areas? The versatility of the bar stools was amazing. Marble baths and showers? It was raining. They need only step outside to freshen up. The extravagance of two telephone lines was completely unnecessary. Nicola had his cell phone. Twenty-four hour room service? The couple had the Buca's pantry at their disposal. All they needed was a box cutter and a butane lighter to cook. Wet bar? The lovers' bar was fully stocked with the restaurant's reserves. Lace-covered French doors opening onto a terrace? They had a cobweb-curtained tunnel leading to il Duomo.

Nicola took her in his arms. Dena melted as his warm lips rained tiny kisses on the sensitive skin of her neck. She moaned softly. "You like?" he teased.

"Si, I like a lot. I wish I could stay forever." The words came out before she could censor herself.

The tiny kisses flitting over her skin ceased. Dena opened her eyes and met Nicola's. His gaze was serious. "Dena? Why you come back to Firenze?" he asked.

I have a feeling this is no time for protestations of undying love, Dena thought. "I told you. Shelby and I are here to buy property," she got out.

His eyes narrowed shrewdly, and bore into her. His hands started to roam her body again. "You sure you not come back for me?"

Mmm, he's disappointed. That's nice. "Well, maybe just a little," she admitted with a coy smile.

He returned the smile with a sexy one of his own. "That's nice. I like you, Dena, but..."

BUT...the most hated word in the English language. It usually doesn't signal anything good in the offing. In matters of the heart, a sentence with BUT generally goes something like this. I like you BUT...I had a good time tonight BUT...I think you're a really swell person BUT...you're perfect in every way BUT...no one could ask for anything more BUT...anyone would be lucky to have you BUT...

What was Nicola's BUT? "Dena, I like you. I can give you fun, I can give you sex, BUT..."

Her heart was pounding furiously as she waited for the knife. She wasn't waiting for it to plunge into her heart. It was already there. Now, he was going to twist it.

"BUT I can no give you love," he finished. His voice registered a sad resoluteness.

Dena's eyes welled up with tears. She struggled to stem their tide, hoping to maintain a bit of dignity. "Oh, oh, that's okay," she warbled, then let out a shaky little laugh. "I'm not looking for love."

No, no. I'm not looking for love. I left my kids for two weeks, conned friends and family, came halfway around the world, and spent thousands of dollars for sex. Just sex. Isn't that every woman's dream come true?

Nicola gently caught a tear with his lips as it traveled down her cheek. This simple caress robbed Dena of any coherent thought she might have had. Within seconds, she was lost in a world of his making...where only his lips, his hands, his voice, his arms, his scent mattered. Mmmm, aahhhh, oohhhh, hmmmm. Feels like love to me.

Two weeks left. The enemy is within sight and in a choke hold. Surely, his defeat is at hand.

Back on the hill, Shelby was explaining to Pasquale that she could not possibly accept his advances because...

"*Bloody hell! Here we go again...changing the subject,*" *India complained.*

"*What?*" *Shelby stopped her story in midstream.*

"*Just when the story is getting juicy, Dena clams up, deciding to exercise some discretion. I want details. What happened in that storeroom, and wasn't the whole experience a bit degrading?*"

Shelby saw red. Jeeezus! Dena, Dena, Dena! Hadn't she gotten enough air time? Wasn't anybody interested in Shelby's story?

"*India, need I remind you that you're asking Dena to disregard an essential Diva Do/n't,*" *Shelby admonished.* "*Why, it's so essential, there's more than one version.*"

Diva Do/n't

Whenever a Diva has a rendezvous, she does not divulge what she did do.

Shelby smiled inwardly. That ought to do the trick. Now, back to me. "*As I was saying, Pasquale...*"

"*Fine, fine,*" *the Englishwoman cut Shelby off. The biting tone in her voice and complete disinterest on her face signaled India's impatience. How she longed to tell the two what they could do with their silly Diva Do/n'ts. Regardless, she was not to be diverted.*

"*Then how about my other question,*" *she grilled Dena.* "*How could you not have found the situation degrading? A storeroom? He can give you sex, but not love?*"

Dena squirmed uncomfortably in her seat. What was wrong with this woman? Who asked these kinds of questions of a perfect stranger? And more importantly, why was Dena answering them? It was like the woman had crawled inside her mind and was plaguing Dena with questions she'd tried to squelch within herself. She'd been able to hide from her own disturbing thoughts. But evading India's penetrating eyes, Dena felt like a criminal trying to keep one step ahead of a bounty hunter.

"*I should have thought it was obvious,*" *she said. Her tone held a bravado she didn't really feel.* "*No, at the time, I didn't feel degraded. Nicola had explained everything. First, his parents*"

160

were in town. Second, he had taken time off work to spend with me. And, third, of course, he would fall desperately in love with me eventually."

India shook her head in defeat. It's no use, she thought. There may be boosters in that brain, but they're not firing. Instead, she turned to Shelby, eyes wide with incredulity.

"You see what I have to contend with," Shelby acknowledged, then quickly seized her chance. "Now can we get back to my story? As I was trying to say..."

Back on the hill, Shelby was fending off the unwanted attentions of Pasquale and even littler Pasquale. It was almost impossible. Hands were everywhere.

"I can't do this," screeched Shelby. "I'm in love."

She hoped the announcement would put a crimp in his plans. With as much contrived sensitivity to Pasquale as she could muster, she explained about Giancarlo...how they'd met six years ago and fallen in love...how she was hoping to marry him.

Confusion clouded his eyes. Pasquale searched for the right words. "But I no understand? I never see you all these years. What happened?"

Well, no sense bringing up the sordid details of being dumped for another woman. A little embarrassing, to say the least. "It was really very sad. I was *molto stupida*," began Shelby.

The wheels of her mind spun, searching for just the right explanation. Well, story actually. Then, it came to her. "I went back to America and met someone else. It broke Giancarlo's heart."

Was he buying this? She raised her head to meet his gaze, struggling to inject guilt and regret in her expression. Pasquale's sympathetic countenance told her that he, and more importantly, little Pasquale had fallen hook, line, and sinker for her off-the- cuff fabrication. Time to go in for the kill.

"Finally, I realized what a fool I'd been. I begged Giancarlo to please take me back."

"And he did?" Pasquale asked with disappointment.

Fake tears of joy and elation glistened in Shelby's eyes. "Yes. Yes, he did. And I am so happy," she lied convincingly.

Then, she let those same eyes cloud with the merest hint of sadness again, sadness and regret at disappointing her companion. "So, you see, Pasquale, much as I like you, and attractive as you are..." Shelby began. What difference were two more lies? "My heart belongs to dear Giancarlo."

And so, as they waited out the rainstorm, Shelby regaled him with stories of her fairy tale romance. Throughout, Pasquale smiled and said "ahhh" in all the right places, proving to be the perfect gentleman.

Just as she was running out of fairy tale fodder, the rain co-operated and once it slowed down, Pasquale drove down from the mountain top and pulled up in front of the hotel. Shelby gathered her things quickly and scrambled from the car as fast as she could, lest the good man changed his mind. Allowing herself to sag with relief at having made a clean getaway with such a brilliant performance, she cursed her luck when she repeatedly pushed on an unyielding hotel door.

Was she locked out for the night? What kind of hotel was this? Would she be forced to prevail on the good graces of little Pasquale and even littler Pasquale to provide her with accommodations for the night?

"It's locked," she squawked in a panic.

It was then that both Pasquales proved to be true gentlemen. "You must ring the bell," he instructed.

And when the night doorman let her in, she turned and with another gentle queen's wave, bade the two Pasquales goodbye, and made her way to her room.

Entering the room, Shelby heaved another sigh of relief. Thank God, Dena wasn't there. Finally a moment alone. If she had to, she'd be willing to slip Nicola a few bills to keep her friend out of her hair for at least a few days. All this together-ness was getting on Shelby's nerves.

Her worry was unnecessary. Dena wasn't thinking about Shelby or returning to the Hotel Machiavelli. It was a few hours before the rain stopped, and she had made the most of them in that storeroom. Dena was saddened to look out and see the last drops had fallen, making a ride on the motorbike possible.

Within seconds, Nicola was gathering his things together and hurrying her to do the same. Leaving their lux accommodations, Dena turned for just one more look. She would never forget their little idyll.

All too soon, Nicola was racing crazily through the near empty Florentine streets with Dena behind latching on to him for dear life. Seemingly within seconds they pulled up, and he deposited her in front of the hotel.

"*Ciao, Bella.* You and Shelby come to the Buca *domani?*" he asked.

Again Dena tried not to appear too eager, but Nicola insisted that they come. With only token resistance, she acquiesced. "*Buona notte. A domani,*" Dena said in her best Italian.

Then, she tiptoed over the sidewalk to the hotel. One shove of the door. It held fast. She tried again, but still it didn't budge. She turned to Nicola, who was waiting to see her safely in.

"I'm locked out. The hotel must be closed for the night," she said hopefully. For effect, she turned back and gave the door another forceful shove.

With a pleading glance, she looked over her shoulder toward Nicola again, praying he would whisk her away to his studio apartment for the remainder of the night. Hope beat furiously in her breast as he dismounted his motorino and marched toward her. She held her breath in anticipation. He can't tear himself away, she sighed, with a sweet smile.

Nicola's movements were swift and sure, the tender lover of a few moments ago gone. Over and over, he punched the bell. If it were human, it would call the *polizia* and file assault charges, Dena couldn't help but think. Finally, the night doorman made an appearance, and she turned to give him a kiss goodnight. Empty air met her lips.

The peal of his tires as he sped off into the Florentine night greeted the diva.

Traveling Tidbit for the Vacationing Night Owl: Small Italian hotels lock their doors at a certain hour. Look for the bell to alert the sleeping, but quite discreet doorman, to let you in. Any knowing looks or raised eyebrows are most probably a figment of your imagination. Saunter to your room, head held high.

Chapter 11

Shelby forced one eye open and peered out from under her blankets. Damn, she was back. Was there no God in heaven? Shelby tiptoed to the bathroom determined not to wake Dena. Her stealth went unrewarded.

When she returned, Dena was up, tweeting happy as a bird.

"Morning, Glory! Our first full day in Florence. What do you want to do?"

Lose you, find Giancarlo, and start my new life. But that's a lot to do on an empty stomach. Instead, Shelby suggested going down to breakfast before the hotel stopped serving.

Even small hotels in Italy provide a continental breakfast consisting of rolls, cereal, juice, and coffee. Breakfast at the Hotel Machiavelli is definitely a cut above. The three-room dining area is spacious and pleasant. Frescoes adorn the walls, lending old world charm to the rooms. Tables are prettily set, complete with tablecloths. If less formality is preferred, guests may eat comfortably in the antique-filled sitting room just off the dining area.

Several buffet tables are laden with a sampling of foods so impressive it would be almost impossible for diners not to find something they like. Mounds of fresh fruit, platters of meats and cheeses, baskets of pastries and rolls, small containers of yogurt, a selection of cereals, and coffee, tea, milk, and assorted fruit juices leave the poor table groaning for mercy.

> **Traveling Tidbit for the Cash-strapped Traveler:**
> Pack zip lock baggies in your luggage, and bring one to breakfast. Without attracting too much attention, stuff a baggie with meat, cheeses, and bread. *VOILA!* You've got lunch.

Bellies full and back in their room, the ladies drew aside their curtains in anticipation. This was the fledgling Divas' first full day in Italy, and Florence was their oyster. To the ladies' utter disappointment, their oyster was still under water. A gray, dismal day with pouring rain greeted the ladies.

Shelby looked at India. The Brit had seemed so nice at first. Accepting of their foibles and not asking too many difficult questions. She could have almost been a diva. Maybe that was going a bit too far, given the poor girl's looks. Still, she had initially seemed fun and carefree when she asked about the hatboxes. Now, she was a bit of a wet rag. Did she and Dena really need another mother or therapist? Shelby was fed up with the woman.

"Seems like it's been a while since you had a DIQ...I mean a DIQ Test question, India. See if you still know what to do with one." A devilish gleam sparkled in Shelby's eyes as she spoke.

How did Dena and Shelby spend their day?
    A) taking in the Uffizi museum,
    B) meeting with realtors,
    C) catching the latest Italian film, or
    D) snoozing the day away.

"You're almost insulting my intelligence with these questions," their pallid opponent accused. "You were just here in April. Nobody leaves Florence without a trip to the Uffizi Museum. So, Answer A is definitely out," she concluded confidently.

Where was Bob Barker when you needed an old, silver-haired man? Well, really they didn't need him, just his game show buzzer, thought Dena. And his money.

"Wrong!" she yipped proudly. "I'll have you know, to this day, I haven't stepped foot inside one Florentine museum."

Shelby managed to stifle a gasp, but nothing could prevent the shake of her head in utter amazement at her friend's inadvertent confession. I'm weary. The girl does tire me out so. But who else would put up with me?

Given that, the warning on Shelby's face as she zeroed in on India was clear. Dear India, don't even think about insulting her, or I'll bury you!

"Well, you know," Shelby dove in to save her friend. "We feel the Renaissance was highly overrated. As I'm sure you do, too." She didn't give the Englishwoman a chance to say yea or nay. "We're big fans of French Impressionism."

And with that, Shelby shoved the purple journal under their companion's nose. "Read for yourself," she instructed.

If you chose Answer A, you haven't learned a thing about our twosome. Turn back to page one and re-read the entire book, you rube. Do you really think the ladies would ever stand in the mile-long July lines in the pouring rain and ruin either their shoes or their coifs?

If you chose Answer B, do you also wear a paper crown sprinkled with gold glitter? Do you refer to yourself in the third person and use HRH in your signature? Let us guess. You think you're Henry XIII or Elizabeth I? Has it completely escaped your attention that buying real property requires capital? About the best that Shelby could manage was to go home and crack open her piggy bank. As for Dena, she'd hidden any excess cash she'd had in her bra. It had slipped out somewhere between leaving her house and getting in the car to the airport.

If you chose Answer C, you should be commended for donating your organs to science. However, we do believe that the Organ Donor Program intended the donation to be made after death. So, how's functioning without a brain working for you? If our tempting twosome were interested in celluloid Italian men, they could have stayed home, popped in a DVD, and saved themselves thousands of dollars.

If you chose Answer D, congratulations to you! You deserve your very own paper crown. The Divas anoint you royalty for a day. Yes, the ladies needed to catch up on their beauty rest before redeployment into the war theater.

Just before crawling back into bed to sleep the day away, Dena gloatingly regaled Shelby with tales of her previous evening. "And he's begged us to come back tonight. He'll be beside himself if we don't. What do you think? Should we?" she finished.

"Fine with me. I wonder which Italian stallion's going to try to bring me home tonight?" To herself, Shelby wondered why they took the risk. Her betrothed would thrash them should he ever find out.

Ten hours and countless dreams later, Shelby and Dena dragged themselves from their beds to get ready for dinner. Dena chose to wear a form-fitting, halter-top sundress of browns and tans that flattered her olive complexion. Shelby wore a white dress splashed with a black floral design. The spaghetti straps showed off the delicate curves of her shoulders.

Little matching purses packed, they looked forward to another exciting evening. As they made their way to the restaurant, neither woman uttered a word. Every bit of concentration was trained on their feet and the strappy heels that clad them...and not falling flat on their perfectly made-up faces.

How to describe the look on Nicola's face when these two visions of supreme loveliness sauntered confidently through the gates of the restaurant courtyard? Now, now, don't get too excited. This is not a DIQ...DIQ...DIQ Test question. Seems the ladies need to work on DIQ, too. Ahem, correction. The ladies really are going to have to work on *saying* DIQ...DIQ...DIQ Test Question without stumbling over it. They seem to have that problem with a hard...uh...a hard...ah...you know, the hard C sound...as in cock...cock...cockles.

Back to the look on Nicola's face when they entered the restaurant gates. How can one describe it? You're walking down the street quite merrily. Your foot sinks into something soft and warm. A putrid smell wafts up over you. You look down, and what do you see? Fresh dog poo all over those new shoes you just purchased. Now, picture being barefooted.

Try this. Junior year of high school. Fifth period, and you're in Chemistry class. Today's project is the infamous "melt the powdered sulfur" experiment. The stench of rotten eggs permeates every pore of your body. You walk out of the classroom and bump into Dash, the senior heartthrob you've had a crush on for years. He thinks that wonderful smell is emanating from you.

Not graphic enough? You've been to church for the christening of your friend's beautiful new bundle of joy. The happy couple invites everyone home for lunch, where they've planned entertainment. The proud papa pops in a video, and there on a fifty-two inch screen is the most horrific sight you've ever seen. Blood, gore, guts everywhere. The howling and screaming of someone possessed. What is it? The joy of childbirth, the new parents tell you. Isn't it beautiful, they ask your back as you race to the bathroom heaving convulsively.

Now, where were the ladies? Oh, yes. Italy, Florence, the Buca, and that look on Nicola's face. They were back, obviously much to the dismay of Nicola, who had a look of undisguised revulsion on his face. Dena wanted to turn tail and run. Better yet, she was standing on centuries old Duomo grounds. Were there catacombs beneath? Please, God, she prayed. Open this Tuscan earth and bury me alive.

Shelby wasn't certain what the deal was. But she had gotten up, gotten dressed, and she wasn't going anywhere until she'd eaten...and had a little something to quench her thirst. Dena would just have to muddle through somehow.

"Buck up, old girl! Square those shoulders, plaster a smile on your face, and do the Diva March!" she hissed at her stricken friend with military severity.

With poise, grace, and a queasy stomach, Dena presented each cheek to her waiter for a kiss. His mouth on her cheeks lacked the familiar soft warmth she loved, instead feeling carved from cold marble. Dena's tentative smile wavered as the ladies followed his stiffened back to a table.

She watched as he walked away, leading them past a table of other diners. His face lit up with animation, and his voice had regained its joking lilt as he smiled and spoke to the party of five. Dena sagged with relief. She had been mistaken. He wasn't in a foul mood.

But somewhere between that table and the ladies', his trademark charm disappeared again. Stone-faced, he stood before them, ready to take their order. Dena waited...a silky nudge of his knee against hers...a caress of his fingers across her back...any sign of affection. At least, a flicker of recognition.

"Pasta all'arrabiata...tagliolini with porcini mushrooms..." On and on, he droned, mechanically listing the evening's specials, each syllable more devoid of emotion than the last.

With each staccato word, Dena sank deeper into her seat, becoming smaller and smaller, her diva confidence disappearing to wherever his charm must have gone. Her heart pounded against her chest, threatening to break through. Frantically, she pressed her hand to her leg, struggling to stop its violent shaking. Try to act normal, she scolded herself.

She wouldn't have believed it possible, but from somewhere she managed to summon a playful smile across her lips. Again she offered up a plea. God, don't let this come out like a frog's croak.

"That's it, Nicola? I was hoping for a dish with a more personal touch. You know, something just for me," she baited the hook. The seductive glimmer in her eye cast out the line. She waited for the bite.

He shook his head. "Nothing more," he answered, a curt dismissal hardening his words. Not even a nibble.

As she watched the contretemps, even Shelby's bitter heart melted for her friend. She hurriedly spoke up to fill the awkward void. "I'll have..."

With every curt reply, each perfunctory smile, and a quite humorless demeanor, Nicola's actions spoke volumes as the evening deteriorated. One thing was abundantly clear. Shelby's and Dena's presence there was about as welcome as that dog dung on one's foot.

"You'd think we were from Texas!" Dena exclaimed.

"Texas?" Shelby repeated, a little afraid her friend was losing it. What the hell did the Lone Star State have to do with this?

"Yes. Nicola says American tourists are as rude as they come. But he particularly despises Texans. Says they're loud, demanding, condescending, and obnoxious, not to mention, lousy tippers."

Surely the former leader of the free world, the esteemed President Bush, would disagree, but just in case he happens to be mistaken...

Traveling Tidbit for the Ugly American Traveler: If you really are ugly, use delusion and pretend you're not. If this doesn't work, consider plastic surgery. If it's your personality that's ugly -- change it or stay home. The rest of the world wasn't put on this earth to serve you!

Corollary Traveling Tidbit for the Texan Traveler: Adhere to the above tidbit. In addition, check your attitude and ten-gallon hat at customs before entering any foreign country.

Shelby would have probed further, but their rather enlightening conversation was abruptly interrupted by a round, foreign object streaking through the air like Halley's comet. Its victim was the woman at the next table. Splat went the airborne missile, coming to a halt in the woman's plate of pasta. Dollops of creamy sauce splattered in her hair, on her expertly made-up face, and in her lap. Eyes bulging and mouth angrily contorted, the poor screaming woman popped up from her seat with Jack in the Box speed.

The attack wasn't over, and soon, brethren citrus missiles followed the first, furiously pelting diners. Along with everyone else, Dena and Shelby ducked and dodged first to the left, then to the right, desperate to evade what turned out to be a hailstorm of oranges and orange peels raining down from an apartment overlooking the Buca's courtyard.

"Looks like someone else isn't particularly pleased with American tourists," Shelby squealed as a squishy peel plopped on her head.

Gathering his wits, Nicola leapt into action. Flailing his hands in the typically Italian manner as he spoke, he stormed up the stairs with a roar. "*Vecchio, Vecchio! Basta!*" Old Man, Old Man! Enough!

Dena and Shelby weren't quite sure how old this old man was. They weren't quite sure why he was using restaurant patrons as target practice. They certainly hadn't the foggiest what Nicola did while he was up there or if the old man was still alive when the waiter left him. What they did know was that no patrons were severely wounded. The barrage of oranges ceased. And of paramount importance, the Divas' bottle of Chianti hadn't been harmed in the melee.

Even with this amusing diversion, how long did this meal seem? Well, how long was the Hundred Years War? When one has a particularly nasty case of the flu with attendant diarrhea, how long does it seem to go on? If one has a cast on the leg, and has developed a persistent itch that can't be gotten to, how long does each second of discomfort seem to last? Multiply any of these by a million. That should give a pretty good idea.

Following Nicola's episode with the old man, Shelby was a bit fearful of the waiter. He was looking and acting a bit un- hinged really.

"Quick, try to focus, Dena. I know you don't do it often, but this is important. Are you sure Nicola really wanted us here tonight? He's giving me the willies, I tell you." Her squealing rivaled the high-pitched tones of a castrated man.

Dena sputtered nervously. "We...we...well, he was speaking Italian. You know the extent of mine is *piu, piu*-- more, more! But Nicola and I speak the language of love. We don't need words..."

Shelby had heard enough. Hastily, she emptied her little purse of any money it possessed and her wine glass of the last drops of Chianti. Throwing the cash down on the table, she fled as fast as her dainty little shoes would allow, without a back- ward glance.

As she watched her friend make a hasty run for her life, Dena was faced with a choice. Stay and take her chances with Nicola or follow Shelby. She chose her friend. In truth, she chose an end to her utter humiliation.

Nevertheless, on her way through the gates, she did slow down long enough for Nicola's kiss goodbye and for him to slip her his cell phone number once again. "Call me later," he whispered smolderingly.

Now, Dena was no stranger to confusion. She'd made its acquaintance long ago, and they'd been almost inseparable since. She'd learn to live with it and function rather normally. But this? This was too much! By all accounts, the man had just spent the last two hours treating her like yesterday's garbage. And now...now... he wanted her to call him? Either she or Nicola was a raving lunatic. She'd have to check with Shelby to make sure that it wasn't she.

"Oh no, you're not confused. Not this time, at least. He *did* treat us like horse dung." Patting Dena's shoulder, Shelby answered, trying to comfort her friend. "Probably stress, dear. You know with that high-powered profession of his."

Dena sagged with relief. "Of course," she agreed. "He's asked me to call later tonight. I'm sure he'll apologize, and everything will be fine." And the bridesmaids dresses? She wondered what color would be best for an Italian wedding.

Shelby didn't answer. If that worked for Dena, let her run with it. Poor girl, maybe it really was time for a psychiatrist's intervention. Something to consider when they got back to the States.

While allowing Dena to maintain her delusion nearly killed Shelby, she knew she couldn't be the one to pop that bubble because of a Diva Do/n't that covered just such a situation.

Diva Do/n't

If you want to stay out of trouble, don't ever burst a fellow Diva's delusional bubble.

Besides, Shelby consoled herself, someone or something else would surely come along and take care of the job. Their friendship wouldn't suffer, and she'd be there to help Dena upon her re-entry to Planet Earth.

Nevertheless, biting her tongue was hard work. Shelby needed a drink. "Let's go to *Caffe Rivoire*[21] for Bellinis," she suggested.

Dena stamped her foot in childish protest. "Shelby, I don't want another man. I want Nicola."

"No, dear. Rivoire is a world renowned bar, and a Bellini isn't a man, but a champagne and peach juice cocktail. They are simply divine!"

Still, if she did happen to find a man to take Dena off her hands...well, that would just be icing on the cake.

Rivoire, long considered the grand dame of Florentine cafés, was founded in 1872 as a steamed chocolate factory. A bit of

---

[21]Caffe Rivoire, Piazza della Signoria 5r

lost elegance in this modern world, patrons can still enjoy its famous hot chocolate and a cornucopia of mouth-watering chocolate confections, as well as savor coffee from elegant silver-filigree cups. Nonetheless, for those like our perennially tipsy travelers, who require something with a bit more kick than hot chocolate, don't despair. *Rivoire* is also known for its exquisite cocktails and aperitifs.

The beauty of an excursion to this little treasure chest is its location in *Piazza della Signoria*, inarguably Florence's most arresting square named after the s*ignoria* or oligarchy that ruled Florence in medieval times. The piazza serves as the crossroads for the city's cultural, political, and social life. Anyone lucky enough to snag an outdoor table at Rivoire should sit down and relax while enjoying the kaleidoscope of international passersby, all viewed against the spectacular backdrop of the Palazzo Vecchio, the Uffizi Gallery, and another very good copy of Michelangelo's Davide.

Bellinis drained and no one showing the slightest interest, Shelby and Dena decided to partake of a free and thoroughly captivating form of entertainment, a leisurely stroll through the streets of Florence, aka people watching.

It didn't take long before the bees started to buzz. As the ladies rounded the Uffizi Gallery, enter stage left two Italian men out on their own *passegiatta,* their evening stroll. Or, more precisely, their evening troll. The two pesky pests quickly zeroed in on Dena and Shelby.

"Che bella!" How beautiful!

"Grazie."

At this point, the gentlemen introduced themselves, as...? Once again, the Divas are not trying to be discreet. The men's names simply escape them. So, let's just call them Mutt and Jeff, or in deference to their Italian heritage, Muttelli and Jeffelli.

If the ladies had been on the streets of New York, L.A., or any other American city, a gentleman passerby might have proffered an appreciative glance their way. If he were really emboldened, perhaps he'd have smiled and gotten out a brief hello. If, by chance, casual greetings were exchanged, that would've been the extent of it. Not so in Italy. If a lady gives an admiring Italian man so much as a sideways glance, he'll attach himself to her like a barnacle on a ship.

Mutelli and Jeffelli were no different. The sauntering sisters had walked quite a few meters when they realized that they were being tailed. Jeffelli and Muttelli hadn't continued on their merry way, but had u-turned and slithered up alongside Dena and Shelby.

"What is that buzzing sound? Mosquitoes?" Dena asked, voice filled with annoyance.

Shelby turned to investigate. "Oh, no. Mutt and Jeff back for an encore," she hissed to her friend.

"You like go to disco?" one of them asked. They buzzed, two Italian bees who had found their latest honey pot.

"Oh no," Dena declined swiftly. "We're just on our way back to our hotel. I have to make an important phone call very soon."

"Oh, to your husband in America?" one of the bees fished.

"No," Dena gloated. "I have a date tonight."

She continued to prattle on proudly to Muttelli and Jeffelli about her impending date with a very important headwaiter, giving Nicola a promotion neither he nor his employers knew about.

Throughout Dena's impromptu dissertation, Shelby was lost in her own thoughts. NASA really should investigate this. A human capable of survival in outer space without benefit of space suit or shuttle. Dena really was quite amazing. Was she, in fact, the missing link? Had she been conceived by sperm and egg, like everyone else? Or had she hatched from some alien pod?

With uncharacteristic restraint, Shelby managed to squelch her usual wisecrack. She was walking a delicate and precarious balance, feeling torn between the need to pull her friend back to earth's reality and the Diva Code of Honor, which brings us to another Diva Do/n't.

Diva Do/n't

When in the company of non-Diva personnel, don't embarrass another Diva or you'll go to hell.

In the end, Shelby was happy to let her newfound proxies fill in for her. Jeffelli and Muttelli were doing a rather good job of their own curtailing Dena's current space exploration. With every roll of their deep Italian eyes and each slick elbow jab they shared, it was as if they were hooking a space tether to Dena and yanking her back into the earth's atmosphere. However, the little moonwalker was resistant to their re-entry path, so the two men offered her a compromise.

"Call him from a pay phone," they suggested. Magnanimously, Jeffelli held out a handful of Italian coins for her use.

Shelby spied in the sly confidence of the men's shared glances what she already knew. There would be no answer to the phone call. She watched on as Dena held the receiver in a death grip, trying to will an answer from the other end of the line. And when, a sad confusion clouded the other woman's hopeful face, Shelby noted the smug satisfaction of Muttelli and Jeffelli.

"There's a recording in Italian. I must have dialed the wrong number," Dena burbled. She hastily snatched yet another coin from Muttelli's outstretched hand.

Even the icebox Shelby called her heart melted for just a minute at the humiliation her friend was inflicting on herself. The second phone call being no more fruitful, Dena finally touched down to earth, anguish distorting her pretty face.

Nonetheless, her brush with reality was short-lived. Shelby, along with Muttelli and Jeffelli, watched in awe as Dena shook off her Diva Down, and fired up her jets once again.

"Oh, I know," she declared, the storm clouds giving way to a smile bright as a sunbeam. "His cell phone battery must be dead. I bet he's sitting outside our hotel right now on his motorino." With a quick farewell, she turned and sashayed away.

Though Shelby could hear the clickety click of her friend's dainty heels on the medieval cobblestones of Florence, she knew that Dena had lifted off once again and was daring to go where no man (or diva, for that matter) had dared go before. Helpless in the face of such lunacy, Shelby turned to the boys with feigned regret.

"So, sorry. As you can see, my responsibilities are endless. Perhaps we'll meet again. Ciao, ciao."

And with a Diva wave, she turned and had to run (oops, glide quickly) to keep up with Dena, who by now had propulsed herself to warp speed.

Shelby's time alone gave her a chance to think, and she made a mental note to herself. It might be time to groom a new friend. Any day now, Dena was likely to enter outer space and any rescue mission would fail. She'd either orbit for eternity or explode upon re-entry. Sad but true, and Shelby did need to look out for herself.

Chapter 12

*I*f the ladies have given the impression that their sole concerns were their faux haute couture collections with matching bras and panties, befriending a charitable vintner who would keep them plied with vast quantities of vino rosso (or better yet, a restaurateur who added in a little food to keep up their energy levels), or conquering their quarry on the ultimate battlefield of the bed, that impression would be woe-fully mistaken.

Theirs was a more pressing, even earth shattering matter. Was it an audience with *Il Papa*, the Pope, to pray for world peace? Helping the heartrending Roma children begging in the streets of Florence? Possibly volunteering to help restore the earthquake-damaged Basilica of Saint Francis of Assisi?

Please! Has there been any mention thus far of the ladies having taken a previous trip to the land of Oz, where Dena managed to secure herself a brain and Shelby, aka the Tinman, got herself so much as an aorta, never mind a whole heart? Yes, the ladies would concede all of the above were quite worthy causes, but theirs was an infinitely more deserving charitable organization. Them and Theirs, Inc.

"Today is Maurice's birthday," Dena announced nostalgically, as she thought back to the day her only son was born. "I have to find something special for him."

To be precise, it was Maurice's thirteenth birthday. In some cultures, this would be his rite of passage into manhood. Had Dena's family been Jewish, Maurice would have been at his Bar Mitzvah. If he were African, he would have been undergoing a quite painful circumcision or receiving gruesome facial scars right about then. Should they have been Aboriginals, the family could have saved thousands in orthodontia work and just waited for the elders to knock out his front teeth with a boomerang.

In other words, it was a landmark birthday. Even by less tradition-bound American standards, Maurice was passing into his teenage years, an occasion most parents consider quite momentous and worthy of commemorating. Indeed, very few would dream of missing this moment in their child's life.

So, where was Maurice's loving mother? Planning his birthday bash? Addressing and mailing the engraved invitations? Consulting with the caterer? Hiring a band? Heavens no. Dena had something special planned.

She had decided the best way to celebrate Maurice's milestone would be to buy him a lovely gift from the land of his ancestral roots. Perish the thought that she would entrust this task to the Internet or mail order. She had to go to Italy herself. And, if she were lucky, while scouring the country for just the right gift for dear Maurice, she'd undergo her own rite of passage with Nicola.

And so it was that on her son's birthday, Dena and Shelby were strolling the teeming streets of Florence doing what they do best. Shopping.

On a quaint side street, they happened upon a small, but tempting shop. As its name, The Writer, suggests, *Lo Scrittoio* is a purveyor of beautiful writing and wrapping papers, as well as exquisite writing instruments. In the shop window, Dena spotted a handsome journal, bound in rich oxblood leather and embossed with the Fleur de Lis, a design used by Florentine armies since the Crusades to identify themselves. The Fleur de Lis, or Flower of the Lily, eventually became the symbol of Florence. The image abounds throughout the city, emblazoned on everything from the official flag to stationery of all kinds.

While at Lo Scrittoio, Dena picked up the journal for her daughter, Giselle, a budding author. She also fell in love with colorful, blown-glass fountain pens and bought a trio, one for each child. Always in a buying mood, Shelby's eyes coveted a burnished siena-colored wood fountain pen with a brass initial stamp atop it. She thought immediately of her sister, who loved to write, and quickly snapped it up.

Next, they were off to the shopping mall, or Florence's medieval version thereof, *Il Ponte Vecchio*, the Old Bridge. Lining each side of this historic landmark are tiny, gold- and gem-laden jewelry stores dating back centuries. By day, the large glass showcase windows display an irresistible array of gems and jewels that sparkle with solar brightness. By night, impressive wood doors with wrought iron detail shutter those windows to conceal and protect the treasures within. The sight instantly transports one back to medieval times, and brings to mind images of Pinocchio's Geppetto hard at work in his woodcarving shop.

The ladies stepped into the little jewelry shop, *Negrin*. Upon noticing a silver Italian horn and chain, Dena had a brilliant idea. "Oh, Maurice has always wanted one of these," she exclaimed. "It will make a perfect gift."

After a few more minutes of browsing, she purchased it, along with a pair of gold hoop earrings for daughter Adie's birthday. For the unvarnished truth was that Dena wasn't missing just one child's birthday. She had skipped the American continent for little Adie's big day, too.

Still, the pleasure the ladies usually derived during their shopping excursions was missing a certain something. Mmmm...what could it be? It didn't take long for the purchasing pals to figure it out, which neatly invites the following shopping caveat.

Diva Do/n't

When you must buy someone else a gift, do buy yourself a little something-something for a little lift.

Corollary Diva Do/n't for Family-less and Friendless: Don't despair if you've no friends or relations. The Divas gladly accept any donations.

"Now what are you looking for?" Shelby asked impatiently. She was ready to move on.

"Well, you know, my cameo bracelet? I haven't anything to go with it."

Shelby laughed. "Yeah, it's lonely and needs a family!"

As Dena was trying to decide on the perfect pendant and earrings, she noticed her friend eyeing a pretty cameo bracelet. "I'll take it!" Shelby told the clerk.

"It's not like you already have any lonely cameos," Dena joked. "So, what's your excuse?"

"It's an orphan and needs a home," Shelby rejoined. With it, she bought a cameo pendant for her mother's fast approaching birthday.

Shopping is not just a pleasant way to spend an afternoon for the ladies. It's a blood sport for the two friends. And as with any sport, to be the very best, it requires keen concentration and intensive training. When out of condition, resumption of the sport taxes the body severely.

It should be kept in mind that the two women hadn't been in a store for quite a time, nearly two whole days now. The thrill of the competition was taking its toll.

"Shopping's hard work," Dena said. "I'm exhausted."

Shelby agreed. The adrenaline coursing through her veins at the outset of their excursion seemed to be waning. Giddy excitement at being back in the shopping saddle could only carry her so far. "Yeah, I think our blood sugar levels are dangerously low. We need..."

"Wine!"

The pair decided to repair to an outdoor café and restore their electrolytes with the Gatorade of the Diva, Chianti by the barrel. Other nutritional supplements included a little cheese and prosciutto for protein, and delicious Italian bread for the carbs. A veritable feast fit for the gods or, in this case, the Divas. But where to find such a repast?

Luckily, just steps away from the Hotel Machiavelli sits a quintessentially Italian gourmet deli, a small, but well ladened gem for any tourist's wallet. Homemade pastas, fresh and prepared meats, assorted scrumptious cheeses, freshly baked breads and pastries, and a respectable selection of wines. One-stop shopping at its best.

The name of this place? Must the ladies toil over every little detail? Just hang a right when leaving the Hotel Macchiavelli, walk down Via Nazionale. You can't miss it.

Upon completing their purchases, Dena and Shelby hurried back to the hotel for a delightful lunch. Still, much as she was enjoying the delectables, the fact that she had yet to make her initial contact with Giancarlo nagged at poor Shelby like an infected tooth.

She'd emailed him from the States that she'd be coming, but hadn't given him specific dates and wasn't quite sure how her return would be received. It was time to call.

"Shelby, where are you?" he asked. After revealing that she was in a Florentine hotel, she was heartened by his response.

"Yes, I know where is. *Senti*, Shelby." Listen, he said with his sexy Italian lilt. "I in Grosseto at the villa. I return Monday. We have dinner, no?"

Shelby was in seventh heaven. He wanted to see her immediately upon his return.

"Is Dena with you?" he asked.

"Oh, yes, she's here." Stuck to me like moss on the shady side of a tree, Shelby thought but couldn't say.

"Good, we all have dinner on Monday."

Normally, Shelby would have been happy at his generosity and willingness to spend time with her friends. However, a threesome wasn't exactly what she'd envisioned for this particular reunion. Best to nip this right in the bud. "Well, I'm not sure Dena will come."

"No, no. Dena must come," Giancarlo said.

Shelby's suspicious mind was awhirl. Why, she wondered. One of her friends hadn't been enough. Now he was going to try his hand at Dena? She kept her thoughts to herself and responded in dulcet tones.

"Well, I'll let her know you'd love to see her, and we'll see," she agreed, struggling to keep the sarcasm at bay.

Anyway, she wasn't unduly worried about Dena horning in on her date. The girl had been babbling on about spending Monday and Tuesday with Nicola. Most likely, as Shelby was having a romantic dinner with Giancarlo on Monday night, Dena would be back at the Michelin three-star accommodations of the Buca's storeroom.

The wine at lunch had given Shelby just the boost she'd needed to call Giancarlo, but it had also made her a bit tired. With nothing more pressing on the rest of the day's agenda than deciding which establishment to bless with their presence for dinner, the ladies decided to get a little beauty rest.

Upon awaking, they consulted their trusty Frommer's and Fodor's guides...yes, Dena had brought her Fodor's with her on this trip. After extended consideration, they settled on *Trattoria Zá Zá.*[22]

Once again, they took great care choosing their outfits. Shelby knew that she would be the envy of every woman who saw her in a fuchsia floral print sundress paired with matching t-strapped sandals. Floral prints were the order of the day, as Dena slipped into a formfitting red and white flowered dress, coordinating it with red leather slides and the cream and red Furla purse she'd bought in Capri.

Feeling certain the proprietors of Zá Zá would recognize them as the Divas immediately, the ladies ignored their travel guides' recommendation to make reservations.

"Okay, India, put on your thinking cap. It's our favorite time, another DIQ coming your way." Shelby gave a sly laugh at her own joke. *That would never happen for old prune face.* *"Uh, we mean another DIQ Test question,"* she corrected.

---

[22]Trattoria Za Za, Piazza Mercato Centrale 26r, PH 055/21-54-11

How were the ladies received upon their arrival at the restaurant?

A) They were immediately shown to the best table in the house,

B) They were asked to pose for a picture to be placed on the restaurant's wall of movie stars,

C) So overwhelmed by the ladies' beauty, the restaurant refused to accept their money and instead paid the dining duo for gracing their humble establishment, or

D) After standing on line for 15 minutes, the ladies were told to wander the streets for the next hour and come back. There might be a bench with dinner trays available for them.

"Look, I've had it with you and your quizzes. Just hand me that book and let me read," India adjured.

If you chose Answer A, you don't get out much, do you? Do you know what the word restaurant means? Learn your ABC's, consult Merriam-Webster, get out of your hovel more, and get back to us. What restaurant do you know gives their best table to two unknown foreigners who haven't bothered to make a reservation?

If you chose Answer B, you know more about the Divas than they do about themselves. Obviously you've seen them in some motion picture they didn't know they appeared in. Please write in with the name of that movie. The ladies will take great pleasure in seeing themselves on the big screen. Thank you in advance.

If you chose Answer C, you definitely suffer with Attention Deficit Disorder. Let's recap. The ladies couldn't manage to get so much as a crust of day-old Italian bread for free in the restaurant where one of them was diddling the very important headwaiter. Given this, please explain how you could possibly have chosen Answer C?

If you chose Answer D, congratulations. You are correct.

"So, let me get this straight," India said as she looked up from the book. "It's your second day of Diva-dumb," she began, smiling at her private play on words. "And where has all this got you?"

Shelby didn't miss the smug, rather self-satisfied smile on the Briton's waxen face. The woman really does need to get out in the sun more. A figure from Madame Tussaud's collection would have more blood coursing through its veins. Why didn't she just shut up and leave them alone?

But the Englishwoman persisted. "Let's see. One of you has been courted in a cobweb-infested storeroom. And if that wasn't enough, the next evening, the gentleman, and I use that term loosely, behaves as if he's never met you."

Okay, it's not so bad, Shelby sighed, sagging with relief. As long as she leaves me out of it. "Oh, India, I think you're being a bit hard on Dena..."

"Oh, I'm not done yet," their self-appointed nemesis interrupted. Then, she trained her gaze on Shelby. "You turn yourself inside out to get back to Italy and Giancarlo, the love of your life..."

Shelby blanched, becoming almost as pale as her inquisitor. Oh no, here she goes. Should've kept my mouth shut and let Dena sink or swim on her own.

"And does he invite you to Grosseto because he can't wait to see you? Oh, no. He's perfectly happy to wait 'til Monday," India landed the lance in Shelby's heart. "Looks like you're going to have to tell them who you are, like your father said. Cause they're sure not seeing it on their own."

Where did this woman come from? And why had they had to meet her? How could someone see so much so soon? Sufficiently chastened, the ladies decided to ignore the wretched woman's comments and picked up their tale.

Dena and Shelby didn't really believe the owners of Zá Zá's were into torture. They could only conclude that the good people sincerely had no idea who they were or the pain they caused by sending the ladies to sally forth through the streets of Florence in new shoes.

By the time the women returned to the restaurant, the spring in their step had deteriorated somewhat. Picture poor Quasimoto, humpbacked and dragging one leg along. Compared to the ladies, his gait looked like ballet. Limping and wincing with pain, Shelby and Dena gratefully fell into their seats at the outdoor table. The throbbing was intense.

Then, Dena came up with one of her brilliant ideas. "I know this sounds crazy..."

"Yes?" Shelby answered tentatively. She looked around, not sure if she should warn the other diners, tell them to run for their lives. Dena had a thought, and even she thought it was crazy. Surely her head was about to explode, and the force would be tantamount to an incoming scud missile, leaving nothing alive in its wake. Should I flee? Do I waste time alerting others or just save myself? It was out of Shelby's hands. Dena spoke before she could make a move.

"My feet are killing me. I have fantasies of asking them to bring the pasta pot, toss in a little Epsom Salt and let us soak our feet for awhile."

Shelby looked up at the sky. No mushroom cloud was visible, and Dena's head was still in one piece. And the truth was that soaking her feet in a pasta pot sounded like a little piece of heaven to Shelby. Well, let's see. Maybe this would be the moment Shelby would credit her friend with being more evolved than a one-celled animal?

"Oh yes, Dena, you're sure to be presented with the James Beard award for culinary excellence." Or maybe not.

Dena smiled giddily. "Oh, Shelby, do you really think so? For what?"

"Why, for coming up with Italian nouvelle cuisine, of course. Toe Jam and Pasta. Light, not many calories, and a lot of protein."

When she saw a little tear form in Dena's eyes, an uncomfortable quiver snaked through Shelby's body. Could this possibly be what guilt feels like? Nah, I'm just hungry.

Fearing they might end up wearing the pasta pot and its contents as a hat should they actually ask for it, the women went to Plan B. "Your biggest bottle of Chianti, my dear man," they begged.

With each sip, the garnet elixir worked its magic as it seeped through the ladies' veins and anesthetized them from head to toe. For their feet, this was a blessing.

Unfortunately, the wine precipitated a similar effect on their gray matter. And so, as for a detailed description...okay, even a rudimentary description of their meal... the ladies cannot oblige.

As their meal progressed, Shelby got a funny feeling. Looking up, she noticed a young man seated at John Torta's, a wine bar directly adjacent to Zá Zá's and under the same ownership. His eyes were trained on her, almost piercing through her, captivating her. She allowed her own gaze to sleek over him from afar. His onyx eyes smoldered. A sexy goatee lent him a dashing presence. Though he was seated, he gave the appearance of tallness, with long lean legs casually crossed.

With each sip of Chianti, Shelby's flirtatious overtures were emboldened. Soon her little smiles became open laughter, their eyes locked in teasing playfulness, and she returned numerous tips of her glass to acknowledge and encourage this latest admirer.

As Dena watched the steamy interaction and encouraged her friend's antics, she couldn't help but be a bit surprised. In reality, she couldn't believe her eyes. Not only had she never seen Shelby flirt before, but certainly not with a younger man. Shelby hated the idea of dating a younger man, didn't she?

Minutes later, a small Roma child approached their table. She presented both women with a single red rose, indicating it had been sent to them by the handsome admirer. Slowly, deliberately, Shelby brought the delicate flower to her nose. Her eyes never left the stranger's face, inhaling him, drawing him in just as she was taking in the perfumed beauty of the rose.

She watched as her handsome stranger rose with graceful purpose and strode to their table. He was indeed tall, and Shelby had to co...co...cock her head sharply to look into those dark eyes. Both she and Dena struggled to stifle twin gasps.

"Ready, India? You know what's coming!"

"You two are testing my patience, especially with what's sure to be a silly question," India said. She grabbed the book from Shelby's grasp.

What about Shelby's admirer surprised the ladies so?

A) His sculptured male beauty, which rivaled that of Michelangelo's famed Davide,

B) He was an Italian rock star and wanted the ladies to star in his upcoming music video,

C) He turned out to be a wealthy Italian prince in search of his princess, or

D) His smoldering eyes and dashing goatee resembled the filmy eyes of a dead fish and the scruffy hair of a flea bitten dog.

If you chose Answer A, make an immediate request to your psychiatrist for electric shock therapy. Twenty-five year old men who look like Davide are not flirting with forty-something year old women whose breasts send off sparks as they scrape the pavement.

If you chose Answer B, put the book down, call your mother and ask if she was on drugs while carrying you. Only hallucinogens could account for anyone believing our two middle-aged ladies could shake their booties down to the ground in a music video and get back up again without the aid of a construction crane.

If you chose Answer C, you're either only seven years old or have the mind of a seven-year old, and you shouldn't be reading this book.

If you chose Answer D, not only are you correct, you also must have experienced the wonders of middle age, where, without glasses, your eyes play tricks on you, and after a few glasses of wine, even a wildebeest can resemble Brad Pitt. Congratulations and have a glass of wine on the Divas!

India let out a begrudging laugh.

"Okay, I have to admit your wisecrack's funny as hell."

"Well, thank you," Dena said. She smiled smugly.

"But, be that as it may, I am still somewhat confused," the Brit continued.

Her smugness suddenly deserted her, and Dena shrank back in her seat. Please don't let this be about me. I don't have anything to do with this. I was just there trying to rest my feet.

"The last I recall, it was true love for Giancarlo," India was just revving up. Then she let her engines rip. "How is it that you found yourself flirting with a complete stranger?"

Now, Shelby really did turn crimson. Okay, maybe Casper did have a point. However, Shelby was still waiting for her engagement ring. "Well India, I do believe we've already had this discussion. Remember that Diva Do/n't about men not being able to fulfill their duties? It has a corollary."

Diva Do/n't

When the man you want is not with you, do find another so you won't be blue.

"And, let's face it. You said it yourself. Giancarlo had not invited me to Grosseto," Shelby added pointedly.

Chapter 13

Sunday in Italy. Home of the Pope, seat of Catholicism, and a country where ninety-eight percent of the population considers itself Catholic. The two Catholic school chums had a choice. Attend Sunday services in one of the most famous and majestic cathedrals in the world, or slip on their bikinis and head to the beach. Bright blue skies, ninety-degree temperatures, seventy-five percent humidity, and no air-conditioning in Il Duomo. Still lost?

"These bags were the perfect choice for carry-on luggage," said Dena.

Shelby smiled at their cunning and foresight. "Yup, the perfect cover. Beach bags by day. And come nightfall..."

Mobility bags for long, hard, strenuous nights in the trenches. Perfect for discreetly carrying sexy negligees for combat fatigues, precious oils as ammo, thongs cum slingshots, and industrial strength helmets for the little heads of the conquered. The ladies' eyes sparkled with devilish delight at the very thought.

Unfortunately, their only cargo today was sunscreen, tanning lotion, towels, cameras, and reading materials. And so, with bathing suits hidden under street clothes and straw hats atop their heads, Dena and Shelby set out for the train station and ultimately the seaside village of Viareggio.

Nicola had suggested this little town, assuring the ladies it was a mere one-hour train ride away. While the waiter's reliability regarding the trip's duration (and alas, quite a few other things) left a lot to be desired, his description of Viareggio turned out to be nearly picture perfect. Stepping off the train two hours later, the ladies were confronted with a perfectly exquisite example of an Italian seaside resort town.

The less than twenty-minute walk from the train station to the beach along Via Mazzini is an experience in and of itself. The street is lined with tempting shops, eateries, and a soon-to-be essential pharmacy.

Shops are to Shelby what casinos are to the gambling addict. As they strolled toward the beach, her antennae picked up a signal. Like a guided missile, she homed in on Applewoods,[23] a

---

[23]Applewoods, Via Massini 84/86, PH 0584/30895

charming British emporium carrying all-natural bath, body, and aromatherapy products, as well as unique gifts for the home.

Dena groaned with disgust. "We're here to go to the beach!"

"I don't need to buy anything. I just need to look," Shelby uttered defensively. "It's in my genes, probably passed down from ancient bartering ancestors. I must come from a long line of shoppers."

Looking around, an unusual lamp with a base of scrolled wrought iron holding a candle caught her attention. Its distinctiveness lay in its shade, made of ecru-colored candle wax etched with black cryptic markings very reminiscent of Egyptian hieroglyphs. Shelby knew this was the perfect gift for her sister and quickly made the purchase.

Dena wasted no time finding a similar, but more colorful lamp for her elder daughter Giselle. As she continued to roam the pretty store, her brown eyes fell upon the men's colognes. Plucking a sampler from its shelf, Dena sniffed the scent.

"And I'll take this cologne for my son," she said to the proprietor, hoping to assuage any leftover maternal pangs of guilt. With a bit of thought, she amended her order. "Make that two bottles."

Shelby swiveled around from the lotion she was sampling. "How much cologne does a thirteen-year old boy need?" she snapped with suspicion.

"Oh, don't forget, I will be spending the next three days with Nicola. This'll be a little token of my affection."

To that, Shelby rolled her eyes in undisguised revulsion. "Lust you mean."

Dena shrugged her shoulders with an uncharacteristic lack of concern for Shelby's opinion. "Ours is a love that will stand the test of time."

A loud hoot of laughter accompanied the next roll of Shelby's eyes. "Yes, you're right. I can see it now. A day, a week, the next ten days we're here. If you're lucky. And that, only if you use a few hundred dollar bills to gift wrap his bottle," she retorted.

Dena, undaunted by her friend's dismal prognosis, happily concluded her purchases. The shop's mother-and-son owners were extremely friendly and accommodating, offering not only to gift-wrap the items, but also to safeguard them while the bathing beauties strutted the Viareggio beach. Should the ladies not make it back before closing time, they promised to leave the packages at the bar next door. Business concluded, Shelby and Dena once again set off toward the beach.

"Look at that, my watch must have stopped. It says 2:30, but that's when the train pulled in," Shelby observed. "Wonder what that means?"

Though they'd chosen the beach over church, the ladies still considered themselves quite attuned to the messages sent from their angels. So, when Shelby looked up and realized that they were in front of a real estate agency, she was convinced her angel had given her a sign. The agency was closed, but photographs of various available properties polka-dotted the window and captured Shelby's and Dena's imaginations. Quietly, each lady stood, lost in her own thoughts.

Shelby could see it clearly. A medieval fieldstone villa on the Tuscan seaside, filled with Italian antiques and family pictures. A portrait of her and Giancarlo, of course, and their twin baby boys, Luca and Giancarlo Jr. Oh, and don't forget his three other children. They'd love her dearly.

Dena's vision was suspiciously similar. In fact, her villa was on the adjoining property. She and Shelby would be neighbors. Yes, she would be in Italy, but her garden would be English. A profusion of color and aromatic scents, a veritable potpourri of herbs, flowers, and shrubs. Nicola and she would start each day amid the delicate scent of honeysuckle wafting in the sea breeze, while sipping espresso. They would enjoy endless hours watching her children romp along the beach with his dog. One big happy family, and if her angel truly shone down on her, they'd be blessed with another little Nicola. This one would have a brain in its head, arms and legs, and more than one eye. And, it wouldn't need a raincoat to come out to play.

While Shelby's fantasy was a short vignette, Dena's was a full-length feature film in Technicolor. Impatiently, Shelby broke through her friend's reverie, asking for a pen to jot down the real estate agency's phone number. Mission completed, they were on their way once again.

One of Viareggio's most breathtaking aspects is the Apuan Alps. The breathtaking mountains can be seen off in the distance, juxtaposed against the white sand and the clear blue waters of the Mediterranean.

As they continued on their way, Dena was mesmerized by the panoramic beauty. "We've found our place. This is surely where we are meant to buy property. It must be; we were guided here by Nicolaaaaaa..."

Not sure what had caused the warble in Dena's voice, Shelby turned, only to discover that her friend had disappeared. She made a searching pirouette. Then, hearing a low whimpering from below, she looked down. There, at her feet was Dena, on her knees in the middle of the cobblestone street, her beach bag and its contents littering the pavement. Her straw hat was cock...cock...cockeyed on her head...clear evidence she had taken a nasty tumble.

"Or maybe not!" Dena exclaimed as Shelby lifted her to her feet. "Maybe my angel's trying to tell me something. Wonder what?"

Shelby was busy reclaiming Dena's strewn belongings. Stooping low, she grabbed each item, throwing them one by one into the waiting beach bag. But this didn't stop her from responding.

"Let's recap. Before being hurled to the pavement, kicked to the curb like last night's drunk, what were the last words on your lips?" She halted for a second, letting her own words sink in. Okay, with Dena, better give it a few more seconds. It was killing her, but Shelby managed to keep a straight face as she continued.

"Hmmmm," she murmured, cupping her chin with her forefinger and casting her eyes upward in exaggerated thought. "Oh yeah. Nicola. Perhaps your angel is saying that you and Nicola will have a long and happy future together."

Dena ignored her friend's sarcasm, more concerned with her injury. Before that unlikely future could begin, her knee, which looked dangerously similar to raw meat, needed attention. And so, the ladies set off on yet another side trip, this time to the pharmacy to purchase first aid items to repair the wounds of her unfortunate incident.

They stood in line for quite a while before realizing they needed to take a number. After a further twenty-minute wait, Shelby became impatient.

"Scusi? Is this a deli? Do you think we need a pound of roast beef? Don't you see the blood running down my friend's leg? Soon her shoes may be ruined. We need to do something quickly! I demand that we go to the front of the line and receive immediate attention," she rattled on haughtily.

No one understood her. She was speaking English. Perhaps this was a good thing; otherwise, they might have been thrown out. But eventually, they were served and Dena was given the necessary cleaning solution, antibiotic cream, and bandages. She found a quiet corner with a chair and began the painful task of nursing her wound.

As she waited, Shelby paced to and fro between the main pharmacy and Dena's makeshift emergency room. Every few seconds, a loud buzzer went off, prizing Shelby from her hectic thoughts. Each time, she nearly jumped out of her skin at the unexpected annoyance. "What is that godforsaken buzzing? An air raid?" she snapped.

Within minutes the short, baldheaded pharmacist was in her face yelling in Italian. He shook an angry finger in her face.

"*Non ho capito*. I don't understand," replied an increasingly agitated Shelby. She took a few steps back. The man looked a touch deranged.

"The alarm, the alarm! It you!" he accused, still waving his finger angrily.

Comprehension slipped over Shelby. Each time she went to check on her friend, she was tripping the alarm guarding the pharmacy's drug supply.

"Scusi, so sorry. Let's get out of here, Dena," she hissed under her breath. As they left the premises, another idea came to mind. Mmmm. Wonder what kind of drugs I could have liberated, she thought too late.

Diva Do/n't

Even when you look like a fool, do make sure to keep your cool.

An hour and a half after having pulled into the train station, the ladies finally reached their intended destination, Viareggio's beach. As far as their eyes could see, a battalion of beach umbrellas, loungers, and deck chairs stood in precision-perfect lines.

"Oh, look umbrellas and chairs for everyone. So much nicer than the beaches in the States," exclaimed Dena. "But why is everyone sitting so far back from the water?"

Shelby shrugged her shoulders in answer, as she cast her gaze over the scene. It was odd that most of the loungers and deckchairs located near the water were unoccupied, while at the back half of the beach, sunbathers were lined up like sardines in a can. Even though the conundrum niggled slightly in the duo's minds, they believed as all divas do, that they deserved the best, and without the slightest hesitation, the two headed straight to a prime location at the water's edge.

Carefully choosing a spot, the ladies spread out their towels and settled in. Both were lathering sun-block on their skin in anticipation of a lazy afternoon of power sunbathing, when a lovely Italian woman appeared before them. "Scusi," she began. "Theeez for my friends."

At first, Dena and Shelby didn't understand. But as the Italian began gesticulating with her hands, they soon got the message. The Divas had chosen already–rented loungers and umbrella.

"Oh, oh, so sorry. All?" They questioned, pointing to the whole area.

The Italian shook her head. "I don't know. You must ask," she answered.

Ask whom was the ladies' next question. Through a combination of gestures and Ital-English, the ladies quickly ascertained that they needed to go the *bagni*, the business office that rents beach umbrellas, deck chairs, and loungers.

Like thieves in the night, the women hastily gathered up their belongings. As they made the long trek back to the service desk, Shelby pushed her hat down further on her head, hoping no one could see her face. "How embarrassing," she muttered.

Preliminaries taken care of, the cashier handed the ladies a paper containing a number and instructed them to look for that space number for their loungers.

"Ah, India, you lucky devil, another DIQ Test question," Dena enthused. *"Try this one on for size."*

> Where do you think the ladies' seats were located?
> A) Next to two very rich, very handsome Italian gentlemen who whisked them off their feet, proposed marriage, and promised a life of happily ever after,
> B) Being told they were too beautiful to be on a public beach, the ladies were escorted to a private beach where their every wish was catered to,
> C) They were given seats at the prime location of the water's edge, or
> D) Their seats were the equivalent of a sports stadium's nosebleed section, roughly one mile from the sea and two feet from the street, where they were forced to dodge oncoming traffic.

> If you chose Answer A, you are too stupid to live. If our pitiful protagonists had managed to dupe two rich men into taking them on, they'd be on a yacht cruising the Greek Isles sipping Bellinis, not wasting their time

penning this drivel and beseeching any and all to line the coffers of their off-shore account.

If you chose Answer B, you can be forgiven your slight error. Yes, the ladies often refer to themselves as visions of loveliness, but have yet to find even one other person who concurs.

If you chose Answer C, your lights may be on, but is anyone home? Do you need directions or a taxi to take you there? Has anything really worked out for the ladies since the beginning of this book?

If you chose Answer D, congratulations. You are correct. We're lovin' it. You deserve a break today. Proceed to the nearest McDonald's, and have a Big Mac on the ladies. And if he's cute (and rich), please tell Big Mac that he is certainly welcome to contact us at www.DelusionalDivas.com. Thank you in advance.

"Carrying matching straw hats and bags, and they still didn't know who you were," India lamented, not without sarcasm.

"Not a clue," Shelby agreed. "But we did find out why everyone was sitting so far from the water's edge. And the Divas' pain is their readers' gain."

"How so?" India asked. She snapped her fingers signaling she had an answer. "Oh, I know. Another terribly indispensable Traveling Tidbit."

The ladies nodded proudly, completely missing the wry amusement in their companion's voice.

> **Traveling Tidbit for Sun-Worshipping Travelers:** Because Italians reserve these spaces well in advance, your best chance of being near the water is to bring your own inflatable lounge chair, and position yourself in the water. When the tide goes out, you will be on the sand. For an umbrella, purchase one of those little umbrella hats.

> **Corollary Traveling Tidbit:** If you insist on wearing that little umbrella hat, be sure to purchase one stateside, because you won't find it in Italy. No Italian would be caught dead in one.

"That bad, huh?" India remarked.

"Well, it wasn't all bad," Dena denied. "What we saw of the place was very nice."

India sat hypnotized as the ladies described the beach...the welcoming warmth of the crystal clear blue-green waters of the Mediterranean...immaculate white sand stretching from one end of the horizon to the other...the length of the beach dotted with national flags, standing tall and proud like sentries on guard.

"Like sentries on guard with broad shoulders and deep green eyes," purred Dena, her eyes with a dreamy, faraway look.

"Dena!" Shelby admonished her friend. She turned back to their audience of one. "As we were saying, national flags from around the world lined the beach welcoming international guests. And a Deejay from a local radio station lent a festive air."

"What a poetic description," India exclaimed. "I can't imagine why the Italian Tourist Board hasn't hired you two and offered pots of money. It's really a shame."

Dena blanched at the thought. "A job?" she screeched. "No, heaven forbid!"

"Exactly," Shelby agreed. Noticing that the blood from Dena's face had run scared at the very idea, leaving her as ghostly white as their companion, Shelby gave her friend a comforting pat on the arm. Her next words were calculated to calm Dena.

"The only shame was our failure to meet men with scads of money to share that picture perfect seaside with us."

"And what was even more pitiful leads us to another Traveling Tidbit."

> **Traveling Tidbit for the Companion-challenged Traveler:** The bagni also provide private dressing rooms/lockers to change and to store your valuables. Now, some people enjoy playing Flipper by themselves while watching others romp in the water with families and friends. If you do, get yourself a ball and go for it! But if you like company, get a locker or one of you will be left behind on the beach guarding your loot.

Unfortunately, when Shelby and Dena tried to rent a dressing room, they were thwarted. Therefore, the ladies cannot provide a description of the Viareggio lockers for their anxious readers. Anyone like the Divas, whose Chianti intake precludes rising before noon can skip this section. All others (i.e., anyone with a grip on their Chianti intake) who manage to land one of Viareggio's dressing rooms, should contact the ladies with a detailed description. They will be sure to include it in the eagerly awaited revised edition. Thank you in advance.

Notwithstanding the dressing room problem, what a wonderful day the two had. The ladies took turns frolicking in the gentle waves of the famed Mediterranean Sea. Alone. They enjoyed a stroll along the sun-drenched beach. Alone. They shook their booties to the Deejay music. Alone.

Though it was Dena who invariably found the bright side of any situation, today it was Shelby. After everything it had taken to finally get to the beach, both women were parched and hungry when they finally settled in. Still, there was the pesky problem of leaving their belongings.

Shelby looked over at her friend. She smiled solicitously and deliberately softened the look in her eyes before speaking. "Don't worry, dear, I don't mind staying here while you go get food." For both of us, she thought to herself, but didn't say.

As she watched Dena's slim back receding toward the food kiosk, alone, Shelby smiled deeply. She leaned back and sighed with contentment. Placing her sun hat over her eyes for a quick snooze, she simply couldn't stifle a quiet chuckle. Well, that worked out very well for me.

After hours of solitary pursuits, the one thing that the bathing beauties could do together was leave. Lazy day at the beach concluded, they ambled back to the train station, making sure to stop at the bar to pick up their packages from Applewood's. It seemed only right to repay the barkeep for his kindness. But how to do so gracefully, they wondered.

"Well, we can't just give him money," Dena said.

Shelby nodded her head in vigorous agreement. Such a gesture would be a bit condescending.

"Politeness dictates that we sit and have a little something. But what?" Dena puzzled.

And once again, that one brain that the ladies often seemed to share kicked in.

"A glass of Chianti," they chimed in unison to the barrista.

Later that evening, the women decided to conserve their money by foregoing a restaurant dinner. Instead, back in their hotel room, they prepared a little picnic made from the leftovers of the previous day's scrumptious lunch. They feasted on thinly sliced prosciutto, parmesan and provolone, crusty Italian bread, and biscotti for dessert.

It's important for budget travelers to be resourceful, and the Divas were no exception. They had needed to keep fresh the food they'd purchased the day before. Many hotels graciously provide mini-bars, as did the Hotel Macchiavelli. When they'd purchased their provisions, Dena and Shelby stood in front of the little box with the door open. It was stuffed to the gills with ten dollar bottles of beer, eight dollar bottles of water, and crackers and cheese snacks that required guests to extract every gold filling in their mouths to pay for them. This dilemma inspired yet another handy Traveling Tidbit.

Traveling Tidbit for the Dollar-Deficient Traveler: Mini-bars work just as well for non-hotel products as for hotel products. Empty that sucker and stock it with more affordable provisions. Before leaving, replace the hotel's items. Your pocketbook will thank you.

Corollary Traveling Tidbit for the Dollar-Deficient Traveler: If you are dollar deprived, most imperatively, do not call the Divas! Thank you in advance.

Having adhered to the aforementioned tidbit the day before, the ladies were ready to tuck into the feast laid out before them. But something was amiss. A disquieting feeling that something had been overlooked niggled at both women. What could it be?

"Let's see," mused Dena. "Have we covered all the food groups?"

"I don't know," answered Shelby. "We'd better consult the Diva Food Pyramid." She reached into her handbag and pulled out a piece of paper, with a scribbled diagram.

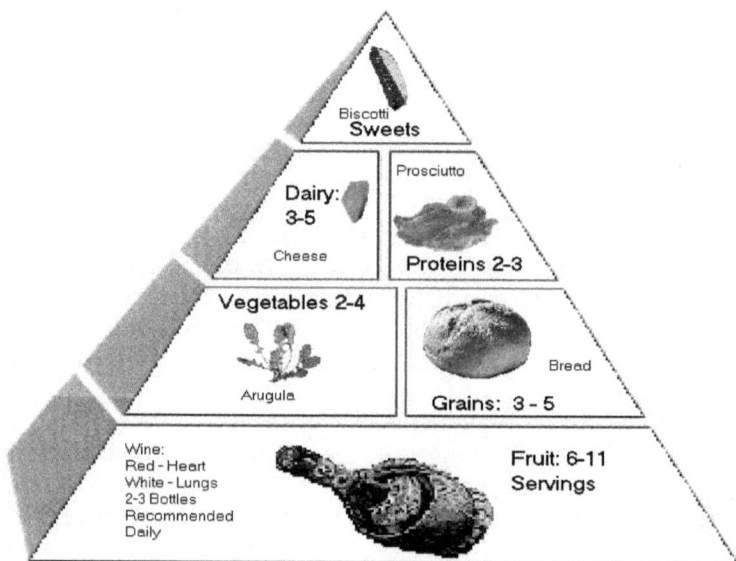

"Well, at the top are our fats and sweets," Shelby read.

"Check, covered by the biscotti," Dena confirmed.

"Next we need dairy and proteins," said Shelby.

"Check, check, cheese and prosciutto," Dena fired back with a mischievous smile.

"I know our grains are covered," Shelby announced. "Plenty of bread."

"So, it looks like we're missing only one thing, our fruits and vegetables. This won't do. It's our largest food group," Dena declared with concern.

"Never fear, we've got veggies," Shelby declared, holding up a bunch of arugula. She thought for a second. "And for fruits, we have two bottles of Chianti and a bottle of Vin Santo for good measure." She held up the booty like a conquering pirate. "But no corkscrew."

Volunteering to go down to the hotel bar for assistance, Dena headed out the door. "Be right back," she promised.

As right back turned into an hour, Shelby's impatience grew. What in God's name was Dena doing? Sucking down the bottle by herself? Or had she found some Italian hottie to share it with? Maybe she'd traipsed over to the Buca with it and was in those deluxe storeroom accommodations going for the gusto.

Just then, Dena burst like a storm through the door. "It took them forever to find their corkscrew," she explained.

And so was born another Traveling Tidbit.

> **Traveling Tidbit for the Tie-One-On Traveler:** To avoid the D.T.'s while vacationing, bring your own corkscrew for several reasons. First, you get more bang for the buck when you buy a bottle of wine in a store. Secondly, you can toss back one or two (hell, the whole bottle if you want) in the privacy of your room whenever you want. And finally, if you happen to throw up and pass out, no one need know but you, and the bed is only feet away.

After drinking their dinner, the tanked twosome decided that the Florentines had been without the Divas' presence for long enough. The warm, starlit evening was perfect for a Diva Stroll. Strutting in the direction of Il Duomo, the two glittering globe-trotters made yet another tactical error when Shelby suggested sitting on the cathedral steps for a bit.

"It's such a perfect summer night," Dena sighed in agreement.

No sooner had they settled themselves on the cathedral's steps than two Italian gentlemen (again, the term is loosely used) approached the ladies. Without invitation, they lowered themselves on the step beside the women...much too close. The Divas, trying to be gracious, allowed themselves to be drawn into light conversation.

"Do you like to dance?" one of the men asked.

Dena popped up like bread from a toaster. "I do, I do!" she squealed in undisguised anticipation.

"We take you to Meccano."

Shelby tried to slink away without being noticed, but Dena, who'd been dying to get to the outdoor disco, wasn't about to let the opportunity pass. Her hand curled around Shelby's arm, holding her friend still, warning that if she moved, sharp fingernails would inflict pain. Shelby, knowing that there was no way to avoid this excursion, remained seated. "Can we walk there, or do we need a cab?" she asked with resignation.

"Oh, no, no, we take you on our motorini," the men offered.

Dena rose immediately, ready to hop on the back of one of the little motorcycles. But Shelby was having none of it. Friendship may mean always being there for each other, but she would just as soon that "there" not be dead or worse at the hands of strangers, or at least, these strangers whom she somehow didn't trust.

"No, no, no. We'll take a cab and meet you there," Shelby politely refused their offer.

The gentleman quickly saw their attempts at persuasion were falling on deaf ears. "Si, si," they finally agreed. "We walk and get you a cab.

This immediately brings to mind a very important Diva Do/n't:

Diva Do/n't

If you want to avoid death or other dangers, do say no to rides from complete strangers.

As they strolled down the street in search of a taxi, one of the men left the foursome. Shelby's eyes followed him like a hawk, finding it extremely odd when he approached two very young men standing on a street corner.

"Where's he going? What's he doing? Is he buying drugs?" she shrieked to the remaining gentleman.

"Oh no, no, they just his friends. Eez okay, come," he replied in smooth tones, trying his best to reassure the ladies.

Somehow Shelby doubted that these clean-cut, thirty-somethings befriended scruffy teenage boys dressed in hip-hop jeans and accompanied by scraggly dogs sporting muzzles. She turned to Dena in a panic.

"It's a drug deal going down. Make a run for it," she shrieked, just before taking off in a sprint. Dena quickly brought up her rear, and the ladies sped off like Olympic athletes.

The narrow winding streets of Florence were perfect for giving the slip to would-be stalkers. Familiar with diversionary tactics (they watched a lot of TV), the ladies dodged and darted up one street and down another, determined to keep the location of their hotel unknown.

After a few minutes, Shelby stopped for a breath of air, reaching into her purse, desperate for her inhaler. Around the corner she cast her eyes, peering to make sure the druggies weren't on their trail. One puff. Two puffs. Blessed air! They were off in a frantic sprint again.

Little did the ladies know that the men hadn't taken one step to follow them. Instead, they shook their heads in amusement at the sight of Shelby and Dena taking off. They watched on until the runners were out of view. Then, they turned and made their way back to the cathedral.

Surely, two more forty-something year old American women would show up soon.

Prossima! Next!

The ladies looked at India, expecting her to commiserate with them on their near escape from death. But their companion was lost in her own thoughts. I've got the best DIQ Test Question of all, India fantasized. One that will put me and anyone crazy enough to buy this loony book (or the freaking revised edition) out of their misery.

How does the Delusional Divas' story end? Dena and Shelby:

> A) Climb on the back of the Italian strangers' motorini, ride off into the night, and are never heard from again. End of story,
>
> B) Get caught in the crosshairs of a drug bust, spend the rest of their rather useless lives languishing in an Italian jail, and are never heard from again. End of story,
>
> C) Running for their lives, encounter Muttelli and Jeffelli. They accept the men's offer of help and are never heard from again. End of story, or
>
> D) While running from that drug deal through the streets of Florence, encounter an open manhole, fall into it, and are never heard from again. End of story.

Just like with their first DIQ Test Question, all answers are correct, as far as I'm concerned, India laughed to herself. But pleasure such as this should be shared. So perhaps, I should get a website of my own, www.DownWithDelusionalDivas.com. Readers could register their vote.

Chapter 14

The Divas awoke to yet another sunny day in Florence filled with hope. Having put the previous evening's nearly disastrous encounter out of their minds, they focused on making contact with the enemy. First, Shelby made her pre-arranged call to Giancarlo. Ever mindful of outward appearances, she managed to quell the sick, bubbling feeling in the pit of her tummy and hold a coherent conversation. When he promptly offered to meet for dinner that evening, she agreed happily.

"And Dena...she come too," Giancarlo prompted.

Shelby's heart sank. Not if I have anything to say about it, she thought. "Oh, I don't know if she can," she prevaricated.

"No, no. She come. Bring Dena. You both come to dinner," he insisted.

What was it with this man and her friends? All these years. All her plans. And he didn't want to be alone with her?

No sooner was the phone in its cradle than Dena quickly jumped in, having heard the gist of the conversation. "Look, Shelby," she began with uncharacteristic sharpness. "I already told you Nicola's taken time off for us to be together. You're on your own tonight."

Not only did Shelby remember, she was counting on it. For this battle, she was going in alone. Dena needn't bother bringing up her rear. Still, Shelby couldn't bring herself to say any of that to her friend.

"I know, but you're certainly welcome," she lied.

Dena was grateful for the offer, but had visions of herself and her company of one troop retreating to their foxhole and being under heavy fire. Deciding to confirm her anticipated plans with Nicola, she placed her own phone call and was buoyed by his eagerness to see her.

"Ahhh, Dena, my parents still here. They leave after lunch. Then, I see you."

"*Va bene*, okay, so you'll call when they leave?" she prompted. But Nicola insisted that she call him.

"Si, si, two hours, I'll call again. *Ciao, bello*," she answered, hanging up the phone with a song in her heart.

And so it seemed that Shelby would have her way and be alone with Giancarlo after all. Dena would call Nicola in the early afternoon to firm up (double entendre implied) her planned tryst. To pass the time until then, she suggested that they finish shopping for gifts for their loved ones back in the Americas.

On cloud nine, the dingbat Divas floated through their toiletries secure in the knowledge that their dreams would be realized in a few short hours. They dressed for shopping with renewed confidence. Dena wore a coral and rose paisley skirt with matching coral shell. Coral sandals set off the ensemble perfectly. She donned a wide-brimmed straw hat to protect her delicate skin from the hot Tuscan sun. Unfortunately, the skirt could not hide the putrid remains of her festering knee injury.

Shelby had a little problem in wardrobe choice. She was still trying to hide the lobster-like color of her severely photosensitive skin brought on by their sunbathing the day before. Finally, she settled on peach linen pants and a floral print peach shell with spaghetti straps. If the clothes didn't hide her skin condition, at least they'd match. A lovely straw cloche, with a matching straw flower on the side, framed her face.

Off they strolled through the teeming cobblestone streets of Florence, headed once again for the *Ponte Vecchio*. As usual, it didn't take long for the first shot to be fired. One purchase made, and the women were off and running. Arm in arm, the comrades stormed their next target. After making a clean sweep of the premises and finding no precious, let alone family, jewels worth taking prisoner, Dena started to tire of these unproductive minor skirmishes.

Let's not forget, this lieutenant of love had been to the front. She'd tasted the sweet thrill of victory, making this enforced retreat an agony. She hungered to be called up, to cross enemy lines, to feel that enemy breathing down her neck. Engaged in a full frontal assault. Aahhhh! Ooohhhh! Mmmmmm! Okay, so sorry, back to the matter at hand.

Shelby had her marching orders for the coming evening, making her quite content to piddle away the afternoon window-shopping, Dena fumed. Finally, she could stand no more.

"Look, if you want to keep shopping, go ahead. I need to get back to the hotel!" she fired out.

"What for?" Shelby asked in confusion.

"To call Nicola, or else I'll be having dinner with you and Giancarlo. Take your pick."

As if it carried rabies, Shelby quickly cast off the eighteen-carat gold ring she'd been admiring. "Thank you, my good man, for all your help. We really need to be going," she said to the rather cute jewelry salesman. And with that, she propelled herself and Dena onto the street and in the direction of the Hotel Macchiavelli.

Back in their room, Dena placed yet another phone call to finalize her plans with Nicola. "Oh, Dena, we still have lunch," he informed her. "I think my parents leave soon. You call back in one hour?"

And if ever there were a Diva Do/n't that should be emblazoned, branded, scarred into the tissue of a diva's brain, here it is:

If you don't want to look like a dunce, don't dare contact that man more than once.

For clarification, contact includes phone calls, visits, emails, smoke signals, Morse code, drumbeat messages, letters, telegrams, or telepathy. There are no exceptions to this rule. One should not kid oneself into suspecting that some grave catastrophe has befallen one's beloved, rendering him unable to respond. No, he's not dead. Not been kidnapped. Hasn't had an accident. Doesn't have amnesia. Is not in the hospital. Nor has he been abducted by little green men.

Get used to it. He has simply chosen not to call. Don't question it. Just get over it. Move on.

So, when Nicola bade Dena to call again, the Helen Reddy female anthem rang in her ears, albeit with a twist. I am Diva. Hear me roar. I won't call you anymore!

"You call me," Dena replied with uncharacteristic resolve.

Between Dena's nonexistent Italian and Nicola's rudimentary English, it took about an hour to convey the hotel telephone number, but finally, he had it written down and promised to call soon. And with that, Dena lay down for a catnap. Her dreams were of suiting up in battle fatigues, charging into enemy territory, and Nicola waving the classic white flag of complete surrender.

Shelby had no time to sleep, having a small errand to run. As a token of her affection, she had bought a small gift for Giancarlo's birthday, but needed wrapping paper and a card.

"Want to take the walk with me?" she inquired.

Dena shook her head, declining the invitation. She couldn't possibly leave. Nicola would be calling any minute.

When Shelby returned an hour later, Dena's confidence had taken a slight hit. While her friend was lovingly wrapping the gift that Giancarlo would cherish for a lifetime, the day was ticking away. And with each passing minute, it became agonizingly apparent that a phone call from Nicola was about as likely as a visit from jolly old St. Nick.

Dena tried to remain hopeful, her fertile mind able to conjure any number of reasons. Perhaps, there was a problem with the phone lines in Italy. She inspected the phone. Looked okay. Had worked fine just an hour ago. But better make sure. Gingerly, Dena lifted the receiver from its cradle and placed it to her ear, listening for a dial tone.

Just then, Shelby looked up from putting the finishing touches on her wrapping project. Her forehead crinkled with confusion. "Did I miss the phone ring?"

"No, just making sure it's working," Dena moaned, with a forlorn look on her face. "It is."

Sadly, this brings to light some additional catastrophes that one might dream up to explain what the Divas like to term the "Poof Factor." What is the Poof Factor? It's really quite simple. One minute, the man's all over you like white on rice, and the next minute. Poof! He's gone. Sucked from the earth's atmosphere.

No, rodents have not eaten the phone lines. A flood did not short circuit the power lines. High winds did not bring down telephone cables. An asteroid has not directly hit his cell phone company tower. It's simply the Poof Factor. Here today. Gone tomorrow. Or, in this case, here today. Gone today.

Shelby buzzed around the room, humming happy little tunes as she prepared for her big evening. Within minutes, she had a backup singer. Dena had chimed in whistling. Shelby turned and saw her friend surveying the contents of her closet.

"Oh!" she began, "did I misunderstand? I thought you hadn't heard from Nicola?"

"I didn't," Dena confirmed. She pulled out a skirt and held it up to herself in front of the mirror.

Wow! I've really got to admire her spunk, Shelby mused. Doesn't even know the language and is still going out on her own. "So where you headed?" she asked.

Dena spun on her heels and faced her friend. Now it was her turn to be confused. "What do you mean where am I going? To dinner," Dena repeated the question and answered it in the same breath.

"That's great," Shelby said encouragingly. "Which restaurant?"

"Well, I didn't think you'd want me sitting here by myself all evening. I'm going with you and Giancarlo."

"Ah...ah...ah," Shelby's voice gurgled in her throat. "Great," she finally managed to get out. "It'll be fun."

Screwed!

There's a fine line between the mainstream sex appeal of Victoria's Secret lingerie and the erotic, somewhat taboo apparel of Frederick's of Hollywood. The Divas didn't consider themselves firmly entrenched on either side of this fence, but preferred to...uhm...to straddle it. The fence, of course.

Tonight, Shelby was striving for demure sexiness. She chose a sunflower yellow silk sheath with simple lines that created an enticing silhouette, hinting at her treasures beneath. Like a silent film flashing in her mind's eye, she envisioned herself and Giancarlo as the leads in a romantic epic by night's end. Therefore, great care also had to be given to her undergarments. The choice was clear. No seedy crotchless panties for this romance, but matching sheer bra and thong trimmed with sunflower yellow lace. Giancarlo would be putty in her hands, and the maddening discomfort of the thong would be worth it all.

Dena was not quite as concerned about her apparel for the evening. It was manifestly apparent that she and Nicola would not be availing themselves of the Buca's basement boudoir this evening. Nonetheless, she took care in choosing a lovely peach silk skirt ensemble. Having no reason to be as attentive to her unmentionables as Shelby, her functional shrimp tone bra and panties were one step shy of granny panties. She would be sitting at dinner quite comfortably in her bloomers, while poor Shelby in her thong would probably develop a nervous twitch as the evening wore on.

One last glance in the mirror and Shelby was satisfied that she was eminently prepared for the evening ahead. Tenderly clutching Giancarlo's gift to her bosom, she whispered a tiny prayer. Let the games begin!

As they made their way through the hotel lobby, Shelby noticed her friend's furtive, then pitiful, glance toward their empty message box. She gave a small, sympathetic shake of her head. Poor Dena, she'd lost that little spring in her step. Shelby gave another little shake of her head to cast off any bad feelings. She was not about to let Dena ruin her plans. This was her night and no other Diva's Down was going to screw it up.

Upon their fashionably late arrival at the gelateria, Giancarlo was nowhere in sight, leaving Shelby in the slightly embarrassing situation of having to inquire of his employees as to his whereabouts. *"C'e Giancarlo?"* she inquired.

"No, non c'e." Barely sparing Shelby a glance, the pretty ice cream scooper informed her that he wasn't there and hadn't been all day.

"Geez, you think she's said those words more than once?" Shelby whispered. "Sounded positively pre-recorded."

Dena chuckled, agreeing that the ice cream server's answer held less spontaneity than the squeals of a trained seal. "Yeah, I get the distinct impression you're not the first woman coming here looking for more than a scoop."

The ladies were stunned to learn that Divahood was not an exclusively female province. Undoubtedly, they were tangling with a diva of the male variety. Giancarlo was even more fashionably late than they. Eventually, they spied him strolling nonchalantly along Via Tavolini as if he hadn't a care in the world. As it had been on their April trip, his cell phone was growing out of his ear.

"I'm surprised the Italians don't sprout roots in their ears from cell phones," Dena laughed.

Without skipping a beat in his phone conversation, he greeted the friends with a *Ciao Belle*. His sexy smile oozed with magnetic charm. While neither diva would ever refer to herself as a sucker, the term did come to mind as Shelby melted like butter at the familiar, affectionate caress of Giancarlo's fingers across her cheek. She was heartened by the sparkle in his eyes as he gazed upon her, indicating he was thrilled to see her. Was it actually possible? Could they recapture the bliss of the past?

Ah, the romantic bubble. So fragile. So susceptible. Shelby couldn't possibly have seen it coming, the first prick (oops, pinprick) to her bubble. Of course, someone more deeply rooted in reality might have considered the events of six years ago, or even this past April, a rather telling clue. But Shelby had forgiven and forgotten. She'd moved on, hadn't she? And what had happened six years ago wasn't the real Giancarlo anyway. No, of course not.

"Shelbeeee," he purred, in his sultry Italian accent as the threesome strode leisurely through the winding, medieval streets of Florence. She preened at the endearing way he placed the stress on the last syllable of her name. Her plans were progressing splendidly.

"I tell Lisa you in Italy. She eez so excited. She want to talk to you. I call her now?" he asked.

Shelby stopped dead in her tracks. Her head felt heavy as iron and steamy hot, like volcanic lava. Had all the blood in her veins backed up to her skull? Deafening sirens blared in her ears. Was Florence under an air raid? Dazed and confused, she bobbed and weaved – a punch drunk prizefighter against the ropes, struggling to stay upright after being dealt the knockout blow. She fought mightily to maintain her composure and dignity. *Hell no, I don't want to talk to that b*!tch... that miserable excuse for a friend.*

Oh my, the situation must be bad. The Divas are not usually given to epithets. But had she said it? Had the words roaring through her brain like a runaway train actually left her lips? Obviously not. Giancarlo was still punching out the numbers on the phone with a brainless, pleased-with-himself smile on his face.

Absolutely incredulous, Dena saw no need to be as circumspect as her friend. "Now?" she sputtered. The shocked look in her eyes matched the disgusted tone in her voice. She was a mother tiger leaping to the defense of her helpless cub.

"Yes," Giancarlo answered. "Lisa wants to say goodbye."

"Goodbye?" Dena spat out his words. "We just got here, and we'll be here for two more weeks!" With poisonous derision dripping from her lips, it took a supreme effort not to end her tirade with "you dope!"

"DDDeeeennnaaa," Giancarlo said with irritation.

"Sounds like a bit of an overreaction to me, Dena," said the Englishwoman.

Dena arched her eyebrows halfway to the sky, but allowed India Wallis to continue.

"Well, I know Shelby wanted this to be a romantic reunion, but you were there, too."

Dena's eyes squinted in confusion. "So?"

"So," continued India, "what was the problem with him calling her old friend? I find it rather endearing."

"Endearing? That's an odd way to look at it," Dena sputtered, just as she had with Giancarlo that evening.

India turned away from Dena in exasperation. "Help me out here. Because I'm lost."

"Shelby? Shelby?" Giancarlo repeated.

She managed to plaster a sickly smile on her face. But words were beyond her capability.

"You do want to speak to Lisa, don't you?" Giancarlo coaxed seductively.

Shelby remained quiet and still as stone, even as her mind was awhirl with flashbacks of her letter earlier in the year to Giancarlo and Lisa. Well, she had written the absolutory note to the happy couple. She had wished them a wonderful life together, hadn't she? And hadn't she told them that she'd be tickled pink to see them both?

Could they be blamed for having the intuition of gnats, the common sense of fruit flies -- for believing that she was actually interested in rekindling a friendship with the two of them, rather than simply trying to reconnect with Giancarlo?

Hoisted with her own petard.

A shiver of disgust and disbelief ran through the English-woman. "Oh, dear God in heaven! The other woman was..." she began wide-eyed. Her voice was a whisper, almost as if she were afraid to utter the name. "Your friend, Lisa?"

A sadness crept into Shelby's eyes, resurfacing whenever she thought of Giancarlo and Lisa. The pain had never disappeared, but it didn't hold court in her heart anymore either. Shelby nodded. "Yes, my friend... Lisa."

"My God, how did you find out?" the Brit couldn't prevent herself from asking.

Shelby's mind drifted to that fateful day six years earlier. Lost in thought so deep, she couldn't speak. Dena did it for her.

"How Shelby find out? Oh, what a beautiful tale," she began.

Feeling a little lonely after Giancarlo's plans to come to New York had been postponed, Shelby phoned one day just to hear his voice.

"Oh," she hesitated, when a not unfamiliar female voice answered from the other end of the line. It can't be, she thought to herself. "Lisa, is that you?"

"Shelby?" Lisa questioned. "Yes, it's me, I miss you so. How are you?"

"This is a surprise," Shelby replied, ignoring the perfunctory question.

Lisa rushed to fill the awkward void. "I'm here doing some translation work for Giancarlo. He's been so good to me and Francesco."

"Translation? What kind of translation?" Shelby asked derisively. Had someone just stabbed her in the heart? She'd have to brush up on her limited vocabulary. Must have missed class the day they'd learned that translation was a synonym for copulation.

Nothing Lisa said penetrated Shelby's consciousness. Her mind was locked in its own painful struggle, desperately trying to keep what she knew was the truth from taking hold.

But finally, Shelby had heard enough of Lisa's babbling on with obvious lies. "Okay Lisa, let's cut to the chase. Are you and Giancarlo together?"

"Stop! For once, I don't need to hear the blow by blow," India interrupted Dena midstream. "No wonder you wanted to hit the man over the head with the cell phone. So, did you actually agree to talk to her that night? Did Giancarlo really call her?"

Through the fog of her chaotic thoughts, Shelby heard a voice from deep within her soul. Get a grip, old girl. Pull yourself together.

Caught in a trap of her own making, she gave a sickly nod of the head, signaling her reluctant assent to Giancarlo's suggestion. She hazarded a glance at Dena, who was well beyond the sputtering stage. Horrified eyes bulging froglike and mouth agape in utter amazement, Dena's engines fired. She was headed for a full-scale liftoff.

Well versed in the carnage left behind by a diva who'd taken off into orbit, Shelby knew if she didn't act quickly, her plans for this evening would be nothing more than the charred remains left in the wake of Dena's booster rockets. Before the girl could utter another syllable, Shelby pounced.

"Leave it alone," she sniped. Narrowed slivers of ice resided where beautiful brown eyes had just been; her mouth was grimly set.

Danger! Danger! Warning bells pealed in Dena's head. Diva turning like a viper on diva friend. Back off before transformation is complete and the rattler strikes. Dena was helpless. Delusion had Shelby tightly in its grasp. The poor girl couldn't see that Giancarlo was the one doing a rather handy job of ruining the evening, not her comrade.

The bitter reality is that sometimes one is forced to abide by a Diva Do/n't under protest. The following is one such example.

When a Diva friend's under extreme delusion, do let her arrive at her own conclusion.

India waved her hands in the air as if stopping oncoming traffic. "Wait a second; stop right there," she ordered, training her eyes on Shelby. "Why would you get mad at Dena? That's the dumbest Diva Do/n't I have ever heard. She was only trying to help you, to protect you. What a friend you were to turn on her like that."

Shelby squirmed uncomfortably in her chair. "We...well, I...I..."

Dena patted her friend's hand. "That's okay, Shelby. Let me explain." She turned to India. "Of course, close friends try to point things out. Try to help a friend see things clearly, but it's risky business."

"I guess so. At least, with Shelby," India accused pointedly.

The British woman had gone too far. Shelby came out of her fog long enough to strike back. "Well, you're a fine one to talk. If you ask me, Annabel was only trying to help you, and you..."

India cut through Shelby's words. "Help? Some help! The woman lied to me."

"Did she?" Dena asked in a quiet, hesitant voice.

"Yes, she lied. She said Malcolm made a pass at her!" India's face was hard with determination.

Again Dena chose her words carefully. "Did you ever consider," she hesitated again, "that Annabel, whether mistaken or not, truly believed Malcolm did what she said?"

"Yeah," Shelby picked up her friend's train of thought. "You'd been friends for thirty-five years. Had she ever done anything to break your trust before this?"

India shook her head. "No, never. We were like sisters."

"So, then, why would she wake up one day and want to bring your life crashing down around you?" asked Dena. "It seems to me her only mistake was miscalculating your reaction. But it's rather obvious to us, Annabel was only trying to help you, just like I did for Shelby."

India's lips parted, a contradiction ripe on the tip of her tongue. Her mouth closed before she spoke. She was deep in *private thought even as she listened as Shelby and Dena continued their tale.*

Saddened, but resigned, to the events unfolding before her, Dena retreated to the sidelines, leaving her friend to her sorry fate.

The cell phone was ringing. During this time, several questions kaleidoscoped at warp speed through Shelby's mind. Does this man hate me? He wants to torture me, doesn't he? Perhaps, he's not playing with a full deck? Maybe both oars aren't in the water, or he fell in headfirst and there was no water. Or, could it be that I've made a scientific discovery: the dimmest bulb on the planet?

Might I win a Nobel Prize for this? Most likely, I'd be the first diva to win the Nobel Prize. Should I wear my navy wool crepe dress to accept the prize, or would the taupe gabardine pantsuit be more appropriate? And what about my underwear? Silk or cotton? But more immediately, what in Sam Hill am I going to say to the one woman I despise more than any in this life?

Sometimes when a diva is incapable of getting out of her own way and won't let a friend pull her out of harm's way, the diva's guardian angel intervenes. Shelby's angel is Asha. Her psychic told her so. And this tidbit brings to mind yet another Diva Do/n't.

Diva Do/n't

When flesh and blood people cannot help you, do contact the spirit world for a different view.

It might help solve the problem. It might not. Even if it doesn't, it makes one feel better for a little while. You know, delusion. Every diva's secret weapon.

Sometimes an angel will let their charge stew a while just to teach her a lesson. Shelby must have been doing something right that day because Asha took pity on her.

Disappointedly shaking his head, Giancarlo flipped his cell phone closed. "Lisa not home yet; she don't answer," he announced.

Shelby allowed herself an inward sigh of relief before replying. "Che peccato!" What a shame! She gave Giancarlo a tiny pat on the shoulder. "Maybe later," she added.

Though her voice held a mellifluous lilt of fake hopefulness, Shelby's private thoughts were very different. Not even in my next life, if I can help it.

Still reeling from Giancarlo's surprise, the threesome arrived at *Il Cantastorie*.[24] The ladies were delighted with his choice of restaurant. Seems impossible, but another Diva Do/n't is upon us.

If you want the best insider information, do be-friend the people of the nation.

Il Cantastorie, which means the Minstrel, is an intimate restaurant situated in the heart of centro. True to its name, it features music, and that night *"il Maestro,"* a colorful (not to mention colorfully dressed) entertainer serenaded diners with his extraordinarily versatile voice. Il Maestro, Signor Santino, drew from a wide musical repertoire, ranging from classical to pop, which offered something for everyone. Well, perhaps not everyone. Il Maestro didn't perform any rap or heavy metal numbers. But the Divas really aren't fans of those musical genres, so it doesn't really matter, does it?

The restaurant has two dining rooms, making it a good idea to request seating in the front room where performances take place. An added bonus is a street-side wall of glass doors that are opened in warm weather to allow diners to see Florence drifting past.

---

[24]Il Cantastorie, Via della Condotta,7/9r, PH 055/239-68-04

The little party had been seated for mere minutes, when Giancarlo, proud as a peacock, announced another small surprise. "I invite a friend to join us."

Il dottore. Dena's ears perked up when she heard the words and her imagination sprouted wings. Could this doctor be the man for me? Tall and handsome with slightly curling black hair and penetrating indigo eyes. A deep voice that speaks English with a sexy accent and endearingly adds an "ah" sound to the end of every word. Intelligent with a keen sense of humor and that classic Italian self-assuredness. Will his name roll like music off my lips? Will he be an Allessandro, or perhaps, a Stefano? Surely he'll fit the bill better than Doctor Dante the Dishrag.

"Your ears perked up?" India repeated. "Thought Nicola was the man of your dreams?"

"India, dear," Dena began, "I'd left my children for the second time in almost as many months, spent thousands of dollars, completely transformed myself...all to get back to Italy and have some fun." Each word left her mouth with rocket-like, purposeful precision. "Think back. You might recall a Diva Do/n't that applies to this situation."

Absentmindedly, the Englishwoman's finger stroked her thin upper lip as she struggled to remember. An exasperated sigh signaled her defeat.

In unison, the ladies began, "One diva don't stop no show...."

"Yes, well, no wonder I couldn't figure it out," India accused. "Nicola is hardly a diva."

Then, the ladies decided to fill her in on the original version of this Diva Do/n't, handed down to Shelby from her dearly departed father. "Yes, whenever my plans were foiled by someone else, Daddy always reminded me that one monkey don't stop no show."

The ladies shared a little laugh, and Dena continued. "And this chimp and his banana weren't the only ones in Florence!"

India couldn't help but laugh, but she was anxious to hear more about this new doctor friend of Giancarlo's.

Having taken a seat facing the wall, Dena could not see the good doctor as he approached. It didn't matter because she had Shelby, who must have been absent on the day that the quintessential diva trait of subtlety was discussed. Within a few minutes of their arrival, Shelby's mouth dropped open so far that her tongue could have mopped the restaurant's terra cotta floor. Her eyes, as they looked upward, popped from their sockets in cartoon-like shock. In that instant, Dena knew the doctor was a toad; no question about it.

Good manners required that she turn to greet the new arrival, but her neck was soldered tight, unwilling to meet her fate. Finally, with immense effort, she managed to wrench her gaze upward toward the new arrival.

Pea-sized, beady eyes magnified by glasses thick as Coke bottles greeted her. Thinning hair was arranged in the hairstyle of complete male denial, the dreaded thatched roof comb-over, and tinted a shade of brown no human being could have come by naturally. In addition, *il Dottore the Sequel* was squat of stature and blubbery of body.

And his name; well, the name said it all. "This is my friend Fausto," Giancarlo offered by way of introduction.

Dena couldn't believe her ears. She wanted to laugh, but squelched the impulse, and offered her hand in greeting. "Oh, oh, nice to meet you, Fatso," she answered, not believing she actually said the name with a straight face.

Dena wasn't the only one who couldn't believe her ears. Shelby was mortified. The girl really did need a hearing aid though perhaps her mistaken moniker was more accurate. "Not Fatso, Dena; his name is Fausto."

For those not familiar with Italian pronunciation, that's FOWSTO, with the "ow" pronounced like *how*. That's how, as in how many beastly doctors did Giancarlo know? How could this be happening to a diva? How could she escape? How many drinks would she need to get through dinner?

Dena was lightheaded. Her breath, at first trapped in her throat like a bullfrog, started coming in quick, shallow succession. Perhaps, she had a touch of the vapors? Could she feign illness and leave? After all, she wasn't feeling well. But alas, another Diva Do/n't was born.

Diva Do/n't

Even if you're about to heave, another Diva you do not leave.

This is such a fundamental tenet of Divadom, that it begs for reiteration. So...

Even if it (or he) makes you puke, another Diva you don't ever rebuke.

Haven't gotten it yet? The ladies will recap.

Even should the situation make you want to hurl, don't ever desert your Diva girl.

Knowing she could not leave Shelby on her own, Dena plastered a smile on her face and resigned herself to a miserable evening.

However, almost every negative has its positive, and dear Fausto was no exception. Dena quickly discovered that while the good doctor might be short on looks and wide of girth, he was very knowledgeable and an interesting conversationalist. So, making the best of a bad situation, she decided to use Fausto's exhaustive knowledge of Italy to the Divas' advantage. Armed with pad and pen, she listened and took notes on his beach recommendations.

The region of Liguria received his highest praise, particularly the towns of Portovenere and Lerici on the Italian Riviera. He also highly recommended the popular Cinque Terre, which in actuality are five small fishing villages.

"Popular?" Dena repeated. "With Italians or tourists?" she asked.

"Both," Fausto admitted reluctantly. "But even with so many people, they are still worth a visit," he said with authority.

Shelby's and Dena's eyes met in amusement at his assumption that they were in the market for a respite from the world. Wide open spaces. Long stretches of unspoiled land. Totally uninhabited beach. Pristine blue-green ocean as far as the eye can see. No one but each other as far as the Divas' eyes could see. Complete solitude. A shudder of horror rippled through Dena's body. Perish the thought!

Again, Shelby was reminded of another of her dearly departed father's motto. As a personal injury attorney, always on the lookout for his next big case, he had constantly told Shelby's mother that it was essential for his business that he go out to bars and clubs. "I have to let my public see me" was his motto.

Ditto for the Divas. What was the sense in being a diva if there was no public to see and admire you? Divas need an audience. Poor, clueless Fausto. Did he actually think the ladies were looking for solitude?

Obviously so. "Grosseto is the place to go if you want to avoid the crowds," he continued.

When Giancarlo piped up in agreement, Shelby's ears stood at attention. "Grosseto? Where your villa is, right, Giancarlo?" she queried expectantly, caressing his arm and letting a coy smile play across her lips.

At his affirmative nod, she continued to press home her advantage. "This Sunday, Dena and I are going to look at a hotel for sale quite near there in Santa Fiora." Surely he'd invite them to spend the weekend there. What a stroke of good luck.

Giancarlo nodded and smiled at this information. Shelby returned his smile with one of her most radiant. Here it comes. Get ready. But act surprised, she cautioned herself. You know, as if the thought of him inviting you never occurred to you. Don't seem too anxious. Play it cool. Hesitate a bit.

They held each other's gaze for what seemed like ages, and Shelby waited. Okay?! Sometime before the next millennium would be good. You know, while I still have my own teeth and haven't regressed to needing diapers again.

"We order our meal now?" Giancarlo encouraged, turning away to look at his menu.

A crestfallen Shelby hurriedly buried her face in her own menu, but the tears stinging her eyes made it impossible to read. Dena's brilliant idea of Divahood was turning out to be just great, she thought angrily to herself. First that cursed phone call to Lisa, and now this.

But just when she was about to curse the day she'd let her friend talk her into this harebrained scheme, Shelby realized her mistake. How silly of me! Of course, he's not going to invite me *and* Dena. So unromantic. Naturally, he'd want to bring me there so we could be alone. That mystery solved, she sighed with relief.

Meals ordered, Dena reintroduced the topic at hand. "Shelby and I are going to Rimini next week. Have you been there?" she asked the doctor.

Fausto, with nostrils flared and brow slightly furrowed, must have just gotten a strong whiff of something quite rancid....the same whiff as Lady Isadora. Had someone thrown a stink bomb into the restaurant? Had one of the ladies forgotten to use antiperspirant before dressing for the evening? Funny, they didn't smell anything untoward.

"I don't really like Rimini," Fausto began. "It's very crowded. Too many loud nightclubs and discos," he elaborated. His face wore a mask of utter distaste.

Sounds like just the place for me. Dena's eyes were dreamy with anticipation. Then Giancarlo weighed in on the matter.

"*Di cattivo gusto!*" Tacky. Tasteless. It seemed he smelled the same thing as Fausto.

The place sounded positively heavenly to Dena, but she supposed it wouldn't do for the newly cultured Divas to show their faces there. Still, couldn't they do a drive by? A hit and run? It pained Dena, but it seemed Rimini was out.

"Well!" she exhaled with as much hauteur as she could summon. "We'll have to contact our travel agent tomorrow and cancel our reservation. I can't imagine why he ever recommended Rimini."

Tomorrow they would head to one of Mr. Web's countless Florentine offices, the underground Internet café at Santa Maria Novella train station, to cancel the Rimini excursion.

Finally, a quiet moment arrived, and Shelby took the opportunity to give Giancarlo his gift. Creamy orange paper with a matching metallic bow tempted him. His eyes held the anticipatory gleam of a little boy at Christmas as he ripped open the gift.

Shelby was as anxious as he, certain her thoughtfulness would endear her even more to Giancarlo. Her searching eyes never left his face. Unfortunately, it wasn't long before the brightness in those eyes was supplanted with a hazy cloud of confusion.

Shelby cringed at the vacant look on his face. He had no idea what he was looking at. It had seemed like a great idea when she bought it. She began to babble an explanation, desperate to generate his interest.

"It's called *Magnetic Poetry*," she started. "They're little tiles, each with a word...you put them together...make sentences out of them... on your refrigerator...you know, to help your English."

He nodded with understanding. "Oh, that's fun," he said. Then, he looked at her with a fake smile. "I like," he said with little conviction.

Shelby pressed on, eager to convince him what a great gift she had chosen. "Some people leave sexy messages to each other," she offered with a provocative little smile. "You know, like...*ti voglio stanotte*." I want you tonight.

A new appreciation filled his eyes. He leaned over and pressed his soft lips to hers, a promise in his kiss that Shelby couldn't mistake. She sighed with relief. He does like it, she told herself.

"I put it here," Giancarlo said. Reaching behind their chairs, he placed the gift in a little alcove built into the wall.

Notwithstanding the addition of Fausto to their party, dinner was a pleasant affair. The women each began with an arugula salad topped with generous shavings of parmesan and olives. Fausto demonstrated the Italian way of dressing the salad by drizzling it with olive oil and sprinkling copious amounts of salt on top.

Oil without vinegar. How novel, thought the ladies, not sure it would be to their taste. But they followed suit, and found Fausto's advice was perfect. The salad was simply *squisita*. Delicious.

True to form, Dena and Shelby cannot describe their entrees with razor sharp specificity. Shelby ordered pasta with a porcini mushroom sauce. However, the dish failed to make much of an impression on her. A few factors may have contributed to this unfortunate circumstance. After all, she was in a tizz over being reunited with the love of her life. Or, at least, the love of her life on this continent. Additionally, her nerves were a tad frazzled after the ill-fated phone call to her dear friend Lisa.

Regardless, Shelby loves her food. She comes from a family of hearty eaters and is usually able to set aside any adversity for a good meal. So, a more likely explanation for her memory lapse was that the dish just didn't have much taste. Under no circumstances did her wine consumption have any bearing whatsoever on the matter.

Dena, on the other hand, was thoroughly delighted with her ravioli with lobster in a cream sauce. She tucked into her meal with the gusto of a big rig trucker.

"Would anyone like a taste?" Good manners dictated that she make the offer.

Shelby looked over at the tempting dish. "Well, mayb..." her voice stopped in midstream.

Dena was holding her fork like a warrior's spear, and her eyes had the protective fervor of a mother bear with its cubs. Shelby was afraid if her hand got too close to one of those ravioli, it might not emerge with all five fingers.

"No, not me," she demurred, pulling her hand back quickly, "but thanks for the offer."

Without a doubt, the hit of the evening was the *bistecca alla fiorentina* ordered by the gentlemen. Il Cantastorie's rendition of this traditional Florentine dish was so mouthwatering, so tender that the Divas have no qualms about recommending this restaurant's steaks even to the toothless traveler. Indeed, Il Cantastorie served the best bistecca alla fiorentina that the ladies have ever tasted.

"Dessert anyone?" Giancarlo offered after the main course was cleared away.

Now the ladies do not consider themselves to be obsessive weight watchers and believe that beautiful women and divas come in all shapes and sizes. However, one of the ladies' preferred methods of limiting caloric intake, and therefore, maintaining their figures, is to pass on dessert. Alas, no sweets for the sweet.

However, when Fausto ordered a Limoncello for himself, Dena's ears perked up. Visions of she and Nicola sipping the sweet liqueur infused with lemon rinds skirted past her mind's eye.

"Oh, I'll have one," she said.

Giancarlo, passing on dessert, likewise ordered a Limoncello. A few sips of the lemony drink, and much to Shelby's delight, her *amore* became very affectionate, placing his arm around her shoulder and pulling her to him in a warm embrace. A few more sips and soon dear Giancarlo was in the mood for a dessert not included on any food pyramid, Diva or otherwise.

With infinite finesse, his hand caressed her knee with soft circular motions that sent shock waves through Shelby. His lips nibbled playfully at her ear in between the tender words he whispered in Italian.

"*Che bella. Ti piace?*" So beautiful...you like? After these words, she was lost, comprehending only half of what he said, but his fingers tracing an erotic path along her inner thigh spoke a seductive language all their own.

Shelby had never been in quite such a situation before. Though a grown woman in her thirties (okay, forties), the sum total of her sexual experiences up until that point had taken place in the privacy and comfort of her or the gentleman's boudoir.

While she and Dena were planning the trip, she'd expressed a desire to spice up her sex life. She had always felt sexually stunted in this respect and was determined to do the deed in more exotic locales. "You know, sex on the beach. Maybe in a car or a hot tub."

Never had the word restaurant popped in her mind as a possibility. So as Giancarlo's hands roamed higher, she was a tad apprehensive. It was so public...the lights so bright. Then again, what could be spicier than that? Hell, why not, she concluded.

So throwing caution to the wind, Shelby did as Rod Stewart encouraged in his little ditty "Tonight's the Night." The Diva spread her wings and...well, surely the rest isn't so hard to imagine.

Meanwhile, Dena and Fausto were completely oblivious to the utterly indecent shenanigans taking place right under their noses, or more correctly, right under their table.

Unfortunately, the attractive young couple at the next table, who were not so unaware, appeared quite surprised to discover that the virtuoso voice of *Il Maestro* wasn't the evening's only entertainment. Shelby was simultaneously titillated and a bit embarrassed when she glimpsed a knowing smile pass between the pair.

Then, Giancarlo's arms gathered her closer. The heady alchemy of his crisp cologne mingled with his male scent, hypnotizing her, evaporating all inhibition.

Her last coherent thought gave birth to another essential Diva Do/n't.

If they don't pay your way, don't worry what they do, think, or say.

And with that in mind, Shelby turned her attention to the matter at hand (or the hand that mattered), snuggling even closer to Giancarlo and enjoying the interlude immensely.

After-dinner drinks and foreplay concluded, the gentlemen were reluctant to end the evening.

"Fausto has a beautiful home. An eleventh-century villa in Fiesole. You really must see," Giancarlo suggested.

Years ago, Shelby had been to Fiesole, a lovely town perched on a hill just a few miles north of Florence, but a world away from the larger city's hustle and bustle. She'd extolled its beauty to Dena, and it was on their To Do list. This was perfect.

Once an Etruscan settlement and later, the ancient Roman city of Faesulae, the town of Fiesole is an important archeological site. Most famous in its archeological zone is the well-preserved and restored three-thousand seat amphitheater complete with Roman baths, which in summer hosts the *Estate Fiesolana*, a festival of music, dance and theater under the star-studded Tuscan sky. Fiesole is also equally well-known for its centuries-old villas used by Florence's well-heeled citizens through the ages as a respite from the city's stifling summer heat and the occasional plague.

"Oh, I'd love to see your home," Shelby agreed with a ready eagerness. After all, these stately, historic residences were rarely accessible to the ordinary tourist.

Ever the faithful friend, Dena nodded her assent with much reluctance. Really, what choice had she? It was Fausto's house or hoofing it back to the hotel. Not that Dena didn't want to see Fausto's villa every bit as much as her friend. She relished any opportunity to get a peek into the lives of people, aware it was the only way to really see a country. And to date, the only home she'd been privy to was Nicola's. And frankly, a hamster cage had more rooms than his apartment.

Yes, Dena definitely wanted to go to Fiesole, but a sick feeling coiled in the pit of her stomach. Wasn't there some way they could see Fausto's home without involving...well, its owner Fatso? Oops, Fausto. Directions, his car, the keys. That was all they needed.

Realizing that even a diva's extensive wiles were not likely to pull off such a feat, Dena resigned herself to spending a few more hours in Fausto's company. Still, she didn't think she could do it without the support of her new best friend, *Cello*...aka Limoncello. How to do it without appearing the lush?

Sometimes, fate aids a distressed diva just when she needs it most. This time fate's emissary was the unexpected arrival of a few of Giancarlo's friends, who popped into the restaurant just as the foursome was leaving.

While he and Fausto were having a rather prolonged conversation with the newcomers, the ladies were left to cool their beautifully-clad heels beside the bar. With a toast to her good fortune, Dena proceeded to order and down two more shots.

Now Shelby wasn't averse to a good buzz, and normally didn't begrudge anyone a tipple or two...or three. But she could feel the blood in her veins bubbling nervously as she grew concerned at the drunken impression Dena might leave with Giancarlo the Near Teetotaler.

"Get over there," she hissed, nudging her friend into hiding.

With Dena safely huddled in a corner with C*ello,* Shelby could once again turn her attention to Giancarlo. As she watched his little tete-á-tete, she realized that her beloved had forgotten his gift, so she beelined it back to the table, convincing herself that her amore's oversight had to be a result of his excitement over spending time with her.

Although total delusion is not a recommended state, Shelby was indeed crossing over into that rugged terrain. She was dreaming of making love with her dear Giancarlo in the baronial luxury of Fausto's estate. Surely, he would realize the error of his past ways and beg her to stay with him forever. They would live happily ever after.

Live happily ever after. Live happily ever after. Live. Live. The word reverberated in her mind.

"Ohmigod," she blurted out. "I forgot to bring condoms."

Shelby was visibly distraught. Much as she looked forward to a night of passion with Giancarlo, she knew she was caught in the throes of yet another Diva Do/n't. And if ever there were a Diva Do/n't to adhere to strictly, this was it.

Diva Do/n't

If you don't have protection, don't you dare touch that erection.

"Oh, don't worry," soothed Dena. "I have two in my purse. You can have them." As her friend covertly handed over the

Diva Lifesavers, Shelby breathed a huge sigh of relief, thanking Dena profusely.

Nevertheless, she was a bit surprised to learn that Dena had the condoms on hand. Was the dear girl expecting an eleventh-hour curtain call from the erstwhile Nicola? For those unfamiliar with this particular diva curtain call, this is known as a booty call for the general public. Poor Dena. It was sad really.

Regardless, Shelby had no time to worry about her friend. Giancarlo had finally wrapped up his conversation and was ready to leave. They were headed for Fausto's home and ecstasy. This was no time to dwell on Dena's delusion. She had her own to play out.

After a pleasant stroll through the streets of Florence, the little group approached Fausto's car.

"Eeeehhhh!" A high-pitched, wailing sound pierced the still night.

Startled, the ladies looked around in panic. "Wh...what?" Dena asked fearfully. Did she need to make a run for it?

Fausto's pained yelp was reminiscent of the squeal of a stuck pig. Shelby and Dena couldn't imagine what had happened. Had he been stabbed? Was he having a heart attack? Was there a full moon, and he a werewolf howling at it? Ergo, the strange hair.

No, it was none of these. Fausto was in good health and ostensibly human. The ladies followed his gaze to the tire on the rear passenger side of his brand new shiny champagne-taupe Jeep. Obviously, the notoriously inefficient policemen of Florence had woken up that evening and harnessed a boot to the tire. Why? The brilliant doctor had illegally parked smack in the middle of *Piazza Santa Croce*, home of the famed *Basilica di Santa Croce*, Michelangelo's final resting place. The Divas were stranded.

Both perplexed and amused at the doctor's folly, Giancarlo quickly whipped out his cell phone, dialed the appropriate number, and used his not inconsiderable influence to have the boot removed. And, for the first time ever, the women gave thanks for his rather unnatural love affair with the cell phone.

Meanwhile, Fausto whined about the exorbitant fine he would have to pay, which did nothing for the façade of the sophisticated, prosperous *medico* with a baronial villa.

Given the customary Italian nonchalance regarding time, the ladies settled back on the Jeep's comfy leather seats, prepared for a very long wait. When a truck arrived within a shockingly short few minutes, they were pleasantly surprised. Two men jumped out, liberated the Jeep, and then, liberated poor Fausto of quite a bit of money.

And soon, the little group was off to Fiesole. Both ladies were looking forward to the adventure. After all, they shared a love of art and history and generally anything that might make them appear cultured.

Much to their surprise and consternation, the boys had a slight detour in mind. After a beautiful drive up into the mountains, Fausto parked in the middle of town. Alighting from the car in their rather precarious high heels, Dena and Shelby found themselves at the foot of *Via di San Nicola*, a steep and winding path which their companions told them led to a panoramic view of all Florence. Also at the summit were the fourteenth-century monastery and church of *Convento di San Nicola*.

Neither woman had ever ridden sidesaddle. Even though dressed to the nines, they were game. "Where are the mules?" they inquired.

The gentlemen were not amused and quickly informed the ladies that the only hooves in sight were their own. A glance of disbelief passed between them, no words necessary. Circumstances were painfully obvious.

Shelby shook her head in disgust. Dena nodded in agreement. Had the whole world gone mad? We're dressed up like Mrs. Astor's pet horses. We have on enough makeup to power a small country. We've engaged these rubes in stimulating, uh, stimulating, uh uh, stimulating conversation, and...

"Unbelievable. Even they don't know who we are," Shelby complained.

Resigned to their fate, the vixen voyagers began the long and grueling trek upwards. Now Dena was a hearty soul, slim but strong. She began her climb with vim and verve, totally confident. But little more than halfway up, the air seemed to thin. She was lightheaded and woozy. Of course, this had nothing to do with the bottle of Limoncello she'd recently put quite a dent in.

Meanwhile, Shelby, who'd always been of delicate constitution, was faring no better. With each excruciating step, her breathing grew more labored. Soon her lungs were wheezing and whistling, and they were not playing a happy tune. How embarrassing! She needed a hit.

What an un-divalike position to be in. Her lungs were about to explode. Did she really want Giancarlo to see her in a lip lock with her inhaler? This is the perfect time for another Diva Do/n't.

**In a choice between your Diva image and death, do
be smart and opt to take that next breath.**

And alas, in a rare display of common sense, Shelby tore open her purse and seized her fast-acting inhaler in a near panic. One puff. Aahh. Two puffs. Blessed relief.

To the ladies' delight, their commendable mountain scaling efforts did not go unrewarded. The view from *Basilica di San Nicola* was simply stunning. High above, the sky lay out in a limitless blanket of velvety blackness. The stars, celestial diamonds glittering brightly, studded the faraway landscape. Below, the view was no less captivating. Seemingly, all of Florence had donned its sparkling finery and staged a dazzling light show.

The beautiful summer evening went to Giancarlo's head. He tucked Shelby into him and whispered in her ear. "We take a walk, no?" he suggested. The deep tones of his voice signaled he was still in a romantic mood.

She followed willingly as he led her along a narrow path that opened onto a glade in the middle of a wooded area. As they sauntered hand in hand, Shelby heard a rustling of leaves along the path. She turned to investigate. Off in the distance, two young lovers were locked in a tender embrace. Hell, they were going at it like no tomorrow. She quickly averted her eyes in embarrassment.

Giancarlo's hand left hers and caressed the sensitive skin at the nape of her neck. She moaned softly when his fingers played with the curls of her hair. Then, another moan reached her ears, but it was not her own. Her eyes focused upward. Up there, another amorous couple going at it, indifferent to anyone or anything around them.

It finally clicked. Giancarlo had brought her to some sort of Italian lovers' lane. They continued on, finally stopping in a secluded spot. He pulled her to him, closing his lips over hers in a sweetly seductive kiss, his arms warm and passionate. *Dio mio*, she swooned inwardly. Another sexual first... seduction under the open sky. She was on a roll.

His kiss deepened; his hands roamed under the silky hem of her dress. She was weak in his arms and her own hands began to explore. Passion overtaking him, Giancarlo started to lower her to the ground.

Oh, he's gone to such lengths... a bed of moldy leaves as my blanket and a mossy rock for a pillow. How romantic. He doesn't really expect me to have sex out here, does he? Kissing, okay. A little fondling even. But sex on the ground? Not quite the exotic locale I had in mind.

What does he take me for? What happened to the villa? You know, the comfort of a down-filled mattress dressed with the finest linen sheets and the twinkle of romantic candlelight. Actually, at this point, I'd settle for an air-filled camping mattress and a kerosene lamp. Okay, even a sleeping bag and a cigarette lighter.

"No, no," she gave him a little shove. "I'm not having sex on the ground." The resolve in her voice was apparent.

Her extreme discomfort notwithstanding, Giancarlo was a man on a mission. Standing, he brought her with him, never loosening his embrace. His ardor grew deeper, kissing her neck and caressing her breasts. Like a blind man, feeling with his hands, he guided her to the support of a nearby tree. His breath was warm and labored.

Shelby's, however, had cooled down completely. The moment had been lost. She knew it, but Giancarlo hadn't a clue. What to do?

No matter how much she had ached for it to be otherwise, he was not the same man she had known six years ago. But she wasn't ready to let that man go. Six long years of wishing and hoping were riding on this moment. The entire evening...cripes, the last six years...had been leading up to this moment. Propelled by bittersweet memories, she reached into her purse to retrieve a condom.

How can one explain delicately the piteous nature of what followed next? Perhaps, it should just be said that Giancarlo, but more importantly, poor little Giancarlo, was not accustomed to latex. And little Giancarlo remained just that. Stubbornly little. Not to be denied, big Giancarlo had a brainstorm.

"Shelby, we don't need thees," he said. "We don't use before." His eyes smoldered with heat, and his voice was husky with desire, reminding her of their passionate history.

That was six years ago before you proposed and then bedded dear Lisa, came the unpleasant thought. When I trusted you.

And, Shelby, delusional or not, was ever mindful of the applicable Diva Do/n't. In fact, this one is so vital that it has a twin to help reinforce its importance. And any diva who disregards it puts her life and others at peril.

Diva Do/n't

If he doesn't don the latex, don't even dream about having sex.

Adamantly, Shelby shook her head and stepped away from the man she'd loved for six long years. "No," she said, reiterating her body language. Love didn't mean much if you were dead. "I can't."

Disappointment clouded his eyes, but her determination was unmistakable. Separately, in an awkward silence, the former lovers hastily straightened their clothing.

Meanwhile, back at the monastery, Dena had been fending off the unwanted affections of Fausto, who seemed to possess more hands than a centipede has legs. Luckily, after a few no hitters, he proved to be a gentleman and took the hint.

While completely repulsed by his advances, Dena couldn't really blame him for trying. She did look especially radiant that evening, and what man could really resist the Diva's grace and beauty. Does the name Nicola ring a bell? Well, she wouldn't think about that tonight.

To pass the time, she frantically engaged Fausto in nonstop conversation, introducing myriad topics ranging from astrology to religion as they sat on the steps of the monastery, patiently awaiting the return of Giancarlo and Shelby. In the midst of their lively discussion, a gravelly, disembodied voice rumbled through the darkness.

"Please leave. Please leave now!"

Dena rocketed to her feet. "Oh, no. We woke the monks!" she exclaimed with dismay.

The doctor, showing no signs of alarm, gave a little chuckle at her concern. He pointed to a shadowy figure lying only steps away. "No, no," he contradicted, "it's just a poor man trying to sleep."

He assured her that they were not being thrown off the monastery steps by the monks, but by a homeless man who was just trying to catch his forty winks. Relieved that they weren't being shooed away by the clergy, Dena apologized to the poor soul and promptly moved away to leave the man to his slumber.

Much to her relief, her AWOL friend put in a reappearance exactly at that moment. It was time to move on to Fausto's lovely home and soak up a bit more culture. But first, they had to get back down that godforsaken hill.

Together the ladies stood at the hill's summit and surveyed the trek ahead of them. It might as well have been Mount Everest. There was nothing to hold onto, no railings to steady one's footing...just Fausto and Giancarlo.

Within seconds, Shelby knew her strappy sandals were no match for what was sure to be a slippery slide down the gravelly path. Her whole body tensed as she teetered on the tiny heels, trying desperately to remain upright. With each step, the earth seemed to roll out from under her as pebbles shifted and scattered in her wake.

One misstep was enough for this diva. If she didn't take precautions, she'd find herself competing in a new Olympic event. Downhill Derriere Slolum, or worse, Downhill Facial Skiing.

"That's it," she announced. "I'm going barefoot." Doffing her shoes, she proceeded bare-, but sure-footed, down the death-defying path.

Dena had her own dilemma as she made her way down the treacherous trail.

"Here, I help you," Fausto offered chivalrously. He held out his arm for her to take.

"No, no, I can make it on my own," she replied, moving a bit away, resisting his help.

The last thing she needed was a repeat of the unfortunate incident in Viareggio brought on by Fausto the Doctor, who incidentally had not offered one iota of medical advice when shown the now green-oozing mess where her once beautiful slim knee had resided.

But dear Fausto was not having his offer of assistance down the mountain denied. He reached over and linked his arm in Dena's. Again, she demurred.

"I really do believe, I'd be better off...aaahhh!"

Shelby's head jerked around when she heard Dena's screeching. She watched on in amazement as Fausto lost his footing and began to ski down the path without benefit of ski poles. Or snow. She feared for Dena, worried her best friend was about to suffer another most unfortunate incident. Oh Lord, poor girl. Not again. Would that gangrenous knee get a twin? Shelby stood there horrified, mouth agape, unable to help.

But Dena wasn't going down willingly. One boo boo was quite enough, thank you. With lightening speed and a freakish strength, she ripped her arm from the doctor's grasp.

"I told you I didn't need your help. Let me go," she ground out with cruel distain. Self-preservation leaping to the fore, she shook the man off like a pesky fly, saving herself at all costs and leaving the doctor to his lonely fate, whatever it might be.

All watched on as Fausto fought mightily and somehow regained his balance, thereby averting a rather ignominious fall. But his poor ego had taken a nasty tumble. Straightening his back, he proceeded down the path in stoic silence.

This day was full of Diva Do/n'ts. While Shelby's removal of her shoes may not have been the most dignified or sanitary choice, and Dena's tactical maneuvers of self-preservation were hardly imbued with the milk of human kindness, the Divas made it down the mountain in one piece. What Diva Do/n't can be gleaned from this experience? For a diva, there is really no choice. Always save yourself.

It's nice to lend a helping hand (or needed arm), but do not if it will cause you harm.

They were back in Fiesole's piazza. It was bustling with activity and happy people on this hot summer evening. Fausto offered to go get the car, and Dena accompanied him. While they were gone, Shelby and Giancarlo found a stone bench to rest on. Seconds passed. They seemed like hours.

She looked over at him and smiled a sad little smile. Again, she was remembering all the things she had loved about him, all the hope he had given her. That was a lifetime ago, she realized, and now...now, she didn't recognize this man sitting next to her.

Her Giancarlo would never have taken her to the woods and expected sex. Her Giancarlo would never have suggested she talk to Lisa. And speaking of Lisa, let's face it, her Giancarlo would never have done what he had done with Lisa six years ago or left her to find out the way she had.

Suddenly, with an uncharacteristically brilliant clarity, Shelby saw that her Giancarlo had never existed. He'd created an illusion, and she had believed it. And this man sitting next to her now? She didn't have anything left to say to this man. Sadly, her dream was over. Or maybe, not so sadly. Maybe now, a new dream could take its place.

Just then, Fausto's Jeep screeched to a halt in front of the quiet pair. Shelby's eyes panned from him to Dena. The doctor's eyes never looked in Giancarlo's or her direction; instead he stared straight ahead as if in some strange trance. Tense hands clenched the steering wheel, and Shelby noticed he had donned driving gloves. Who did he think he was, Mario Andretti, she mused.

Dena's eyes widened in warning. Almost imperceptibly, her head shook from side to side. Her lips were moving, but no sounds were audible. One too many hours with Fatso, Shelby giggled privately.

They'd barely closed their door before the Jeep made a violent lurch forward. Like rag dolls, Giancarlo and Shelby were thrown back into their seats. Shelby jerked worried eyes toward their chauffeur. His shoulders were hunched as he leaned over the steering wheel, his lips almost kissing the windshield. The expression on his face was frightening. Even his windowpane glasses couldn't mask the slightly demented, glazed gleam in his eyes as he pressed the pedal to the metal.

Fausto didn't seem to notice his passengers being tossed about like a Waldorf salad. First sliding to the right, only to be flung to the left seconds later. Upfront, Dena grabbed her neck, hoping to stave off whiplash.

Down the hill the car hurtled, taking hairpin turns at eighty miles per hour. Dena turned back to her friend, about to suggest they bail. Jump and roll. Wasn't that what they said to do in a carjacking? But she couldn't get Shelby's attention.

The other woman was frantically groping for her seatbelt, as was Giancarclo, who himself looked a little green around the gills. Suddenly, Fausto's Dr. Jekyll had transformed into a scary Mr. Hyde, in a sudden display of misplaced manhood.

Why were they going down the hill? Shelby didn't understand. Wasn't Fausto's villa in the opposite direction?

Meanwhile, Dena had questions of her own. What could possibly have brought about such a drastic metamorphosis in the mild-mannered doctor? Surely his nose wasn't out of joint (any more than usual) because of the rather sharp tongue-lashing he'd gotten for almost dragging her down with him on his slippery mountain descent? She was perfectly justified in being preoccupied with her safety. Lord knew one oozing knee was enough. Or, could he be a bit miffed at not having gotten to first base, never mind third?

The Divas would never know. Truthfully, they didn't really care. As they came to yet another screeching halt in front of the Hotel Macchiavelli, it was quite apparent that they would not be repairing to Fausto's historic, and perhaps mythical, they now suspected, eleventh-century villa. There would be no furthering of their cultural pursuits tonight.

The best they could hope for was to make it out of Fausto's one-man bumper car race with body parts intact. In short order, their prayers were answered, as Fausto rather precipitously and unceremoniously dumped them at their hotel's front door.

Dena flung open her door as if a prisoner making a break. Her goodbyes trailing behind her, she made a run for it. When they heard footsteps following the click of their heels, the ladies were very surprised to find that Dr. Jekyll had staged a come-back. Fausto had alighted from the car and was graciously escorting them to the hotel door. Had he finally figured out who they were?

Giancarlo, on the other hand, displayed little gentlemanly courtesy. Rather than seeing them safely to the door, he jumped from the back and ensconced himself in the front seat. With a slight wave of his hand, he bade Shelby to call him.

The Diva returned the offhand wave with one of her own. "Oh yes, I will," she agreed with a smile.

As she turned to make her way into the hotel, Dena was sure she heard her friend mumble under her breath. She wasn't altogether certain, but she thought she heard something about when pigs fly or when hell freezes over.

Having made their way to the welcome sanctuary of their room, the ladies were silent as they prepared for bed, each lost in their solitary thoughts. For Dena, it was quite the body blow to yet again amble past the woefully empty message box for Room 105. The poor girl, still without a firm grasp on the Poof Factor. Once again, she'd allowed her mind to wander into catastrophe-conjuring mode.

Should anyone else also be afflicted with this particular malady, let the Divas clear it up once and for all. No, he hasn't had a mishap on his motorino. There's been no death in the family. He's not undergone emergency surgery. He hasn't run off to join a monastery and taken a vow of silence. The earth is still round, and he hasn't fallen off the edge. In short, he is simply not interested in further communiqués. Now, repeat after the Divas. Accept it. Deal with it. Move on.

While Dena remained happily within the safety of her delusional cocoon, Shelby was not so lucky. Undoubtedly, the universe in its infinite wisdom deemed six years more than enough time for the diva to operate under any single delusion. Hence, as she stripped the makeup from her face, any remaining fantasies about a romantic reunion for her and Giancarlo were similarly cleansed from every corner of her soul. Reality was finally rearing its ugly head.

Both exhausted, the ladies slipped into the sensuously soft silk negligees they'd purchased in anticipation of their romantic vacation and crawled rather forlornly into their lonely beds.

As Shelby drifted off to sleep, having finally accepted the true state of her relationship with Giancarlo, any lingering doubts were decisively squelched by a most unexpected ghostly visitor. This experience is best described in a little poem that the Divas like to call *'Twas the Night after Giancarlo*. They consider it their contribution to the arts.

'Twas the Night After Giancarlo

*Twas the Night after Giancarlo and all through the room
Not a creature was stirring, not even a loon.
While visions of Limoncello lemons danced through her head,
Diva Dena was dreaming of Nicola all snug in her bed.*

*When up from poor Diva Shelby, there arose a bloodcurdling cry,
A black specter loomed over her,
She thought she might die.*

*And frightened Diva Dena, torn from her dreams,
Was yanked from her fantasy by the other diva's screams.
She yelled oh so loud "Why all this clatter?"
"Tell me, tell me, what the hell's the matter?"*

*"I thought I saw a man in this very room,
dressed all in black, full of dark gloom and doom.
But he was a dream with meaning so deep,
I'll explain to you tomorrow,
For now, go to sleep."*

*Soon Diva Shelby again began to snore.
The dream held no power over her anymore.
But a cowering Diva Dena was awake for the night.
That scream had given her a helluva fright!*

"Wow, that was some night," India concluded. "After six years of keeping a glimmer of hope alive, it must have been devastating to realize it was really over."

Shelby shook her head in denial. "Oddly enough, it wasn't. Yes, I was sad, but it was also a relief."

The wordless question evident in the Englishwoman's eyes demanded elaboration.

"I was finally free from my delusion. I didn't need it anymore. At least, not that one," Shelby obliged.

"The delusion that you could conquer Giancarlo and get him back?" India continued.

Shelby shifted in her seat, the questions making her a bit uncomfortable. "No, like I said earlier, I could probably have kept seeing him, and who knows what would have developed again?"

India hazarded another guess. "Then you didn't need the delusion of being a diva anymore?"

"Oh, no, that's still alive and well even now."

India was out of theories. "What then?"

Shelby decided to take pity on her. "No, my biggest delusion was that I even wanted Giancarlo anymore. That we could be happy together after everything that had happened."

She fell quiet, lost in a morass of the past six years. Then, she continued. "My God, he asked me to marry him and move to Italy. Then he picks up with my friend and was too weak to even tell me himself."

India made no comment. She was only half listening, as snippets of her life with Malcolm reeled like a movie through her mind. Late nights at the office…the scent of an unfamiliar perfume on his shirt…phone calls with no answer at the other end.

"It all became perfectly clear with my dream that night," Shelby finished.

"Wh…what became clear?" India asked, coming out of her fog. "I didn't quite get that poem. Who was that dark specter?"

Shelby shrugged her shoulders. "Who knows for sure? To me, he was the Grim Reaper. My Giancarlo was dead. And so was the life I'd envisioned."

A comprehending light crept into India's eyes. Maybe mine is dead too, she acknowledged, but only to herself. Then, another question came to mind.

"And that was a relief?" India wasn't so sure she bought it.

"Yes, I didn't need the delusion. I could go home and get on with my life."

Again, India was silent. Is it possible I don't need my delusion anymore either, she asked herself hesitantly.

Chapter 15

*P*oised in front of the open armoire deciding what to wear the next day, Dena had a thought. She was feeling a bit strange. Not bad strange, but good strange. What could it be? She hadn't done anything differently from her normal routine.

"Yeah, now that you mention it, I feel quite refreshed myself. Rather unusual," Shelby agreed when her friend voiced the little mystery.

"I definitely drank enough for at least a Level One hangover," Dena continued. "But this morning, I'm feeling right as rain."

After their first trip to Italy, the ladies had developed a rating system for their hangovers.

DIVA HANGOVER-OMETER

	Symptoms	Activities	Next Drink	Cures
Level One	Cotton Mouth Headache Puffy Eyes	Able to Function almost normally	Lunch, Dinner or Abstain	Good breakfast
Level Two	Level 1 symptoms plus: Upset Stomach Shakes/Tremors	Rise Later. Eat grease immediately. Avoid carnival rides and other fast transports.	During Breakfast	Hair of the Dog
Level Three	Levels 1 and 2 symptoms plus: Inability to open eyes without pain, move without pain, or communicate without pain	None Hire someone to shoot you and put you out of your misery.	Turn over in your bed. Reach for bottle of Chianti on bed stand Suck on the straw	The Dog AND Its Puppies

Dena and Shelby like to think of this as their own little Step Program. No, certainly not a twelve-step program to stop drinking. Heaven forbid the ladies sober up and face facts. Theirs was a three-step program with a twofold purpose. First, it helped determine precisely at what meal the Divas would next down that first drop of lifesaving Chianti. Second, it controlled their level of activity on any given day.

Dena was mulling over a rather novel theory. "Do you think Dr. Jekyll-Mr. Hyde had anything to do with it?"

"Yeah, who needs Paolo and Fabrizio?" Shelby asked. "Even *my* hair was straight last night. Scared straight. It's got to be Fausto."

Agreeing the answer lay with the cadaverous cardiologist, the ladies decided their discovery called for another category on the Hangover-ometer... Hangover Prevention.

One gander at Fatso...Fausto, and a person could dive head first into a wine cask and come out stone cold sober.

"I think we have a duty to alert Alcoholics Anonymous," Shelby joked.

In her amusement, Dena fell onto her bed and banged her knee. She let out a scream of pain. Unfortunately, the wacky doctor's powers hadn't extending to scaring her knee straight. Overnight, it had turned an even more disturbing shade of green and was weeping profusely. Something had to be done.

If Shelby heard the words impetigo and gangrene one more time, she wasn't sure she could be responsible for her actions. Thoughts of amputating the damned leg herself started to flitter through her fertile mind.

"Okay, okay! We'll go to the emergency room," she humored her friend. "I'm sure they'll want to perform immediate surgery. Should I notify your next of kin?"

"Emergency room?" India screeched. *"You've got to be kidding me."*

Shelby's eyes widened and fixed on India. Blinking them furiously like Morse Code in a disaster, she tried to warn the woman to drop the subject and save herself. It was too late.

Dena practically shoved her knee in India's face. "Look at it, look at it!" she ordered.

If she's any representative of the British, Dena fumed, the Normans ought to ransack their godforsaken little island again.

"My knee's a mess! I still think it really could be impetigo."

Shelby couldn't help herself. Enough was enough. "Or maybe..." She paused and leaned forward. Suspense hung in the air.

She struggled to keep a straight face as she continued. "Maybe it's that flesh-eating bacteria."

"Exactly!" Dena agreed, the sarcasm completely lost on her.

India guffawed at the suggestion. "Well, what happened at the emergency room? Did they operate?"

Shelby shoved the little purple book at the Englishwoman. "Not another one," India groaned.

What did the emergency room doctors do when confronted with Dena's booboo?
A) Immediately prepped her for surgery,
B) A studly Italian medico laid her on a gurney (and we do mean laid her),
C) Professionally cleaned and bandaged her wound, or
D) Informed her the knee hardly constituted an emergency and sent her on her way.

If you chose Answer A, you're not fit to walk the streets alone. Nothing happens immediately in Italy. Does the word even appear in Italian dictionaries?

If you chose Answer B, you can be forgiven. It is a well-known fact that the Divas are the object of every man's desire. However, you must have forgotten that Dena was practically engaged to dear Nicola, and her name is nearly synonymous with the word fidelity. What, she's already married? No!?

If you chose Answer C, is your name Alice? Have you fallen through the looking glass and is Wonderland your place of residence? Little Deenie took a tumble and scraped her knee. Millions of five-year olds do it every day. Do you really think their mommies are ferrying them to the emergency room?

If you chose Answer D, congratulations. You're correct.

"I knew it," India blurted out with an air of supreme satisfaction.

"Oh please. Those doctors were a bunch of charlatans," Dena decreed, waving her hand dismissively. "And I still intend to see a real doctor when I get home."

As well you should, India concurred silently, but not for the knee.

All the way to the hotel from the hospital, Dena limped and sputtered. She would not be silenced.

"Well, I never! This knee is infected. I need a doctor," she fumed. "Who do they think they are? And they certainly didn't seem to know who I am."

Shelby had to disagree with that last statement, even if she chose to keep her opinion to herself. She was pretty sure the hospital staff knew exactly who, or at least what, Dena was. A nut job.

Regardless, Shelby sensed the rest of her trip would be a living hell if Dena didn't see a doctor. After all, Giancarlo was history, and it didn't look as if Nicola would be taking gimpy off her hands any time soon. Like it or not, Shelby was stuck with her, and if she didn't find Dena a doctor soon, she'd be hearing about that damned knee morning, noon, and night.

More for her own peace of mind than her hypochondriac friend's, Shelby linked her arm in Dena's to comfort her. "Don't worry. Soon as we get back, we'll ask the hotel for a doctor," she promised.

Within the hour, a young female doctor with a ready smile appeared at their hotel door. The poor woman barely made it over the threshold before Dena pounced on her, swinging her leg in the woman's face.

"It's impetigo, isn't it?" she shrieked.

The pretty doctor stifled a smile, and shook her head in the negative.

"Gangrene then?" Dena continued hysterically.

Again, a negative shake of the doctor's head. "But it is infected," she answered.

As she cleaned Dena's "wound," the doctor was in the mood to chat, wanting to know why the Americans were in Florence.

Dena, always forthcoming with way more information than necessary, revealed Shelby's Italian romance.

"Your boyfriend's in Florence?" the doctor queried.

Shelby nodded in the affirmative.

"Ouch!" Dena yelped, grabbing her knee. The doctor's gentle ministrations as she cleaned the wound had turned a bit rough, almost as if she were angry about something. "Careful! That's an open wound you're cleaning, not the kitchen floor."

The doctor muttered an apology, but her eyes never left Shelby. "Your boyfriend, he's not from Florence, is he?" she asked. Couched as a question, it was more a statement.

"Well, actually, no," Shelby admitted warily. Giancarlo had been born in Brindisi, but so what?

Her assumption confirmed, a smug smile crept across the doctor's face. Her condescension irritated the travelers, but also piqued their curiosity.

"How did you know he wasn't from here?" Dena piped up.

"Because true *Fiorentini*...Florentines...would only date other Florentines," she answered with haughty confidence.

Suddenly, the pretty doctor had turned rather ugly. Dena and Shelby were flabbergasted and not a little disbelieving. Both sets of eyes arched in suspicion.

The doctor answered their unspoken question. "*Si, si, veramente.* It is true. A real Florentine man would never speak to you," she elaborated with thinly veiled glee.

Who the hell did this woman think she was, Shelby stewed. Some doctor. Do they have the Hippocratic Oath here? You know, the one that says first do no harm? She probably cut worms in half as a child and watched them squirm. No, she looks like a cat woman. Bet she's thrown her share of furry felines into the Arno River to see if they could swim. Her microwave? Not for food. For cats. Wants to know if they heat up evenly or if the tails are done first.

Dena was similarly disturbed. What was wrong with the doctors of Florence? First, Dante the Dish Rag. Next, Fatso the Fruitcake. Followed up by Emergency Room Doctor the Evil. And now, here was House Call Doctor the Haughty. Did the screening committee in Italian medical schools only accept severely dysfunctional candidates?

One loaded look between them, and our duo swept into action. Time to get Dr. Frankenstella out of there before she whipped out a scalpel and started harvesting human body parts. Dena fumbled for money, as Shelby artfully edged the demon doctor towards the door. They took great care to lock it once she had left.

Though they had banished the harridan, Dena couldn't banish her assertions from her mind as easily. "Do you think she's right?" Dena asked. "About the Florentine men?"

Shelby waved her hand in the air dismissively. "Sounds like the rantings of a jealous, middle-aged spinster to me."

"Yes, but have you ever gone out with a Florentine?" Dena refused to let the subject drop. "Where's Brindisi?"

Reluctantly, Shelby admitted that Brindisi was nowhere near Florence, but in the south of Italy.

"And Nicola's from the south also," Dena added thoughtfully.

Seeing Shelby was bored with the subject, she dropped it. But Dena wasn't about to let it go for good. If it killed her, she would prove Dr. Frankenstella wrong, she promised herself. But first, she needed to take care of her knee.

Prescription in hand and hats on heads, the ladies made their way to the pharmacy. After picking up Dena's medicine, they decided that their ten-minute walk was quite enough exercise for one day.

It was lunchtime. Luckily, they were in Piazza della Signoria. Michelangelo's original Davide once stood there in all his naked splendor for legions of women to look and drool...*scusi*...dream. In 1873, Davide was moved to the *Galleria dell'Accademia*[25] for safekeeping.

Nevertheless, as mentioned previously, ladies the world over need not despair. A quite magnificent copy now stands in its place in the piazza.

Conveniently located in the piazza is a wonderful outdoor café,[26] which features much-needed canvas umbrellas to shield patrons from the near brain-sizzling rays of the Florentine summer sun. Lush potted plants edge the perimeters of the café separating diners from holiday strollers on the piazza. With the heat index approaching spontaneous combustion levels, its oppressiveness had taken a visible toll on Dena and Shelby. The maitre d' quickly showed them to a corner table surrounded by oxygen-supplying plants.

"Why did he put us here?" complained Dena, a frown crinkling her brow.

"What's the matter with this table?" Shelby asked.

"I can't see a thing, and no one can see me. I'm moving," Dena answered testily. "Divas don't people watch. They watch people watch them."

For the quick of mind, yes, this actually is still people watching, but for quite a different purpose. For the dull of mind, it may help to read slowly and aloud. When Divas watch people watch them, they *are* people watching.

With laser beam precision, Dena's eyes scanned the layout of the café searching for a more auspicious location for the ladies. Water glass, napkin, and place setting in tow, she pounced on an available table leaving Shelby to follow behind or dine alone. Dena's choice was perfect. If they had been at tennis match, the ladies would have been center court, which brings to light another Diva Do/n't.

---

[25]Via Ricasoli 58-60

[26]Ristorante Il Cavallino, Piazza Signoria 28, PH 055/215818

**If you want everyone to see your pretty face, don't
let yourself be seated in an obscure place.**

Notwithstanding their relocation, the waiter had no trouble
finding the ladies and quickly arrived with the carafe of Chianti
they'd ordered before being seated. Dena started to pour the
wine and then stopped midway, a question forming in her pretty
brown eyes.

"Do we have anything to toast to?" she pondered.

"No successes, but plenty of failures," Shelby pointed out.

Dena raised her glass, reflecting aloud on their state of
affairs: first, having dipped into their retirement funds to
finance this excursion, and second, most likely ending up
subsisting on Kibbles and Bits and the kindness of strangers in
their old age.

Shelby laughed and joined in the fun. "My fellow Derelict
Diva, raise your glass again to spending the complete spring
season alternately ignoring friends, family, and job while shopping to impress men."

The lyrical ring of their clinking goblets filled the air. "And
let's not forget to toast the Disabled Divas, courtesy of every pair
of shoes we purchased."

"Here, here," Dena concurred happily. "Raise your glass a
third time to our own personal torture chambers. Leaving burns
and blisters wherever leather meets flesh."

The restaurant's canvas umbrellas were no match for the
humid ninety-five degree day. Scorching heat, along with the
suffusing warmth of the wine, went straight to the ladies' heads.

Shelby straightened her shoulders and sat tall and proud.
She raised her head in a regal fashion and continued with the
silliness.

"The Duchess Divas would like to salute their royal milliners
whose unparalleled craftsmanship has bestowed upon them
their gorgeous sun hats." As she spoke, Shelby raised her voice
a few octaves and swallowed the R sound in her words, doing
her best to imitate a British accent.

Dena giggled at her friend's new brogue, which sounded as if
Shelby were channeling a cross between Julia Child and good

Queen Bess. "Please continue, my Divining Diva!" she encouraged.

Shelby readily obliged. "No matter that these hats, meant to shade our ladies from harmful UV rays, have turned into portable greenhouses. Or that if things continue unabated, plant life will start sprouting from their ears."

As they chortled with merry abandon, the waiter appeared with a basket of bread. He refilled their glasses much to the women's delight.

A look of mischief filled Dena's eyes. "Oh, oh, I've got one!" she exclaimed. "Here's to the 'The Donald' Divas. Conning those aforementioned friends and family, not to mention themselves, into believing this was a business trip that would make them millionaire moguls."

"Bloody good one," Shelby concurred. "To 'The Donald' Divas." Then, she thought for a second before amending that. "Only with hair meant for humans."

And so, a mere ninety-six hours after The Divas had touched down on Tuscan soil (that's four days for the mathematically challenged), the ladies were forced to admit that their campaign against the men of Italy had boomeranged and their military offensive was a hopeless failure.

"The world should be so lucky," Shelby declared before taking another sip of wine

Dena answered with a quizzical stare at her friend's cryptic remark.

"To have wars where barely a shot is fired and the only casualties are those of the heart, which..." Shelby elaborated.

"Which will eventually heal," Dena finished the thought, nodding her head in agreement. "So, what exactly is the bright side of this whole thing?"

"Beats me," Shelby answered.

And so, the ladies wrote their own breaking news story. This just in from the front: The Deployed Divas' offensive has ended in a dismal defeat. The campaign to shock and awe has shocked and awed no one more than the Disarmed Divas themselves.

Shock at the speed with which their war commenced, was waged, and a ceasefire declared. Shock at the enemy's retreat with barely a shot fired. Awed that the only male species that might actually take pleasure in their cache of sexy lingerie was the attic moths hungrily awaiting the ladies' return. And finally, awed by the fact that they would be practicing the safest sex of all. Abstention.

"So, when the passersby below my apartment get too rowdy on a Friday night, I can use my condoms as water balloons," Shelby quipped.

Dena grabbed her purse and held it to her protectively. "Well, you're not getting mine. We're here for another ten days, and it's not over 'til the fat lady sings."

Shelby turned her head and pointed a polished finger off into the crowd. "Is that Aretha I see coming down the street?" she returned sarcastically.

An unsuspecting Dena let her eyes follow in the direction of her friend's finger. Shelby shook her head in disbelief.

"I don't think we've found your Diva name yet. Maybe Dipsy Diva," she continued. Then, she reconsidered. "On second thought, make that Delusional Diva."

Dena was saved from further humiliation by the waiter's return with their lunch, a lovely mélange of arugula, sliced ripe pears, and shaved parmesan cheese drizzled with an aromatic olive oil. As she enjoyed her salad, Shelby was forced to reveal that she'd be enjoying it a lot more if there were a strapping young Italian gentleman across from her.

Dena nodded her head in wholehearted agreement. "You're not exactly my first choice for a lunch companion either. Not to beat a dead horse, but what could Nicola possibly have been thinking? Encouraging me to come back here, telling me he'd taken time off from work to spend with me, and then disappearing like Halley's Comet, not to be seen for the next seventy-six years?"

"Yeah, well, if you can explain to this diva how a man could lead her to believe she was the next best thing since sliced bread, ask her to marry him, wind up diddling her friend..."

"That's right. He diddled your friend," Dena interrupted Shelby midstream. "And here you sit, back for more. Maybe Delusional Diva should be plural."

Shelby's eyes bulged from their sockets. She tried to form coherent words. "Bb, bu, bu," was all that came out, as her mouth gaped convulsively like a fish out of water gasping for air. Drawing in a deep breath, she composed herself.

"Well," she blew out finally, her voice dripping with indignation. "He did call me. Asked if I'd ever come to Italy again."

Dena decided to concede the point and forego mentioning the little matter of Shelby's initial letter to him and Lisa. "So we've determined that Italian men are just as crazy as American men. Where are we going next time?"

This time, Shelby forsook the British affectation and the royal we. "I'm beginning to think it doesn't much matter. North, south, east, west. No matter which latitude or longitude they're on, crazy is crazy, nuts is nuts, insane is insane."

"So what do we do then?" Dena asked.

"Well, I don't know about you, but the first thing I'm doing is taking off this pressure cooker they have the nerve to call a hat!"

With devilish delight, Shelby yanked the straw cover from her head and breathed sigh of relief. "And beyond that," she continued, "we are in Italy. You know, the place normal people come to sightsee. The home of the Titiano, Michelangelo, Botticelli. Perhaps we should concentrate on the dead men."

"Yes, they are easier to predict," Dena laughed. And much as she longed to imitate Shelby and rid herself of her cheese-curding chapeau, instead she gave it a little pat and kept it right where it was. After all, dear Nicola could be right around the corner.

And so the ladies happened upon perhaps the most pro-found Diva Do/n't of all.

Diva Do/n't

Unless you would like to be as crazy as they, don't try to figure out what men do or say.

Having come to the unanimous conclusion that breathing men should no longer be the focus of their trip, the women began charting the remainder of their day around Florence. But first, Dena needed to make a little pit stop. Back to the Hotel Macchiavelli.

Her friend eyed her suspiciously. "What for?" Shelby interrogated.

"These shoes are killing me," Dena answered, in the most convincing voice she could affect.

It wasn't good enough. Shelby had known her too long to be fooled. "Yes, and so is being away from the hotel message box for more than twenty minutes," she shot back.

Still, Shelby knew it wasn't so long ago that she'd been afflicted with the same delusional disease. Okay, she'd just gotten over it last night. And there was still Rick back home. So, she decided to cut the poor girl some slack.

Back to the hotel they limped, only to be confronted with a cavernously empty message box. That being the case, the travelers decided to do something novel. They were going sightseeing.

On to the Boboli Gardens and the Pitti Palace.

"Sightseeing! That is a new one for you two," India interrupted the ladies' tale yet again. "How were the palace and gardens? I've been to Florence several times, but never made it there."

"Oh, they were beautiful," the women concurred.

"Well, that will make scintillating copy for your book," India joked.

Shelby relented, even as she had the uncharitable thought that it surely wasn't a man's attentions that kept the Brit from visiting those landmarks. "Well, Dena does have a little tidbit to share regarding the Boboli Gardens, a guard, and a tree," she offered.

"We'd been wandering along the graveled walkways admiring the splendid statuary dating back to the Renaissance..."

Lost in thought, Dena turned to Shelby, only to discover the other woman nowhere to be found. Fifteen minutes, a few grottoes, and countless stairs later, Dena had had enough. The heat was stultifying. She was sure she could griddle a pancake on the top of her hat. Then, she felt something trickling down her leg. She didn't know knees could sweat. But when she looked down, it wasn't sweat Dena saw.

The powdery white medicinal spray Devil Doctor had prescribed was supposed to act as its own bandage, and under normal temperatures, it may have done just that. However, this being a typical Florentine summer, i.e., heat and humidity up the wazoo, upon closer observation, Dena discovered the white bandage had melted and mixed with the underlying green puss. My, what a lovely shade of mint green gunk trailing down her leg.

Spinning around, she found a seat on a bench in the middle of the gardens, where she plopped herself unceremoniously. Shelby would just have to find her. As she attended to her leg, thinking how unappealing it looked, Dena heard a deep Italian voice.

"Scusi, bella, you alone?" it asked.

She raised her head and looked up into the most beautiful pair of green eyes she'd ever seen. He was tall, he was dark, he was gorgeous, he was young. Perfect! So, Dena flashed him her prettiest smile.

"Nn...no, no," she got out with a stammer, "with *mia amica*."

Looking around and seeing no one, the stranger inquired as to her friend's whereabouts. When Dena admitted they had lost each other, the man's face lit up like a Chinese lantern.

"I help you look," he offered.

Dena couldn't miss the unmistakable evidence of wheels dangerously turning in his head. Still, he was adorable. Why not, she convinced herself.

They walked for a few minutes before coming to a giant tree whose leaf-laden branches fanned out and knelt to the ground creating a secluded bower within. The handsome guard, whose name Dena never found out, suggested they take a brief respite from the heat within the tree's shady environs.

Lord! He wants to diddle under a tree in broad daylight? What kind of woman does he think I am? Okay, there was the alleyway tryst with Nicola. But it was dark. I was drunk.

"No, no, I can't. I have a boyfriend." She knew she was breaking the poor man's heart, but hers belonged to Nicola.

"Che peccato!" What a shame. He shook his head, regret in his voice and a wistful look his eyes.

Dena wanted to reach out and comfort him. Her hand moved toward his arm, then stopped abruptly in midair, when confronted with his back. As fast as he'd uttered his words, he'd spun around and headed in the opposite direction. Dena's eyes followed as her handsome stranger sped away without a backward glance.

Minutes later, the two friends spotted each other. As they ambled toward the exit, she regaled Shelby with the details of her encounter with the guard. "I'm sure he was crushed," Dena said as she finished her tale.

At that very minute, the ladies were passing the infamous tree. They heard a rustling of leaves. It couldn't be the wind. There wasn't a breeze to be had that day.

Then, from under the tree, a woman's giggle floated through the air. "Oh, yes, I'm sure he's simply inconsolable," Shelby agreed.

"And so, India, the moral of this little vignette," Shelby began, "is that our readers should beware of the green-eyed guard and the trysting tree at the Boboli Gardens."

She stopped, then had a laughable thought, which she voiced. "And so should you, of course."

"Unless, of course, you'd like to diddle beneath its branches," Dena amended with giggle.

The ladies shared a knowing smile. Fat chance of that ever happening.

The ladies' victory was short-lived as the feisty English-woman volleyed back. "Well, I'm sure your readers will love that story, but isn't your book a travel guide, too?" she asked pointed-ly. "Aren't you going to describe the places?"

She thinks she's so smart, Shelby seethed before going on to explain that though she and Dena knew their readers would love the Divas' refreshingly unique description of these sights, they had decided that the world hardly needed another boring tome describing a bunch of over-discussed landmarks.

"And besides, Messrs. Frommer and Fodor do such a splendid job that we've decided to let them do it for us," Dena finished, smiling proudly at their brilliant idea.

"I believe they call that plagiarism, Divas," India remarked. "I can see it now. The Delusional Divas at Alcatraz. Do you think they'll let you wear your hats while you're cleaning toilets?"

But the ladies were already one step ahead of dear India. They'd had a difficult choice to make, and there'd been much to consider. Plagiarism (and an all expense paid trip to an island…Riker's Island, aka the Big House) or give due credit to their dear friends, the Messrs. Fodor and Frommer.

They'd heard the accommodations at Club Fed prison were not too bad. But still, they'd worried. What color were the prison uniforms? Would they be complimentary to their skin tones? Did the prison guards dole out matching shoes and hats to prisoners? Would Chianti be served only with dinner or with every meal? And what about their toilette? Had the prison barber received his tuition in hair design from Louis Licari or Vidal Sassoon? Was he schooled in the fine art of color, subtle highlighting, and cutting? Did he have a manicurist and wax specialist on staff? And, most importantly, with what frequency were conjugal visits allowed?

Now, delusion waxes and wanes for the ladies, and every once in a while, they have a burst of common sense.

"Please India, we may not have much sanity regarding men, but we do have a tenuous toehold on reality," Shelby averred.

She ignored the exaggerated roll of the Englishwoman's fishy eyes. "Even we realized that the chance of Club Fed having such amenities is about as likely as our chance of walking down the aisle with Nicola and Giancarlo."

"Well now, wait a minute," Dena interrupted her friend. "Per-haps, we should say walking down the aisle SOON."

If they had been talking to anyone other than the sanctimonious Brit, Shelby would have had a field day with her friend's comment. Instead, she ignored the remark.

"As I was saying, deluxe accommodations at Club Fed were about as likely as hell freezing over. Therefore, for a quite lovely description of both the Pitti Palace and the Boboli Gardens, we're going to refer our readers to Frommer's Italy from $70 a Day[27] and Fodor's Up Close: Italy." [28]

"Okay, okay," India conceded. "What about the Pitti Palace? Can you describe any of it?"

"Yeah, yeah, yeah, the Pitti Palace," Shelby began. Her voice droned on with the boredom of a tour guide who'd given the same spiel a thousand times...a superb collection of Renaissance and Baroque art...the largest building in Florence, formerly the official residence of the Medicis, the city's medieval rulers.

Having heard quite enough, Dena put into words what the tone of her friend's diatribe conveyed. "Who really cares? It wasn't our palace and..."

Lord knows there is only so much time or activity that a diva can tolerate that doesn't have at least a tangential relationship to shopping, the male of the species, or alcoholic beverages. Two hours at the Pitti Palace and the Boboli Gardens had stretched the limits of both women's endurance. They needed a quick fix and weren't too particular about the details.

Dena and Shelby chose the very convenient strip of shops and restaurants directly across from the Pitti Palace. Hopefully, they could kill two birds with one stone. Possibly three, if the waiter was good-looking and willing. Strategically choosing a prime location next to a very chic gift shop, the ladies settled themselves at an outdoor café and promptly ordered a carafe of Chianti.

Shelby was uneasy and couldn't seem to enjoy the wine until she'd made at least one purchase. She was suffering from the shopping DTs. For those untutored in this malaise, some of the symptoms include sleepwalking to the nearest mall, salivating at the mere mention of a clearance sale, the uncontrollable urge to

[27]Reid Bramblett, Shelen Brewer, and Patricia Schultz, Frommer's Italy from $70 a Day (2nd Edition): (New York: MacMillan, 1999), pp. 245 – 247)
[28]Nancy Smallvan Itallie, ed., Fodor's Up Close Italy (2nd Edition), (New York: Fodor's Travel Publications, 2000), p. 217

steal the shopping bags of strangers no matter the contents, and constant phone calls to ascertain credit card funds availability.

Now, Alcoholics Anonymous and similar programs lead the public to believe the only course of action is abstention from the offending activity, i.e., a twelve-step program. The ladies may concur for drug addictions. However, if afflicted with the buying bug, abstention simply isn't an option. Everyone needs food to eat, clothes to wear, and wine to lower the cholesterol.

Given this, the Divas had devised a one-step program that worked quite well for them and quite possibly for their readers. Give in. Surrender your addiction to the universe. Shop 'til you drop. Rest a bit...with a glass of wine. Then, pick yourself up and make your way to the shoe department.

Okay, admittedly this is more than one step. But the ladies do it so effortlessly that it seems like a single step. And with practice, anyone can be just as proficient.

So, Shelby strolled into an alluring gift shop and promptly found religion, the Diva way. Immediately upon entering the emporium, a vision appeared unto her, filling her with peace, joy, and everlasting love. Was it Mary, the Blessed Mother of Jesus? Had the Holy Spirit descended upon her, filling her with newfound religious fervor? Perhaps, it was the Archangel Gabriel come to proclaim the second coming of our Lord? No, no. Not quite.

Rather, smiling at her with a rather demented grin from every nook and cranny of the little shop was Bacchus, the Roman god of wine. Shelby nearly fell to her knees in adoration. Finally, a god she could relate to. Among the many wares for sale were wine corks, ceramic dishes, and wine bottle caddies, all sporting the grinning image.

The impish smile on Bacchus' chubby face, along with hair made of grapes on the vine, symbolized all that was sacred to the Divas...the pursuit of carefree amusement and a life of leisure. Shelby felt an overwhelming impulse to kneel down in gratitude for the good times a few fermented grapes had provided her. With great effort, she resisted and satisfied herself with buying several items. When she got home, she would build a little altar to her new lord and pay homage daily.

Returning to the table, she found Dena all atwitter, sputtering something about a strange man, a kiss and just who did he think he was. Shelby, still in her beatific state, barely listened, but that didn't stop Dena.

"He just leaned right over the railing as I was sipping my Chianti and tried to kiss me on the lips. Have they lost their minds here in Florence? Now, if he had been good-looking, okay. But he was old and ugly."

"This is Italy. These are Italian men. Calm down, Dena. Go buy yourself a little something," Shelby advised.

Religious conversion is an exhausting experience and requires rest and reflection. And so, draining their carafe of wine, the ladies paid their bill, idled back to the hotel, and collapsed on their beds for their midday nap.

The Englishwoman was dumbfounded. "Your own religion, you're kidding right?"

"Oh no, we're Bacchus' prophets. Just like Moses and the tablets, we recorded the tenets of Bacchusism as the Great One instructed us," Shelby said with complete sincerity.

"Here, read for yourself." Once again, Dena shoved the little purple book under India's nose.

Bacchusism is a monotheistic religion worshipping the Roman god of wine, Bacchus. Founded in the early twenty-first century by the Delusional Divas, the religion consists of one commandment. *Thou shalt toss back at least one glass of vino daily.* Luckily, failure to do so does not damn one's soul to eternal hell. However, one is consigned to living in the hellish state of eternal sobriety.

Bacchus, being a beneficent and forgiving god, has decreed that a pilgrimage to any vineyard or liquor store offers immediate redemption for any devotee breaking his commandment. For anyone who absolutely needs a prayer in order to consider Bacchusism a formal religion, recite the following:

Bacchus is great. His religion divine.
Thank you, Lord Bacchus, for da wine.

India had to laugh. The ladies' new faith certainly sounded like more fun than the Church of England. Maybe the Archbishop of Canterbury should take notes.

Sometimes, the most delightful food can be found in the most unlikely places. Just a stone's throw from the Hotel Macchiavelli on Via Nazionale is Oktoberfest.

"I didn't come to Italy for bratwurst and sauerkraut," sniped Shelby. She started to walk away, but Dena hung back studying the outdoor menu. Discovering that the restaurant's fare was not German at all, but Italian, she called Shelby back.

They walked into the cozy, wood-paneled restaurant decorated with a potpourri of German beer steins. Alas, that is the extent of any German influence. Oktoberfest is run by a classically gregarious Italian family, consisting of a middle-aged father, his son, and daughter.

"Where do you think the mother is?" Shelby mused aloud.

"If she's lucky, with a handsome masseuse. But probably right back there in the kitchen knee deep in tomatoes and pasta," Dena joked.

Oktoberfest's business card advertises itself as a beer, fast food, and snack bar establishment. While primarily open for breakfast and lunch, dinner is also served. Anyone considering venturing there should not let the fast food and snacks description deter them. This is not prefab McDonald's hamburgers or KFC chicken. Upon entering, patrons are tantalized by home-style Italian cooking presented cafeteria style behind a glass deli case. The assortment of appetizers, pastas, grilled vegetables, and main dishes are tempting and varied. One can also order from the menu.

As Dena and Shelby pondered the menu, Papa Oktoberfest suggested they try the dish he and his family were about to enjoy, assuring them it would be *magnifico*. Flattered by the friendly proprietor's generosity and eager to sample indisputably authentic Italian cooking, the ladies accepted enthusiastically.

As they waited for dinner, the movie *Hidden Dragon, Crouching Tiger* started to air on the restaurant's big screen TV.

"Hmmm. That title remind you of any men we know?" Dena asked.

"No, I think ours are more like *Fleeing Dragon, Running Tiger*," Shelby declared.

As the ladies shared the joke over a carafe of splendid house red wine, their meal arrived. It was hard to believe, but the homemade tagliatelle in a delicate cream sauce was arguably one of the best dishes the ladies had during either of their Italian tours. And the price was ridiculously low.

"Great place," Dena enthused.

And she was correct. Good food and a friendly atmosphere make Oktoberfest perfect for the cash-strapped and not so cash-strapped diva.

Properly nourished, Shelby was ready to seek the comfort of her bed once again. But Dena had other ideas.

"Let's go dancing," she suggested.

Shelby wanted to scream. Sure, back in the States, she had promised Twinkle Toes they would go dancing. She never dreamt she would have to make good on it. Damn that Nicola! He was supposed to have taken this harpy off her hands. Instead, he was nowhere to be found, and Shelby was cornered like a mouse. Trapped in those talons Dena manicured and called fingernails, she fumed.

"We could try out the club Nicola mentioned, Meccano," Dena coaxed hopefully.

Before Shelby knew what had hit her, the pair were in a cab wending their way to the popular disco, which in summer abandons its indoor facilities and operates in the open air on the southern edge of Cascine Park. Dena happily paid cover charge, made her way to the outside bar, and ordered herself a complimentary drink.

Looking around, she located a premier table at the dance floor's edge. Soon, the Disco Diva was tapping her feet to the music, bopping her head, and snapping her fingers.

Meanwhile, Shelby was still standing at the entrance deciding whether she should part with her money or use it for a cab ride home. After reluctantly paying the entrance fee and making her way in, she noticed that the tables surrounding the dance floor were practically empty. Seeing the place was dead as a doornail, her mood changed abruptly. She was elated. A few minutes of this and Dena would be ready to leave. Shelby could almost feel her fluffy pillow under her head. But she hadn't bargained for her friend's tenacity.

"Wanna go look for that other club, Central Park? The cab driver said it was just across the street," Dena cajoled.

Like a lemming, Shelby followed, wondering when the agony would end. Dena had no idea how to get to the next club, but when she noticed a crowd of Florentines all heading in the same direction, she followed. Reaching their destination, the long line waiting to enter gave Dena hope. Counting her chickens before they hatched, she was certain this club would be worth the entrance fee.

Designed to resemble a park, the nightclub boasts tall, lush potted trees and plants surrounded by park-like wooden benches. The sprawling nightspot offers several dance floors and bars.

That evening, the place was teeming with people. Packed tighter than a can of sardines, breathing was a luxury. While an overflowing crowd was just what Dena was looking for, it turned out those chickens she'd counted were newly hatched chicks, young enough to be her and Shelby's offspring.

While both women looked absolutely fabulous in skimpy, formfitting, floral sundresses and matching sandals that branded and practically set fire to their feet, they hadn't succumbed totally to delusion yet. They were no match for the young, nubile teens pulsating on the dance floor like natives doing a fertility dance.

This experience yielded another Diva Do/n't.

To feel like a Diva through and through, don't frequent places where all are younger than you.

Squaring their shoulders and holding their heads high, the middle-aged hot mamas strolled straight to the exit vowing never to darken the doors of Central Park again.

"Perhaps, Meccano has picked up a bit," Dena ventured.

"Oh, ya think? In the last fifteen minutes?" Shelby replied with derision. Her bed was calling.

But Dena was determined. With precision calculation, she pulled out the one thing she knew would push her frugal friend's buttons. "We did pay all that money to get in. You don't want to waste it, do you?"

Much to both women's surprise, the club had gotten a jump start since their departure. Before long, Dena was out on the dance floor with a studly, young carabiniere. This wasn't the same police officer Nicola had wanted to decapitate at Full Up, but he would do. His name was Marco, and Dena was entranced. Every once in a while, she spared a look at Shelby and waved heartily with a demented grin on her face.

Shelby couldn't help wondering if Dena was channeling Bacchus, their newfound god. What she didn't know was that her friend's crazed look was actually the beginnings of a devious plot hatching in that by now, somewhat pickled brain.

"Oh, you have a friend? Where?" Dena asked Marco. If she acted quickly and kept Shelby occupied, she could buy herself some quality time with this delicious policeman. On the dance floor, of course.

And so it came to pass that Shelby found herself being pawned off on Alberto, a twenty-six year old shoemaker, in whom she had absolutely no interest. Conversely, he seemed so taken with the diva's dainty feet that she feared he might whip out a Brannock shoe measure device, a bit of leather, and a large needle to craft a pair of fine Italian shoes.

In the meantime, Marco had spirited a self-satisfied Dena indoors to show her a thing or two. No, no, no, you dirty minded devils. The only thing he whipped out was his wallet to produce proof of his identity.

"See, I really am a carabiniere," he said, proffering his work ID. "You safe if you come with me to the car."

Yes, Dena was pickled. Yes, the two had danced themselves into a sexual frenzy. Yes, Marco the Cop was a tall, good-looking hunk. And, yes, her beloved Nicola had been kidnapped by a band of marauding Romans and was MIA. All good reasons, in her estimation, to follow Marco wherever he chose to lead.

And then a voice came unto her. Was it her guardian angel? Some unknown patron saint of fools and simpletons? Or was it Bacchus? No, no, Dena thought to herself, this voice sounds familiar. Shrill and scathing. Ah, of course, her dear friend Shelby.

Dena could easily imagine what her friend would have to say. Have you lost your cotton pickin' mind? You don't have the sense God gave birds, do you? Are you really going to walk off with a man you don't know from Adam? And Shelby would be right.

"I can't leave my friend," she managed to croak out. At least not this trip.

Still, when Dena reluctantly told the hot cop that she could not accompany him to the splendor of his car, he refused to accept defeat. He escorted Dena back onto the dance floor and swung her around until she was quite parched and in desperate need of water.

"The bar's closed, but I have water in my car," he tried once again. And once again, Dena demurred, refusing to leave the club.

But Marco was determined. Eager to get in Dena's good graces (and no doubt into something else of hers a little later), he graciously offered to fetch the water from the car. Apparently, it was actually a pail of water that poor Marco couldn't manage on his own, so he enlisted the help of Shelby's shoemaker, and off they set.

Shelby looked at her watch, cursing the moment she had agreed to come out. The men had been gone for quite a while, and she secretly hoped Dena's fictitious band of Romans had kidnapped them. She wanted to go back to the hotel.

"What are they doing? Digging for water?" she complained.

"Oh, don't worry. They'll be back. They've offered us a ride to the hotel," Dena assured her friend.

"You won't need them for a ride," Shelby began with a sneer, "because I'm going to give you a ride on the end of my foot. What in Bacchus' name makes you think I'm getting in a car with total strangers?"

Tired and irritable, she strode off without a backward glance. "I'm getting a cab."

Once again, Dena was confronted with a choice. Stay and take her chances with a man. Or follow her friend. Shelby was not at all surprised when she heard the pitter patter of strappy sandal-clad feet tipping behind her.

They were waiting at the entrance for a cab, Dena all the while scanning the horizon for the return of her new beloved. Off in the distance, she saw a strange little man frantically waving at them.

"Who is that?" she asked, poking Shelby to get her attention.

At first, Shelby had no idea who it was. She just prayed it wasn't the flat foot and the shoemaker. As the little man got closer, both ladies smiled with recognition and Shelby with relief. It was Nicola *Due*. They walked down the driveway of the club to greet him. "Where are you going?" he asked.

When he heard they were waiting for a cab to ferry them home, *Due* objected vigorously. "I'm with a friend. We drive you," he insisted.

Noting their reluctance, *Due* moved in for the kill, offering to take the ladies for cappuccino. He smiled to himself when they agreed, knowing Shelby couldn't refuse the creamy java.

And as they pulled away with Nicola *Due* and his friend, Dena spied a taxi pulling up to the club, followed by another car carrying none other than Marco the Cop and Alberto the Shoe-maker. She couldn't help but feel a pang of regret for what might have been with the new love of her life.

With the promise of a cappuccino for their trouble, Shelby yet again found herself looking down on Florence from atop Piazzale Michelangelo. Couldn't they meet just one man in Florence with an original thought in his head? And what about that cappuccino?

Which leads to another salient Diva Don't.

**If an Italian man says he will see you to your door,
do expect at least one unscheduled detour.**

Dena rather than being annoyed was entranced, as this was her first visit by moonlight. Too bad the view came with the unwanted attentions of Nicola *Due*'s friend, whose name escaped the ladies as soon as he said it. However, because he seemed to have more arms than a tree has branches, Dena christened him Ottavio the Octopus.

Up on the hill, Shelby had her own problems to contend with. The unwanted but nonetheless flattering attentions of poor *Due*. The more she rebuffed his advances, the more determined and, dare one say excited, the little man got.

"You a strong, hard woman," he began. "You know what you want."

Yes, and unfortunately, it was not *Due*. But even Shelby wasn't heartless enough to say that.

"If only things were different, there might have been a chance for us," she sighed regretfully. "But remember, Giancarlo and I are in love."

Most men would have thrown in the towel after the third humiliating rejection, but not *Due*. "Well, you come to my restaurant before we close for the summer," he begged.

Handing her the restaurant's business card, complete with a map on the reverse side, *Due* and Ottavio bade the ladies *Buona Notte* at their hotel door and drove off into the Florentine night.

The ladies are still waiting for their promised cappuccino.

Chapter 16

Since she had been in Italy six years earlier, Shelby had desperately wanted to see the much-loved old town of San Gimignano. On and on she would chatter about the place until Dena wanted to scream.

"I know, I know. A famous Tuscan hill town," Dena parroted, having heard the story for the umpteenth time. "The place with all the towers, right?"

As soon as the question left her lips, she mentally kicked herself for encouraging Shelby. Here she goes again. Another blasted history lesson. Home to a stunning array of medieval stone towers. Built in the twelfth and thirteenth centuries by two feuding families to gain prestige and defense. There used to be more than seventy of these structures. Imagine. People could actually walk across town via the rooftops. Now only fourteen towers remain.

Time for my own little history lesson, Dena thought. "Fifteen. Fifteen towers remain."

Determined to prove herself correct, Shelby flipped through her Frommer's guide. "Just like it says right here in my book," she exclaimed, her voice laced with haughty superiority. "Fourteen!"

"Well, what made me think fifteen?" Dena wondered aloud.

Just then Shelby noticed a sneaky smirk stealing across India's face. She could practically read the Englishwoman's mind. Fifteen...well, let me see...how about the number of brain cells actually firing up in Dena's head. Or the number years younger she likes her men, Shelby telepathically finished India's thought for her. My God, no wonder this witch gets on my nerves...a bit too much like me for my taste. Who does she think she is insulting my best friend? That's my job.

"So that's when we found out that dear Messrs. Fodor and Frommer had conflicting information on the number of towers still standing in San Gimignano," Dena cut through the thoughts of both women.

"So which is it?" India inquired. "Fourteen or fifteen?"

"Oh, we couldn't be bothered trying to count them," Shelby answered. "We had more important things on our agenda."

The Englishwoman arched her eyebrow. What could be more important than travel writers giving their readers accurate information? Oh, what's wrong with me, she chastised herself. With these two, it surely has something to do with men or wine.

Fourteen? Fifteen? Neither woman really gave a hoot. Right then, both were looking forward to sampling the *Vernaccia* they had read about. Sampling...laughable really. The ladies never just sampled wine. And although neither preferred white wine, they felt it would be a shame not to try the wine that Dante wrote about. Not Dante the Dishrag Doctor, but Dante Alighieri, the famed author of the *Divine Comedy*.

And with that, the history-buffs left their hotel headed for SITA bus station for transport to San Gimignano.

The ladies boarded the bus to Poggibonsi for the first leg of their journey, but not before Dena downed the requisite tablet to calm her queasy stomach. Once in Poggibonsi, they caught a connecting bus taking them to San Gimignano. This bus deposited them outside the stone wall enclosing the tiny town, which is as far as vehicles are allowed in San Gimignano.

"Geez," Shelby exclaimed as she looked around. "I've got this eerie feeling...like I've been here."

Her body followed the slow scan of her eyes, doing a 360-degree turn. Her gaze clouded with puzzlement. "Damn this is familiar. How could that be?"

Just then, her face brightened with revelation. "I bet I'm having a bleed through from a past life. I probably lived here."

Dena looked at her friend with undisguised skepticism, but it didn't faze Shelby as she continued to babble. "I always told you I was practically Italian. Maybe I really was!"

They proceeded through the town's arched doorway and stepped onto a narrow, upwardly inclining street. As far as the eye could see, medieval stone and brick buildings lined either side. Both ladies experienced the sensation of skyrocketing centuries back in time.

Haunting visions flitted through Shelby's mind. Visions of herself as the wife of a wealthy Sangimignese aristocrat swirled past her. She could almost feel herself in medieval garb. Long, flowing gowns, elaborate headdresses.

Her life was fabulous, living in a medieval castle, arranging glittering banquets, a patron of the arts, being presented at court, surrounded by serfs at her beck and call. Unbelievable!

Unbelievable is right, Dena thought. The girl has gone mad. Wiping away hot beads of sweat trickling down her brow, Dena's throat was parched and her head throbbing from the relentless rays of the Tuscan sun.

"Well, if you're having a bleed through, could you please have one of your serfs fan me with peacock feathers and bring me a goblet of perfectly chilled Vernaccia?" she snapped. "If it's not too much trouble, Your Highness, would you fast forward to the twenty-first century, and let's get a move on. It's hot and I'm thirsty."

They meandered through the throngs of fellow visitors, stopping here and there to browse in quaint shops brimming with art, traditional Italian ceramics, housewares and linens, clothing, and foodstuffs. Dena turned just for a second to look at a sidewalk display of local artwork.

"Oh, isn't thiii..," she began, intending to show her friend a particularly unusual rendering. But all she caught was a distant glimpse of Shelby heading around a corner and down a side street. Now where was she going, and why hadn't she said anything? Damn, she was acting strange. Dena hurried to catch up before the teeming streets swallowed Shelby and they were separated.

"Shelby, Shelby!" she called out. No answer. With hurried steps, Dena finally reached her side. "Where're you going?"

And still, no response. Shelby's face had a faraway look, her body moving with a sleepwalker's lethargy, as if she were being led by a phantom guide.

Finally, she spoke. "I swear. I just can't shake the feeling I've been here before."

Dena, worried for her friend, was a protective shadow by her side.

"If we walk a little farther, I am certain we'll come to a view of a large valley." Still, there was a questioning tone in Shelby's words, sure but not sure.

Suddenly, she stopped dead in her tracks, her feet glued to the pavement. Below lay *Val d'Elsa*, a lush green valley pregnant with silvery green olive trees, rolling hills, and venerable vineyards.

Despite the day's intense heat, a chill shimmied its way along Dena's spine. Could Shelby possibly be right? Was she truly having a bleed through from a past life? Did such things really happen? Would her friend be all right? Dena certainly wasn't equipped to handle someone having a psychic experience. Whom should she contact?

While Dena was contemplating this unsettling turn of events, Shelby walked off, once again leaving her friend on her own. Again, Dena hastened to follow, every few seconds casting a worried, furtive glance in Shelby's direction. This was getting creepy. She was relieved when Shelby finally spoke again.

"I think if we keep walking, we'll come to the main square and a gelateria on the corner."

Gelateria!? Dena's antennae rose sky high. She cleared her throat before speaking, not sure how she was going to couch what she had to say. "Ah, Shelby, about this bleed through thing..."

Shelby's smile beamed with excitement. "Yeah," she began with a deep sigh of satisfaction. "I've always suspected I had psychic tendencies."

Dena had had enough. Circumspection was simply no longer possible. Unable to control her laughter, she snorted with glee. The girl wasn't having a bleed through. More like a brain bleed.

A derisive click of her tongue gave evidence to Shelby's irritation at her friend's apparent amusement at her expense. "Experiences like this happen when one is on a spiritual path," she said with condescension.

"Oh, like the path you were on with Giancarlo and little Giancarlo the other night," Dena shot back. "Was that your spiritual path? Or did you wander a bit? Because I think you've just taken another little detour."

Shelby hunched her shoulders and turned her hand palm upward, wordlessly asking what the hell her friend she was getting at.

Dena's eyes gleamed with undisguised mirth. She wondered if *Shelbyanini il Magnifico* had seen something else in her crystal ball. Then, she let the words drip out one by one for effect.

"A gelateria, huh? In medieval Italy? How interesting."

Realization of her foolishness dawned on Shelby. She was crestfallen, but not enough to let Dena get the upper hand. Okay, regroup, she told herself. How to get out of this humiliating situation? Think...think. A few seconds and she had her answer.

"Had you going there for a while, didn't I?" Shelby poked her friend's arm playfully. "I must be slipping though. You caught on much too fast."

"This was all a practical joke?" Dena was flabbergasted.

"Not completely," Shelby denied. "I really do have a feeling of déjà vu. This town reminds me so much of a place Giancarlo and I once visited."

A disturbing sadness stole into her eyes. She shook her head to cast off the sudden depression. "But I don't want to think about him right now. Let's go shopping."

Tucked away on one of many hidden side streets is *L'Angolo dell'Alabastro*,[29] a charming little gift shop featuring craftware all made from alabaster. Alabaster, a hard, translucent, calcium-containing mineral, is usually white, but sometimes has veins of other color running through it, depending on the other minerals it contains. Colors range from grays and pinks to greens, raspberry, and earthy mustard tones.

Everywhere the ladies turned, a unique object more delicate and beautiful than the last greeted them. There were candlestick holders, chandeliers large and small, perfume atomizers, decorative bowls and platters in various shades. With enough money and a little more room in their luggage, both women would have been quite happy to relieve the storekeeper of her entire inventory.

"We could ship things home," Dena suggested as her gaze fell longingly on a boudoir lamp.

But visions of those cherished Mammy and Chef cookie jars flickered through Shelby's mind's eye, the ones that had arrived in a gazillion pieces instead of the original four. She wasn't about to have a repeat performance.

"If my purchases don't fit in the space your condoms previously occupied in my hatbox, they'll stay right here," she proclaimed.

Consequently, both ladies made small token purchases, each buying diminutive candle stands in a distinctive smoky golden tone. Dena's eyes fell on a raspberry perfume atomizer that was perfect for her mother. "She'll feel like a princess," she declared.

The temporary high the ladies invariably experienced from shopping disappeared the moment they stepped out of the little shop into the suffocating heat of the July Tuscan summer. Dena moaned, complaining that it must be time to eat. By her calculations, she was in the throes of a Level One hangover.

Shelby readily agreed. It was definitely time for a respite and some good food.

"And, let's not forget that Vernaccia you've been talking about," Dena reminded her friend.

Before setting out for San Gimignano, the ladies had promised to treat themselves to a gourmet lunch. Pouring over their guide books, they'd chosen the only restaurant listed as a favorite by Frommer's Italy.

---

[29]L'Angolo dell'Alabastro, Via del Castello 29, PH 0577/907183

Bel Soggiorno[30] was relatively empty when Shelby and Dena entered, affording an unobstructed view. Brick walls and vaulted wood ceilings give the enchanting restaurant an Old World ambience. Punched copper chandeliers lend a soft, romantic lighting. Juxtaposed to this period decor is an ultra-modern wall of crystal-clear windows overlooking a panoramic view of Val d'Elsa.

The ladies were escorted immediately to a coveted window table. Before her derriere hit the chair, Dena bade the handsome waiter for two glasses of Dante's wine.

"Well, Mister Frommer certainly knows whereof he speaks," Shelby decreed in her by now ever-present British accent. "This place is simply exquisite."

Similarly, the food was fit for royalty and divas. The ladies started with a shared *Crostatina di Pomodori e Olive Nere con Salsa di capperi e premezzolo*, a tomato and black olive tart.

"Mmmmmm!" Shelby rolled her eyes in appreciation.

"Ahhhhhhhh!" Dena sighed, savoring the delicate pastry. "In the words of Chef Emeril, my mouth is happy, happy."

A vigorous nod of Shelby's head signaled her agreement. It also signaled that she wasn't wasting her time on conversation. Without missing a beat, she continued eating.

For their entrees, both women chose selections from the grill for which the Tuscan restaurant is known. Dena feasted on rabbit, while Shelby, whose tastes are far more pedestrian when it comes to meats, favored the grilled pork chops. Their side dishes of *Peperonato*, vegetable goulash, and *Fagioli bianchi all'olio*, white beans in olive oil, provided the perfect light accompaniment.

Meal eaten, Dena perused the dessert menu. Everything sounded delicious, rendering a choice nearly impossible. Needing help, Shelby chose to see what Mr. Frommer had to say on the matter. The good gentleman recommended the *Crostata di Ficchi con gelato di vaniglia,* a scrumptious fig tart with vanilla ice cream.

"He's been spot on so far. I say let's just go ahead with his suggestion."

"Spot on? Spot on what? Where?" Dena began inspecting her clothes for unsightly food stains.

"It's an English expression. It means Mr. Frommer's been correct, my dear," Shelby explained, still in Brit mode.

---

[30]Bel Soggiorno, Via San Giovanni 91, PH 0577/940275, www.sangimignano.com

"Okay, Queen Diva Julia Child, fig tart it is," Dena agreed readily.

They knew they had made the right choice when a few minutes later, they surveyed the remains of their dessert plate. Not a crumb to be found, giving ample testimony to the chef's expertise and Mr. Frommer's unerring sweet tooth. Both pushed back their chairs from the table.

Needing to walk off the thousands of calories they had just stuffed into themselves, the ladies plodded up San Gimignano's main thoroughfare to the *Piazza della Cisterna*.

"Jeez this place feels familiar!" Shelby remarked again, unable to shake the feeling she'd seen it before. "First the town wall, and then, the overlook to the valley. I'm telling you, if there really is a gelateria up here on the corner, then this has to be the place that Giancarlo brought me."

Dena looked at her friend with utter amazement. How the hell wouldn't someone remember if they had ever been someplace before? A few more steps, and sure enough, on the corner, stood a gelateria. Dena did not even try to conceal her self-righteous grin as she spoke.

"Just for the record, let's recap here. First, I've been listening to you yammer on since April about San Gimignano. You just *had* to get there. Second, you practically wrestled me to the ground this morning and dragged me on not one, but two buses, knowing that on a good day I puke at the mere mention of bus travel. Third, this isn't a good day. I have a Level One hangover. Fourth, in case you haven't noticed, all my diva shoes have turned my feet into two festering blisters."

Shelby had to admit, if only to herself, that Dena had a point. Perhaps, a few points. Regardless, she didn't intend to stand there and continue listening to her friend rattle them off like darts at a dart board. "B...but," she tried to interrupt.

It was impossible. Dena was just getting started. And she proceeded with her seemingly endless catalogue of complaints.

"Fifth, it is so hot that if the temperature rises one more degree, there will be an unscheduled fireworks display here starring me. Sixth, I am sure that I've missed several phone calls from Nicola while on this little excursion. And after all this, you have the gall to tell me that you let a man drag you around this town six years ago without bothering to find out the name of the blasted place?"

At this point, Dena had to stop to take a breath, and Shelby thought she might be spared a final insult. It was not to be. Dena's mouth was off and running again.

"Now, you tell me. Which one of us needs to see the Wizard about a brain?"

A good friend can admit her failings, and acknowledge when she's wrong. Surely after more than thirty years of friendship, Dena's and Shelby's relationship had progressed this far. So naturally, the next words out of Shelby's mouth would be an admission that finally Dena had hit the nail on the head.

Shelby's eyes narrowed as she considered her options. "This is wonderful. If I've been here before, this is where Giancarlo bought some fabulous *salsiccia di cinghiale,* wild boar sausage. You really have to try it. I think I remember exactly where the shop is located."

Had this simpleton heard even one word? *Cinghiale?* What the hell was Shelby talking about? Dena shook her head in wonderment.

And with that, Shelby headed off in search of cinghiale, a sly smile on her face. She had succeeded in confounding her friend once again and all was right with her world.

La Buca,[31] a specialty foods shop, is located on the main thoroughfare and hard to miss. A wild boar that had evidently lost its fight with a taxidermist stands at the entrance luring curious patrons inside. La Buca specializes in wild boar salami, wines such as Vernaccia and Chianti, and olive oil from the San Gimignano olive trees.

Immediately upon entering the tiny establishment, Shelby made a beeline for the meat counter. Her eyes gleamed when she saw the object of her desire, *salumi di cinghiale*, wild boar salami. She tried to maintain her composure, but the drool dribbling down her chin gave her away. She simply had to buy some for friends and family back home, but wondered aloud if the delicious meat would pass through customs.

"Well, it doesn't matter. I'm going to try," she decided. She began sizing up the various flavors, lengths, and thicknesses of the meat. Soon it was her turn to order.

"Si, si," she began, "*Vorrei questo.*" I would like that one.

When the clerk indicated he was unsure of which salami she desired, Shelby pointed again. "Yes, that's right, that long, thick one. I'll take him...uh, I mean, I'll take that one. Can't wait to wrap my lips around that."

"Yes, I know what you mean," Dena innocently remarked.

---

[31]La Buca, Via San Giovanni 16, PH 0577/940407, www.labucadimontauto.it

Shelby wasn't done shopping. She also wanted to buy the tiny sausages that Giancarlo had purchased years ago, which come fresh or vacuum-packed. Both ladies bought some of each.

> **Traveling Tidbit for the Carnivore Connoisseur:** If in San Gimignano, don't pass up the chance to sample this distinctive delicacy. If you are going to attempt, as the ladies did, to smuggle some home, we recommend the vacuum-packed variety. Warning: This tidbit will self-destruct in five seconds. Should you be detained by U.S. Customs agents, the Divas will disavow any and all knowledge of your activities.

Purchases completed, the ladies headed for the walled outskirts of the town and the bus home. The day had been long and exhausting. The stratospheric degree heat, unrelenting sun, and high humidity had taken their toll. All either woman wanted was the comfort of her bed and a nap.

After a couple of hours shuteye, Shelby awoke to the sensation of floodlights burning into her retinas and a strange clicking sound on the terracotta tiled floor. Reluctantly, she peered out of one sleep-heavy eye to find Dena prancing to and fro, obviously readying herself for an evening on the town.

"Oh, good, you're awake," Dena said with enthusiasm. "Get up. It's time to boogie."

Shelby was afraid to ask, but she knew she'd have to find out sometime. Dena answered the question with a beaming face.

"Space Electronic Disco,[32] of course. Mr. Frommer says it's quite popular. Even has an imitation space capsule that sails back and forth across the dance floor!"

Before Shelby could stop herself, the words shot from her mouth. "Oh, yes, do let's go," she said with saccharine sweetness.

Then, her lip curled into a sneer as she continued. "And when we get there, I am going to put you and that infernal Frommer's guide in the space capsule and launch you both into outer space. Probably won't be a new experience for you, will it?"

---

[32]Space Electronic Disco, Via Palazzuolo 37, PH 055/29-30-82

"You actually went?" India questioned Shelby in disbelief.

Dena snorted before her friend had a chance to respond. "India, if the dynamics of our friendship haven't become apparent yet, let me clue you in," she said. "I knew if I didn't consult Frommer's for something altogether different, that man everyone thinks shines down from the moon would be a woman...named Dena. My all-expense paid trip courtesy of Shelby. The tides going in and out? That would be ME. The werewolves howling at what? ME!"

The Englishwoman allowed herself a chuckle in appreciation of Dena's wit before inquiring where the ladies did end up that evening.

Shelby's vote was for either *Chiodo Fisso*,[33] a wine cavern with folk music, or *il Barretto*,[34] a piano bar billed as a nice quiet place with an older crowd.

"Whooppee," Dena scorned. She couldn't believe her choices. She could spend her evening six feet under listening to music that would make her wish she were dead. Or, in a piano bar, with octogenarians. They didn't call them lounge bars for nothing. The mere thought of either place made her yawn, but what choice did she have?

An hour later, they were standing in front of Chiodo Fisso. Dena tried the door, but it refused to give way to the gentle pressure of her hand. She pushed a bit harder. It wouldn't budge.

"I do believe the place is closed," she tossed the words over her shoulder. She was careful to hide the tiny smile of delight, but somehow the triumphant lilt in her voice refused to stay undercover. She could almost feel the poison daggers from Shelby's eyes stinging the flesh of her back.

"That's ridiculous. Messr. Frommer distinctly said they're only closed for two weeks in August. It's July."

Dena shifted her body to the right. She didn't utter a word. She didn't have to. The sweep of her arm toward the door said it for her. Well by all means, be my guest. You try it.

Shelby pushed at the door with all her might. She tried again, rattling the doorknob. Nothing. "I'll be damned," she exclaimed. "It *is* closed."

---

[33]Chiodo Fisso, Via Dante Alighieri 16r, 055/23-81-290
[34]Il Barretto, Via d. Parione 50, PH 055/2394122

Dena heaved a sigh of relief. "What a shame," she lied with ease. "Guess that means we're off to Space Electronic."

Shelby turned to her friend with a devilish smirk. She mimicked Dena's earlier gesture, raising her arm and ushering her friend off to no place in particular. "You go right ahead. But tell me, will you be following the stars to Space Electronic? Because I'm going to find Il Barretto."

Dena hesitated as she watched her friend's back fade into the inky night. She flashed back to April and their endless odyssey in search of the restaurant *Belle Donne*. The click of Shelby's heels on the cobblestone streets was growing fainter with each step. Dena's uncertainty lasted a full...well, let's see...almost three seconds before giving way to stunning clarity.

"Wait up," she called out. Then, as fast as the shoes that had her feet in a vise grip would allow, Dena hobbled down the street to join her friend. After all, she couldn't let Shelby go alone. It could be dangerous.

Il Barretto was not easy to find. Both women swore that Italians really needed a lesson or two in cartography. One and a half hours and two more blisters on each foot later, they stood in front of the piano bar's door.

In silent answer to Dena's prayer, this door also refused to give way. She hung back and watched her friend pounce on it, using her shoulder as a battering ram, but the door held fast. Il Barretto was closed for the summer.

"Oh, oh," Dena's voice was heavy with sarcastic disappointment. She shook her head in mock distress. "The injustice of it all," she lamented.

"What are you talking about?" Shelby sniped.

"To think that we traveled all this way only to have my fondest hopes dashed."

Shelby knew she was walking into a minefield, but somehow she couldn't stop herself. "Your fondest hopes dashed. Give me a break. You didn't want to come here or hear folk music."

"Oh, Shelby, how wrong you are. I was so looking forward to doing the Italian Do-si-do. You know, the Do-si-do-ini!"

Shelby looked at her friend suspiciously. But Dena wasn't at all finished. She grabbed Shelby's arm, linked it with her own, and began to swing her around. "Don't worry, Shelby, you can *Swing Your Paesano Round and Round* out here with me."

Forcefully, Shelby yanked her arm away, ordering Dena to let go of her. Her face was etched in seriousness.

"I'm not interested in any Swing Your Paesano," she barked.

But then, she couldn't control the smile that crept up. Her eyes twinkled with merry abandon. Suddenly, she grabbed

264

Dena's arm and spun her around in a frenzy. "Everyone knows that Skip to My Luigi is the authentic Italian folk dance."

Round and round the friends twirled, laughing and cavorting like children running through a sprinkler on a hot summer day. Soon they realized that it was a hot summer night, there was no sprinkler water, they'd left childhood behind a decade ago...okay, a few decades ago. And if they didn't settle down, they would collapse from dehydration and exhaustion.

"So, on to Space Electronic," Dena suggested, figuring she had nothing to lose.

"Dena, we've been wandering the streets of Florence for two hours. Even my feet are hungering for that pasta pot from Za Za's. It's hot and muggy. It's late, and we're the only ones out here. Just face it!"

"Face what?" Dena eyes questioned.

"Frommer fu..fu..fu..." Shelby stammered, "fumbled the ball. We should've listened to Pasquale when he said all the clubs were closed for the summer."

Traveling Tidbit for Tripping the Light Fantastic Travelers: Notwithstanding the expertise of the good Messr. Frommer, most of Florence's indoor clubs are closed for the month of August, and some for the entire summer. Call ahead. Your feet will thank you.

Standing in front of the locked doors of il Barretto, it dawned on the dejected duo that not only was this club empty, but indeed, the streets of Florence seemed deserted compared to their April trip. Odd, but they were practically the only people on the street, leaving them to wonder where everybody was. Florence was a ghost town. What to do now?

And as if thinking with one brain, which many suspected was all the Divas had between them anyway, a light bulb went off in the minds of both ladies simultaneously. They turned and met each other's gaze with gleeful grins.

"Chianti!"

Once again, through the streets of Florence they trudged, finding restaurant after restaurant locked tight, their closed doors taunting the parched and woefully sober pair. Finally, they happened upon a lone restaurant open for business that evening in Florence.

La Bussola[35] proved to be an oasis in the urban desert. Choosing to eat al fresco, they had their pick of any table.

"This really is very strange," Dena remarked. She couldn't shake her curiosity about the empty streets. "We've been trekking through the streets of Florence for over two hours now, and how many people have we seen?" She stopped to calculate. "Maybe fifty?"

"Not even," Shelby contradicted. "But who needs 'em. As long as there's one restaurant still open with a sufficient cache of Chianti, I say good riddance...especially to the men."

"Well, we do need *some* men," Dena contradicted. "Him, for starters." And with that, she signaled the waiter and ordered a carafe.

Not wanting to drink on an empty stomach, but not being overly hungry due to their heavy meal in San Gimignano, the tuckered-out twosome ordered a light salad. The chilled shrimp, served in an avocado half with Russian dressing, was pleasing to the eye and a delight for the palate.

When the waiter came to clear away their plates, he asked if the women desired anything else. Shelby immediately declined the after-dinner drink he suggested. But Dena wavered, tempted to order a Limoncello. "But it's so strong," she said indecisively.

The waiter had the perfect solution. *Crema de Limoncello,* a shot of the liqueur with heavy cream that he promised was not very strong.

Dena's first sip was tentative. "Mmmm," she murmured, her eyes widening with enjoyment. It was delicious. She wondered about the ingredients.

Just then the waiter returned. "You like?" he asked.

"Oh *si, molto buono.* How do you make it? Only Limoncello and crème?" she asked skeptically.

He gave a nervous little laugh, like a child caught with his hand in the cookie jar. "No, no," he admitted. "It also have *un po' di*...how you say?" The English words escaped him. Finally, he ran inside and returned with two bottles in tow.

"Oooohh!" Dena said when she surveyed the bottles. "Oh, it's not Limoncello. It's a *Crema di Limone* and brandy."

"*Si, si,*" the waiter nodded his head vigorously. "And a little *latte*...milk."

---

[35]La Bussola, Via Porta Rossa 58, PH 055/293376

Very little milk, Dena thought to herself. But still delicious. And when the waiter offered to bring another, she readily agreed.

Quietly, Shelby sat, taking in the little exchange. She was worried for her friend, but not more than she was for herself. She hoped she wouldn't have to carry Dena home on her back.

"I've never heard of that drink," said India. "What's it called, so I can try it next time I come to Italy?"

Dena shrugged her shoulders. "The waiter said it doesn't have a name. You just have to remember the ingredients."

"But you liked it better than Limoncello alone?" India wanted to know.

"Of course she did," Shelby interjected with a smirk. "She got it on the house."

Chapter 17

Once again, an empty hotel message box mocked the ladies. Left to their own devices yet another day. What to do? What to do?

Shelby had heard that Perugia was a sweet little town. Her once dear friend Lisa had lived there at one time, and extolled its virtues more than once. Notwithstanding the source, Shelby suggested going since she'd never gotten a chance to see it.

Dena gave a little smirk. "Now, let's not too be hasty, Shel. It's a cinch I've never been to Perugia. But you, well the jury's still out on that. Sure you weren't there in a past life?"

Choosing to ignore the snide remark, Shelby started rifling through her wardrobe furiously. Dresses and skirts were being flung around the room at an alarming rate, a torrent of colors and materials.

"What are you doing?" Dena asked as an airborne skirt's button nearly put out her eye.

Shelby didn't stop to answer. She was a woman on a mission. She'd had enough. Spending thousands on a new wardrobe, putting her feet in shoes that a CIA agent could use for interrogations, cooking her head with a furnace posing as a hat, smothering herself in makeup and perfumes that made her itch and sneeze, and probably needing a hip replacement from doing that damned Diva Stroll.

Finally, Shelby stopped her frantic search for the perfect outfit. A big blue vein pulsed in her forehead. She trained angry eyes on her friend.

"All this time, energy, and money, and not a soul has recognized who I am. Jeezus, not even a stray dog has tried to hump me since I've been here."

Dena hurried to contradict her friend's assertion. "Now, Shelby, that's not true. You've had a few men who've tried to hump you."

Shelby had to concede the point. "Well, true. I guess that's not really what I mean. I'm not just talking about men."

She flopped dejectedly on the bed. For a moment, she hesitated as she contemplated the true source of her discontent. Then, it poured out like an oil gusher. How all her life people had made fun of the way she looked.

Dena stared at her friend in disbelief as the sad tale unfolded. It was all so very hard to believe. How could Shelby's father have possibly told the nurse that she must have made a mistake when Shelby was born, that the nurse must have brought them the wrong baby? Could he really have been mean enough to tell the nurse to take the baby back, that the child was too ugly to be his?

"Yes, really," Shelby answered her astonished friend. "He and my grandmother actually argued over it in the hospital."

But he hadn't been the only one, she recalled. When she was little, her two older sisters used to tell her that she was adopted, taking perverse pleasure in laughing at her buck teeth, flat feet, and leathery skin courtesy of her eczema.

"And the nasty nicknames were endless," she remembered. Bugs Bunny, or Mary Grace, that hideous maid on TV, or Scratch 'n Pick.

Dena knew she shouldn't ask, but her curiosity got the better of her. "Scratch and Pick? What was that?"

"The name they made up for me because of my rash. I was always scratching it and picking off scabs."

Dena tried not to shudder at the thought. "They really did all those things?

"If you say *really* one more time, I'll scream. Who could make this stuff up?"

Tears pooled in Shelby's eyes. She sniffled. "But even with all that, I never believed them. I don't know how or why, but I never truly in my soul thought I was ugly or unattractive. So this Diva thing was my chance to prove it. And still, nobody has recognized me or who I am."

Her friend's tears were contagious, welling in Dena's eyes. She hated seeing Shelby hurt this way. All these years of friendship, and she never knew any of this. They had more in common than either of them ever knew.

Shelby snorted with disbelief. "What are you crying about? Who ever called you ugly?"

Dena gave a sigh of exasperation. Was Shelby kidding, she asked herself. The shorter list would be those who hadn't laughed at her looks. A faraway look clouded Dena's eyes as she slipped back into the past.

"My name was Don, as in Don Knotts. You know, the skinny, bug-eyed, big nosed, jittery screw-up Deputy Sheriff on the Andy Griffith Show. Try going through life with that mirror."

"Yes, I can see the resemblance," Shelby joked. "Just kidding, my dear."

The friends shared a poignant laugh through their tears, both wondering how the people they loved the most could be so hurtful.

Shelby got up from her bed and gave her friend a hug. Their touch communicated what words could not. Neither had thought there was anything left to learn about the other. Or that their friendship could become any deeper. This shared pain proved them both wrong.

Still, the sentimental moment didn't last for long. Perugia was waiting, and the ladies didn't want to waste a minute.

"Cheer up, my friend," Dena encouraged. "Today's the day. We're gonna be the Drop-dead Gorgeous Divas. And if Italy doesn't know who we are today, we'll have to conclude they're all blind, deaf, and dumb."

Determined to turn heads, the two set about choosing their outfits. Shelby settled on an oatmeal beige dress made of delicate linen. Its empire waist gave way to an A-line skirt that accentuated the curves of her body. She paired the dress with matching sandals of oatmeal raw silk outlined with a border of tiny silk violets. Completing her ensemble, she chose a beige and white straw hat with a bouquet of violets and a matching straw bag. And, on the off chance that a breeze should catch the hem of her dress, all of Italy would be treated to a glimpse of her lacy violet thong.

Dena's choices weren't so easy, especially for her feet. The blisters were fast becoming open sores matching the one on her knee. If she made the wrong shoe selection today, the only thing anyone would notice would be her battle wounds. Mindful of this, she voted for the closest thing she had to orthopedic oxfords. She would just have to build her outfit around them.

Once dressed, Dena twisted first in one direction, then the other, surveying the result in the mirror. She had slipped into a form-fitting peach sundress with a red and orange tropical floral print. The halter-top design showed off her sun-bronzed shoulders. And atop her head, she'd placed a wide-brimmed crimson straw hat as the perfect finishing touch.

Finally, on her feet, she gingerly placed buttery soft red leather sandals. The ladies' shoe stresses and feet fiascos bring to mind the following.

Diva Do/n't

Do break those new shoes in on someone else's feet, if you don't want yours to be raw meat.

The trip to Perugia is a two-hour train ride. Tickets purchased, the ladies boarded and found choice accommodations. They settled in for the ride and waited for their beauty and charisma to be noticed. They were gratified when it happened so quickly.

"*Scusi, Signore...*ladies," came a sexy Italian male voice.

Dena and Shelby looked up into the eyes of two gorgeous men standing over them. Tall, dark, and handsome. Were they dreaming? Dena pinched herself, but it wasn't necessary. Shelby gave a tiny, surreptitious jab with her elbow. The gleam in her eyes said what she couldn't in words. Finally, we're being recognized.

"*Buon giorno*," Shelby answered with a breathless whisper. "*Vi aiutiamo?*" Can we help you?

"Si, we sit here," one of the gentleman said in his best English.

"Oh, you want to sit with us," Dena's voice bubbled over with delight. Her eyes lit up in invitation.

"No, no. These our seats," the Italian Adonis explained.

The ladies looked at each other in confusion, and then, back up at the men.

"*Non abbiamo capito*," Shelby answered. We don't understand.

Giving up on his limited English, the gentleman pulled out his ticket and stuck it under the women's noses, pointing to the words *prima classe* – first class. Then he indicated some numbers, which coincidentally matched the ladies' seat numbers.

A dreadful comprehension washed over Shelby. She looked over at her friend with a face a more sickly shade of green than if she'd had a Level Three hangover. How to break the news to Dena, who was busy preening, looking for her lipstick?

"You won't need that, Dena. Just gather your things and come along. These are their seats, and they want them."

Like rats, the ladies scurried to gather their belongings. Heaven be praised for their hats; plopping them as far down on their heads as possible, they hid the ruby redness spreading over both ladies' faces.

"But how does anybody know which cars are first class?" Dena asked no one in particular.

The walk back to the second class cars was akin to being led to the electric chair, the gas chamber, the guillotine, or the hanging tree. Take your pick.

"Dead Divas Walking. Now there's a brilliant title for your book," the Englishwoman offered.

"India, you never did tell us what it is that you do for a living? What are you in? Publishing?" Shelby cracked.

"No, no, my dear. I'm a Public Relations Specialist, but right now I'm between jobs."

"No kidding," Dena remarked facetiously. *"Well, don't worry. With all your tact and diplomacy, I'm sure you'll find another job quite soon,"* she elaborated with wide-eyed innocence.

India wasn't sure whether the comment was a dig or not, so she decided to let it pass without comment. But her largesse was not without its limits. "Now, back to this first class/second class dilemma. Did you ever figure it out?"

"Not a chance," Shelby answered. *"We figured we'd..."*

India nodded her head; she knew where this was going. "Publish it in the revised edition, naturally after your readers do all the work for you."

"Exactly," Dena agreed.

"C'mon, ladies, I figured out the train thing on the first day," the Brit boasted.

Dena opened the little purple journal to a clean page and poised her pen expectantly, waiting for India to impart her vital snippet of knowledge.

Figure it out for yourselves, my budding Misses Fodor and Frommer, the Englishwoman thought uncharitably. "So tell me," she began, *"were you at least on the right train. Was it going to Perugia?"*

It was obvious India had no intention of clueing the ladies in. Shelby glanced at Dena as she sheathed her pen, but not before the point of the pen had come dangerously close to the Englishwoman's bum.

Perugia is a hill town, and once they had disembarked, the ladies realized that the train stops at the bottom of that hill. Decisions, decisions.

Both women's eyes fearfully followed the main street's ascent up the mountain. "The exercise might be good for us, and we can stop along the way and take in the view," Shelby offered.

Dena bowed her head slightly. That, along with an exaggerated sweep of her arm toward the hill, made words unnecessary. Still, she decided to make her point perfectly clear.

"The last I shook my family tree, neither a goat herder nor a yak fell out of it. The only thing I'm climbing is aboard that bus."

And with that, she turned on her heel and made for the bus stop. Shelby followed, giving wordless thanks that the decision had been taken out of her hands.

Perugia's town center is graced by *Fontana Maggiore,* a two-tiered, thirteenth-century fountain that resembles an elaborate wedding cake. Instead of a bride and groom atop, three nymphs adorn the fountain. The lower tier consists of fifty hand-carved panels depicting such diverse subjects as Aesop's Fables, the months of the year, and biblical stories. Encircling the upper tier are twenty-four statuettes.

"Mmm...a wedding cake fountain. The perfect place for a wish that the love of my life proposes marriage soon," said Shelby.

"You have got to be kidding? I thought you were done with Giancarlo."

"Dena, you really do have to keep up. You know how I feel about Rick."

More importantly, Dena had a pretty good idea how Rick felt about her friend. But she bit her tongue as Shelby closed her eyes, and tossed a few coins over her shoulder.

Dena shook her head in pity. Poor girl. She really does believe that snake will slither away from his wife and marry her. Nevertheless, she decided to keep her opinion to herself and changed the subject, suggesting they visit Perugia's Duomo. She had read that one of the chapels housed the wedding ring of the Virgin Mary.

Shelby was instantly game for the proposal. If the ring were nice enough, perhaps she could have her wedding ring custom made in its image.

Again, Dena kept her own council and humored her friend. "Stunning idea," she agreed, upon hearing the ridiculous notion.

Perugia's town center is quite compact, so locating the cathedral should have been a simple endeavor. Actually, in Italy, almost nothing could be easier. Tourists can just look up at the town skyline, find the church with a massive dome, and follow it.

The ladies were already in the square where the church was located. So, finding it would be a cinch. They swung their gaze skyward. No dome. Must be the other way. They pirouetted. No dome.

While Shelby sized up passersby to ask for directions, Dena continued scanning the skyscape in search of the elusive dome. Her eyes rested on a particularly beautiful building. Its size, lovely pink-tinted façade, and impressive staircase made it a likely suspect in her estimation.

Shelby left her people-vetting long enough to follow the direction of her friend's pointing finger. When her eyes focused on the building, she raised her brow in skepticism. No dome.

"Look around you. Do you see a dome anywhere?" Dena retorted, insisting they at least give the building a try.

Up the grand staircase they trudged. Halfway there, Shelby was struggling for her next breath. She rummaged through her purse for her inhaler.

"Y..ahh, y..ahh," she drew in a ragged breath. "You keep going. I'll catch up."

When she made it to the top, Dena gave a healthy tug on the entrance door. At its refusal to give way, she pulled a bit harder. Still, no luck. Locked tight. She turned and started to call down to Shelby.

Stopping herself, not wanting to further disturb the peaceful setting of the little town, she used sign language. Silently, she swept her hand back and forth across her neck, signaling her friend to abort the mission. As a breathless Shelby took another puff of the inhaler, she struggled to banish the image of something sharper sliding across Dena's scrawny neck.

Next, they tried a small street-level entrance to the building. Stepping across the threshold, they found themselves in a massive rectangular room with a vaulted ceiling and huge Romanesque arches. The walls were bejeweled with frescoes. Rows of dark wood chairs filled the space. Tall windows let in the summer daylight.

"That must be the altar," Shelby said, indicating a large wooden bar dominating the front.

Dena wasn't so sure, wondering why the altar had no cross. "And those frescoes certainly don't depict any religious story I've ever read."

Just then, they heard footsteps behind them. "*Buon giorno,*" came a deep voice.

"*Scusi,*" Shelby started in Italian. "*Quest'è il Duomo?*" Is this the Duomo?

A little smile played across the Italian's face. "No, no, eez Palazzo dei Priori." Pointing to his right, he continued. "Il Duomo eez there."

Yet again, the ladies set out in search of the cathedral. When confronted with the next choice, they were sure a mistake had been made.

"Look at this building. Does this look like a church to you? It can't possibly be the Duomo," said Dena.

"Look, that's what the man said," Shelby answered. "At least let's have a look."

Once inside, their eyes had to adjust to the darkness. A quick survey told the ladies they were in the right place. The Chapel of the Ring awaited them. As they took in their surroundings, the women noted that several chapels lined both sides of the interior, each with a statue of a saint protecting the tiny altar within. Which one was theirs?

Shelby tore out her guide book looking for an answer. She read...the first chapel on the left. Twin pairs of eyes looked around and counted more than one entrance, leaving them both with the same question. On the left of what?

"Thank you, Messr. Frommer, for such precise directions." Shelby stopped short of cursing, but only because she was in a church.

"Look, it shouldn't be that difficult," Dena said with sunny optimism. "We just find the chapel with a box."

Shelby was worried. Dena was beginning to be the voice of reason. Still, she couldn't offer a plausible contradiction, so off they trotted.

Around the cathedral they tiptoed, halting at the first chapel. No box. On to the next. No box. From chapel to chapel, the duo plodded peering inside each. On and on they proceeded, stopping in front of the next chapel. No damn box anywhere.

"Do you see a plaque? Anything with the name?" Dena asked.

Shelby shook her head. "Must've missed it," Shelby said.

They were back at the spot where they'd begun. "Let's try again."

They would give it one more go, but this time they decided to split up. Separating, the women headed off in opposite directions.

Five minutes later, they bumped into each other again. "Find anything?" Dena asked.

"Yeah, I found a lot of things. But if you're talking about Mary's ring, hell no," Shelby answered, all intentions of clean language abandoned.

"Well, what in blazes are we supposed to be looking for exactly?" Dena asked.

The search had gone on so long, Shelby had forgotten herself. Once again, she pulled out the guide book.

"Well, once we find the chapel, supposedly there's a locked box. In that locked box another locked box. In that locked box, another, and..."

"All right, all right, I get the point," Dena hissed.

Messr. Frommer promised that once they found the chapel, there would be a box. Actually, there are purportedly fifteen locked boxes in all. Rumor has it that nestled in that fifteenth box is the Blessed Mother's wedding ring. The keys to the fifteen boxes are held by fifteen different church officials.

However, not a word of this was proven to the Divas that day. They never found the box. They're not quite sure they located the correct chapel. However, the crackerjack team does believe they did manage to make it to the appropriate cathedral.

To this day, the two are left with a host of nagging questions? First, why doesn't the Duomo have a dome? Wouldn't it make it so much easier to locate? Next, why aren't the chapels identified? Another thing, where are the locked boxes? And, are they see-through? And if they're not transparent, how can anyone be sure there's a ring in there? For that matter, how do we know there are fourteen more boxes inside? And the Divas' questions don't stop there.

Once one sets eyes on the ring, how does one know it is truly Mary's ring? Is there a legal chain of custody to verify it is in fact the Virgin Mother's ring? Or, is it engraved? Does it say, "All my love, Mary Mother of God. Your loving cuckolded husband Joseph"?

Furthermore, how did the ring make its way from Jerusalem to Perugia? Who had the cohones to steal the Mother of God's ring? The ladies would like to meet that man. Oh, please excuse the Divas. And finally, what about those fifteen church officials with the keys? Does anyone know who these men are? Is a scavenger hunt necessary to gather them together? And what happens if one of them hides their key and dies?

Tears were rolling down India's cheeks, unable to speak.

"You see our point, don't you?" Shelby asked. "We're just supposed to take all this on faith?"

India nodded her head in agreement, still struggling to speak. "B..b..but you two are going straight to hell," she finally managed to get out.

"Oh, no we're not," Dena disagreed. "We are now devotees of Bacchusism, where one needn't take anything on faith."

"You can see the wine," Shelby added. "You can taste the wine. And if you drink enough..."

"You will surely feel da wine," Dena finished her thought. "Thank you, Lord Bacchus."

The three ladies shared a hearty laugh. Then, a serious thought distracted India from her laughter.

"How come no one's ever heard of this?" she revealed. "I never knew Mary's ring even existed. Did you?"

"Nope," answered Dena. *"Which gave us a brilliant plan!"*

Her eyes shone with excitement as she told how she and Shelby had hypothesized that the story regarding Mary's wedding band was probably the biggest fraud perpetrated by the Catholic Church on its followers. The budding detectives had considered contacting the Vatican and promising to keep their findings, or lack thereof, under wraps if they could have a date with two Swiss Guards of their choosing, an overnight in the Vatican, and a substantial deposit in their offshore account.

Shelby tapped Dena's hand to interrupt. *"You forgot our most important demand, dear."*

Dena went over the items she'd mentioned, but for the life of her couldn't think of what she'd left out. She stared blankly at her friend.

"How could you forget some of that great wine they use for Mass?" Shelby asked, dumbfounded by Dena's oversight.

Dena clapped a hand on her thigh. Shelby was right. How could she forget the wine? The Pope probably used the best vintage Chianti. Probably was a little tipsy up there on the altar.

The Englishwoman laughed. *"Hopefully, it'll be before he and his parishioners think it's turned to the blood of Christ,"* she added.

The ladies shared in India's joke, laughing with devilish glee. *Sometimes the old bag's not so bad* Shelby thought before picking up where Dena had left off. *"But in the end, we decided our theory was too important not to share with the world in our upcoming New York Times bestseller,"* she concluded.

"Don't forget the blockbuster film," Dena reminded her friend.

"And the rest of your day in Perugia?" the Englishwoman asked, changing the subject quickly.

"A big fat bust as far as I'm concerned," Shelby lamented.

Dena nodded in agreement. *"Yeah, Shelby was pretty much done with the place when we couldn't find the Blessed Mother's ring."*

"Well, surely you didn't miss the Perugina chocolate factory and museum?" India prodded.

"Why waste our time?" both ladies chimed in.

"We can buy Perugina chocolates at any Marshalls or TJ Maxx at home for half the price," Dena informed India.

Quickly the travelers outlined the rest of their day, which included a lunch not worth mentioning and the purchase of a few tchotchkes.

"Then we high-tailed it back to Florence for an evening concert."

They had tickets for a classical music concert being performed at the *Chiesa di Orsanmichele*, Church of St. Michael's of the Garden. An evening of high culture awaited Dena and Shelby, and they were quite looking forward to it. And, if perchance, some refined gentleman looked their way, well all the better.

Back at the hotel, the ladies reviewed the day's events. It goes without saying that it didn't take much time to conclude that they had miserably failed in their mission to wow the men of Italy. Any fool could see why. They hadn't chosen the right outfits. Not a soul had recognized the Divas. Time to bring out the big guns.

Bearing all this in mind, Shelby chose a Tahari white silk pantsuit paired with a violet paisley shell and her purple silk slides. Dena looked quite lovely in a peach silk sheath with matching strappy heels. As they did the Diva Stroll through the Florentine streets, the city was exceedingly quiet. Again, the nagging question. Where was everybody?

Several possibilities came to mind. Had the town been struck by another Bubonic Plague? Maybe everyone had fled Florence for the countryside without informing the ladies that packs of rats were out to get them. Alternatively, perhaps the medieval rival city states of Florence and Siena were in conflict again, causing Florentines to head for the hills. Truthfully, even these pea-brained pretties thought this was unlikely, so they continued to speculate.

"It is the middle of July," Dena stated the obvious. "Think it could be the heat? Maybe everyone's at the beach."

Shelby thought her friend might just have something there. "You're probably right, and that's exactly what we should do tomorrow. Head to the beach."

Just then, the ladies heard music wafting through the night air. When they realized it was coming from the direction of their destination, they quickened their pace. No time to wonder about the people-less steam bath that Florence had become. The concert had already started, and they loathed being late.

Hateful as the thought was, being fashionably late proved to be a blessing for the culture-questing couple. The church was full, and the only seats to be had were in the back pews. Slipping in quietly, the ladies sat down to enjoy the orchestra.

Strains of slow tempo, soothing notes wafted through the air, casting a spell over the audience...a sleeping spell. Unable to keep her eyes open, Shelby's head nodded once. It nodded twice. She jerked awake. Opening her eyes, she looked around and found she wasn't the only one afflicted with sleeping sickness. Here and there, scattered throughout the audience, were dozens of slumbering spectators. Between the heat, the somnolent music, and the low lighting, they were dropping like flies. Shelby succumbed again to the sickness.

A little while later, an elderly neighbor's knock against her shoulder jolted her awake again. In turn, her jerking movement startled a slumbering Dena. The ladies gave each other a bored look. With their shared brain, they knew what must be done.

Without so much as a word between them, they rose in unison. Like seasoned soldiers in formation, the women advanced toward the door and the freedom of the night air.

Having cleared the exit, they burst into laughter reminiscent of their perennially giggling teenage years. So much for the Divas, high culture, and the performing arts.

"The only art I want to see performed is that of the culinary variety. A plate of pasta in front of me," laughed Dena. Then she remembered the most important thing. "And the musically delicious tinkle of wine being poured into my glass."

Trattoria Sostanza–Troia[36] was Nicola *Due*'s place of employment. Coincidentally, the establishment was listed as a Frommer's Favorite. From her purse, Shelby retrieved the business card he'd pressed into her hand and studied the map on the reverse side.

For the better part of an hour, the women wandered through the streets of Florence, twisting the map first one way, then the other. They could never agree. If one suggested turning right, the other thought left was correct. Fifteen minutes later, no nearer to their destination, realization hit that they were both wrong.

"Look how hard can it be? Here's the Duomo on the map. That's where we're standing," Shelby steamed, pointing to a spot on the map. "We just follow this street."

Wrong again. In the end, they were dizzy. Make that dizzier than usual. Knowing they had to be close, but fearing the restaurant would stop serving before they arrived, the bumbling bimbos finally succumbed to the inevitable. They hailed a cab.

The welcoming smile on Nicola *Due*'s face more than made up for their trouble. Still, Dena thought it was their obligation to break it to the restaurant that their business card was almost criminally off the mark. Settled at their table, she did just that, shoving the damnable card under *Due*'s considerable nose.

---

[36]Trattoria Sostanza, V. Porcellana , 25r, Ph 055/212691

"See, it's wrong," she informed him. "You're nowhere near the Duomo."

"No, no," *Due* argued, pointing to the landmark on the card. "This not the Duomo. Eez train station!"

And so it was that for a complete hour, Dena and Shelby had stumbled from pillar to post using their beloved Duomo as the starting point, but what they had assumed was the Duomo on the map was not. It was the *Santa Maria Novella* train station.

So the ladies gave new meaning to the phrase, "You can't get there from here."

> **Traveling Tidbit for the Cartographically Challenged Traveler:** When choosing a landmark from which to navigate, it's a good idea to make sure that landmark is in actuality what you think it is.

Dining at Sostanza is a communal affair. Groups of patrons are seated together at tables, depending on their numbers. *Due* had led the ladies to a table where they joined a rather handsome father dining with his teenage son and daughter.

After following their waiter friend's advice, and ordering the restaurant's trademark *Bistecca alla fiorentina* along with a green bean side dish, Dena turned her attention to the teenagers, smiling and greeting them in her best Italian. They responded with their own smile, and Dena needed no further urging. She was off and running.

Before long, the ladies found out everything they needed to know. The children lived in Germany with their mother. Their parents were divorced. They were out to dinner with their very available father.

Ah, another light bulb in that collective brain. Which of the them should set their sights on the poor, unsuspecting man? Would this ruin their friendship?

Dena reached into her considerable bag of social tricks, and tried to engage the man in conversation. Shelby gave him a pretty smile, following Dena's lead.

Before long, the pair knew their friendship was in no danger at all. The taciturn gentleman did not spare so much as a smile, let alone a spark of interest in either of the Divas.

Halfway through Dena's and Shelby's meal, the family rose to leave. The children bade them goodbye, and the father grunted his farewell to the ladies.

"Not so much as a by your leave," Shelby lamented.

No, he hadn't given them a smile, he'd barely given them a hello, and by no stretch of even our ladies' vivid imaginations, had he handed them his calling card. However, he had graced them with something far more valuable.

"Who cares, Shelby? Look," Dena whispered with a conspiratorial smile.

She pointed to the family's half-filled carafe of wine and nudged her friend. "Quick, slide it this way before they clear the table."

Traveling Tidbit for Dollarless Diners: Communal dining is an art. The hand must be quicker than the waiter's eye. Immediately upon your fellow diners' departure, scan their leftovers for any tempting untouched consumables.

Their own and anyone else's food they could commandeer eaten, our ladies bade goodbye to *Due*, who promised to meet them later that evening at Meccano.

"Ha, ha, ha!" Shelby's maniacal laughter filled the taxicab two hours later as they pulled away from the outdoor nightclub.

But Dena hardly shared her amused point of view. She didn't see a blessed thing funny about the whole day. First, they'd gotten kicked out of First Class by two good-looking men. Next, looking for the Virgin Mother's ring had been a bust. Their big concert should have been billed as a Sleep-in. Later, they were totally ignored by that father at dinner. Meccano had been scads of fun. They'd ended up doing the Do-si-do-ini with each other. And to cap off the whole evening, even *Due* had stood them up! He'd never darkened Meccano's door that evening.

When her friend put it like that, for just a second, Shelby wondered what indeed she found so humorous. But it didn't take long before another giggle bubbled up inside her. Not just today, she thought to herself. Who would believe the craziness they had put themselves through these past four months?

Dena waited for her friend to elaborate.

"Think about it. I come here looking for a man who dumped me for my supposed friend," Shelby obliged.

"I get here and meet a waiter who's ten years my junior," Dena countered.

"After so many years of dreaming and hoping, I envision a romantic reunion in a villa, and my Romeo plans a tacky roll in the hay... literally," Shelby recounts with embarrassment.

"I nix our trip to Rome to hurry back to my Italian Jeeves, only to have him pat the asses of other women in front of me," Dena added.

Shelby's thoughts continued, but one thing she refused to tell to her friend, even if she was finally ready to admit it to herself. Dance at each other's wedding! How could he say such a completely insensitive thing to me after I had laid my soul bare to him, she fumed.

She covered her eyes with her hands. Her shoulders started to shake as a wave of tears racked her body. And still, she had loved him. Had thought there was a reason to return to Florence a second time in one year. How stupid could she be?

Dena hated to see her friend in such pain. She reached into her purse for a tissue and handed it to her. She knew she shouldn't ask her next question, but the curiosity weighed on her, and the words were out before she could stop them.

"Shelby, you're not crying because you still want Giancarlo, are you?"

That brought a strangled laugh to her friend. "Hell, no," Shelby denied. "I'm crying because I've been making really bad choices. Lying to friends and family about a business venture, draining my savings to buy hats, shoes, lingerie, and condoms to become a diva. And for what? To entice a man who treated me like the dirt under his shoe?"

Shelby shook her head in complete wonderment, incredulous at her foolishness. It was all so ridiculous. Maybe, she really should consider going back into therapy.

Tears welled in Dena's eyes as she listened to her friend chronicle her mistakes. She knew she wasn't without her own misdeeds.

If Shelby had made bad choices, what about her? Losing twenty pounds mooning over a man who had stood her up her last night in Florence on their previous trip. Going just as wacky as Shelby with the shopping. Only she had spent Luke's hard earned money. And leaving her kids again to come back and hear that the idiot could give her fun, but not love!

A lull descended over the cab as each woman took a solitary trip through the events of the past few months. Shelby broke the silence.

"Divas? What a farce!"

How could they have been so crazy? So delusional?

282

Chapter 18

When consulting Frommer's on Viareggio, Shelby had come across a blurb about another seaside resort. *Forte dei Marmi is tonier, less developed, and more picturesque than Viareggio.*[37]

As Shelby read, Dena listened attentively. She was certain it was just the place for the Divas.

"More Tonys? Yes, indeedy, let's go there."

Shelby giggled at her friend's play on words. Tonys, Frankies, Sals, or Vinnys. Dena could take her pick as far as she was concerned. Shelby had had enough of men. Still, it did sound like a place the ladies should check out.

Although only a bit farther from Florence than Viareggio, no direct trains service Forte dei Marmi. So, the ladies hopped a train to the *Pisa Centrale* station, not to be confused with the *Pisa Aeroporto* station. Then, they caught a connecting train heading to *Torino* (Turin), getting out at the Forte dei Marmi stop. The name means marble fort, and the area is the site of vast marble quarries.

"Oh, yeah. This looks real tony," Dena sniped. She threw her friend a look of sheer disgust.

It looked as if they were in the middle of a Flintstones cartoon, downtown Bedrock to be precise. The train station was in the middle of nowhere. Nothing to the north, nothing to the south, nothing to the east or west. Shelby knew it didn't look good, but she wasn't about to admit to a mistake.

"I bet we can walk to the beach. Let's just ask that cab driver which way," she said, pinning a smile of false optimism on her face.

At their question, the man shook his head back and forth. "No can walk...long walk," he answered.

Shelby was skeptical. Her ego was still smarting from Guido the Crooked Cabbie of Naples and the promised two-hour tour of Pompeii that lasted for fifteen minutes.

"Here we go again," she hissed to Dena. "Another slick as olive oil cabbie trying to take the Divas for a ride."

Dena nodded in agreement. This time, they weren't going down without a fight. "Which way? We want to walk," she said forcefully.

---

[37]Frommer's Italy, p. 278.

"*Pazza,*" the driver muttered under his breath. Crazy! He pointed far off into the distance. He stood shaking his head with bemusement, certain the women would not make it far.

Off they trudged, resolute heads held high. Soon those heads started flagging, and their feet started throbbing. Both women squinted into the horizon. Not a drop of sea water was in sight. Their heads and egos were willing, but their feet were staging a mutiny.

Reluctantly, they backtracked, making their way up to the cabbie. Approximately ten minutes later, he dropped them off at the beach's edge.

"Fancy that," Dena mused in amazement. "He was telling the truth. The beach is too far to walk."

And with that the ladies dubbed the good man Tommaso the Trustworthy Taxi Driver.

Though rare, every once in a while, Dena and Shelby managed to apply what they had learned previously to a new situation. For most people, this is easy. It falls under the heading of common sense. Common sense and the Divas. Two mutually exclusive terms. But that day? That day was different.

After their humiliation in Viareggio, they had managed to limit their Chianti consumption the night before and had risen before noon. Not only did they arrive at Forte dei Marmi's beach early, but they knew enough not to head straight for the water's edge and risk being shooed away like a couple of bothersome sand fleas. Instead, they headed directly to the *bagni* to rent loungers, an umbrella, and a changing room.

The changing rooms are quite convenient and comfortably spacious. Beachgoers can leave valuables in a clean, secure environment, which comes equipped with hooks for clothes, a bench, and a mirror. Just what every diva needs -- a bird's eye, and sometimes sobering, view of her luscious body in a swimsuit. Nearby the changing rooms, bathers may use outside showers to remove sand and salt.

Early arrival also garnered the ladies another benefit. They managed to secure a spot near the water's edge where they could stay without fear of being unceremoniously relocated. Sunscreen applied liberally, towels laid out on their loungers, hats and sunglasses to protect their delicate skin, and they were ready for a pleasant day at the beach.

Shelby gave a sigh of contentment as she lay in the sun. "Ahhh, now this is nice. Only one thing missing. A little nip to start the afternoon off right," she said as she rose from her lounger. "I'm headed to the bar for wine. Want anything?"

"I'll go with you," Dena said. This was their last day in Florence, she thought with a bit of sadness. Her wedding to Nicola was apparently off. Maybe the bartender here was a hottie.

Once at the bar, Dena and Shelby decided to mix it up a bit and have a good cold beer instead. Beer and the beach just seemed to go together.

Back at their little oasis in the sand, Shelby reached into her bag and pulled out the necklace of mini cinghiale sausage she'd bought in San Gimignano. Twisting two off, she offered one to her friend before beginning to gnaw on one of the hard salamis herself.

Dena bit in eagerly. Damn, it was hard as a rock. But the flavor was delicious, making it impossible to resist. Yes, it was delicious, but she wasn't about to lose a tooth for it. So, she sucked on the link to soften it up a bit. Seeing the usefulness of her friend's method, Shelby followed suit.

There the women lay, gnawing and sucking on short, thick pieces of meat in between swigs of their brewskies. It may not have been quite the self-portrait the Divas had had when planning this trip, but this was actually the happiest, not to mention most satisfied, they'd been in days. Besides, when they quickly perused their surrounding, they quickly concluded there really was no one to impress.

"This tastes great, but all this fat will go straight to my thighs," Dena worried.

"Well, if it does, you'd better pull a towel over you and hide from the beach police or you'll be evicted," replied Shelby.

She had heard there was some idiotic mayor in Italy who'd had the brilliant idea of banishing women with flabby butts and cellulite thighs from the beaches. His rationale? Ugly women in bikinis detracted from the natural beauty of the area, which hurt tourism.

"And the ugly men?" Dena asked. "Are they banned, too?"

With a sharp swat of her hand in midair, Shelby dismissed the question. "I'd bet anything the law was enacted specifically for their benefit. Undoubtedly, the mayor's a toad," she laughed. "This way, ugly men can go out on the beach, leave their long-suffering, pasta-cooking wives at home, and run wild and free among the hot babes."

Dena straightened her posture and tightened her tummy muscles. "Well, they wouldn't throw us off. We're hot."

"You just keep telling yourself that, Dena. But in the meantime, take this towel. Cover yourself, for gods sakes. Here comes a policeman."

Stomachs satiated, it was time for a dip in the ocean. The day was hot, the sun was shining, and the water was an inviting shade of blue-green. With guts sucked in so nothing would jiggle, the ladies walked slowly down to the water's edge.

"It's heavenly," Shelby declared when she hit the warm Mediterranean seawater. But she didn't get the answer she expected.

"Ooh, ooh, ooh," she heard coming from Dena's direction. Turning, Shelby saw her friend doing a great impression of Mr. Bojangles in the water. Hopping first on one foot, then to the other and back again.

Eyes big as flying saucers popping out of her head, Dena kept reaching for her legs, smacking at first one and then the other. "Ooh...ooh...ooh," she kept screeching.

"What the hell is your problem?" Shelby asked.

Those eyes really were something. Together with her skinny arms and legs, Dena looked like a bug-eyed frog. I was wrong. Her sisters were right, Shelby revised her assessment. There really is a resemblance to Don Knotts.

"Something's attacking me. Don't you feel it?" Dena shrieked frantically.

"No, I don't feel a thing."

Soon her shrieks turned to screams, and Shelby became concerned. Not enough to help her friend, just enough to inch slowly out of harm's way.

In mid-performance, Dena switched from a tap dance to a jaunty Irish jig, with each step slipping further and further into hysteria.

"A school of jellyfish must be attacking me. I'm out of here. Save yourself!" she yelled over her shoulder as she made for shore.

Shelby followed her friend back to their spot to see if she could help. Dena could have serious injuries. She may need medical attention. What were friends for, after all? Perhaps I'll need to find a doctor to help her. Maybe he'll be cute, maybe he'll be single, maybe he'll fall in love with me. She'd better be hurt! But not too badly, of course. Hopefully, just a few welts or a bite or two.

When she reached Dena, Shelby looked down to inspect the damage. Much to her disgust, but not at all to her surprise, Dena didn't have so much as a pinprick on her legs. No welts, no bites, no cuts, no chunks of missing flesh. Her legs were smooth as a baby's ass. Or, in this case, as smooth as the ass' ass.

Satisfied that her friend was not at death's door, Shelby didn't say a word. With deliberate movements, she shook her head and turned away, returning to the water.

So, even though they had managed to secure a dressing room for their valuables...well, valuables might be a stretch for the Divas on a budget; let's just say personal items...it looked as if Shelby would be cast in the role of Flipper once again, frolicking in the water all by her lonesome.

As the sunny day wore on, Dena sat roasting in the heat looking longingly at the inviting blue waters. Feeling sorry for herself and for her friend being out there all alone, she decided to attempt another foray into the sea. She waded in tentatively, making her way to Shelby, who was playfully catching the waves.

Dena had just started to relax and join in the fun, when she was seized by another fit. "There! There they are again. What is it?" she yipped.

Shelby looked around her. A sea full of sunbathers enjoying the warm Mediterranean waters. Not a one of them seemed plagued by mysterious sea creatures feeding on their legs. No screaming, no other eyes bulging, no hippity-hopping from foot to foot, no flailing arms. Just happy people enjoying a tranquil, summer afternoon.

Shelby's eyes panned back to her friend. It was time. She'd been trying to avoid it the whole trip. Shelby looked but didn't see even one light bulb on in that house. No knives in the drawer. Dena was in the water, but she didn't have a paddle never mind any oars.

Shelby cast her eyes around again. Any fisherman nearby? One with a net? Perhaps they could capture her friend as she skedaddled for land. But Dena was too fast. She didn't stop at their umbrella, but kept running.

Where the hell was she going? Shelby wondered if she would have to spend the rest of her vacation alone. Then, she saw Dena wasn't making a getaway; she was making a pit stop at the bar.

By the time Shelby made it back to their spot, Dena was safely ensconced in her beach chair taking a deep gulp of another beer.

By her side was a little purple cloth-covered book. She picked it up and started writing. Shelby had noticed Dena writing in it before and been mildly curious. She decided to satisfy her curiosity.

"Writing in my journal," Dena replied to the question.

Shelby was shocked, unable to fathom why her friend would want to record any of their experiences. "Damned if I'd ever memorialize our humiliations for posterity," she said.

"Maybe, but you have to admit this trip has been pretty damn unusual," Dena argued.

"Insane is more like it," Shelby countered.

Dena couldn't argue with that, and both women fell silent, each lost in their thoughts. Like a vintage film reel rewinding, their escapades flickered like movies in front of both women's eyes. *Driving the Divas* starring Fausto the Fatso. *Diva Down in Viareggio* starring Dena's knee. *The Disserviced Diva* starring Little Giancarlo. *Deity of the Divas* starring Bacchus. *Deserting the Diva* starring Nicola. *Undercover with the Diva Detectives* starring Mary, Mother of God's ring. And last, but certainly not least, *Diva in Dreamland* starring the Black Specter.

With each shared memory, the ladies laughed longer and more loudly. Tears streamed down their eyes.

"Stop!" Shelby grabbed her stomach with one hand and raised the other in a plea. "I'm gonna wet myself."

"We could write an article about this," Dena said, excitement bubbling inside her. "Send it to travel magazines. You know, something like the travels and travails of the Divas."

"There's enough material in that for a trilogy."

Then, Shelby stopped laughing. Eying the purple book, she considered her friend's idea more seriously.

As they swigged down more beer, the ladies batted around ideas.

"Ah hah," the Englishwoman puffed loudly, startling the ladies from their tale. "So that's when you got the idea to write."

Dena and Shelby nodded their heads affirmatively. You go to the head of the class, Shelby thought snidely.

"So, your delusions actually had an upside?" said India. Her words were more statement than question.

Grudgingly, Shelby gave credit to India's insight. Again the ladies nodded their agreement.

"Exactly," Dena said excitedly. "Delusion may not..."

She hesitated and revised what she had planned to say. "Most likely, will not lead you where you originally intended, but instead in a direction totally unexpected."

Shelby picked up her friend's train of thought. "And hopefully, that direction will take your life on a new and exciting path that leads you exactly where you are meant to go."

Now, it was India's turn to acknowledge a grudging respect. Maybe these two bumbling bimbos really had stumbled onto something. And bumbling bimbos or not, the British woman did have to admit one thing. Dena and Shelby had stumbled on one thing she had thrown away. A deep and abiding friendship.

With their day at the beach effectively in shambles, Dena suggested a walk through the town. Forte dei Marmi is a delightful little place. In the main square, stands a stone fort with a bell tower built in 1788. Cars are not permitted in the center of town. Many people, young and old alike, tool around on bicycles. Fountains and inviting wooden benches tempt one to take a rest and watch the comings and goings around them.

"I smell something fabulous. Don't you?" Shelby asked Dena as she pretended to sniff the air.

"I don't smell food?" Dena replied questioningly.

"No, this is a rare, wonderful scent. One I've caught a whiff of only in passing," Shelby answered with a broad smile. "You know, when I've gone past Gucci, Versace, or Prada. Or the time I went by the Cipriani Hotel."

"Oh, I know what it is." Dena's eyes widened with sudden comprehension. "You smell ducats, dear. The fine bouquet of money."

Shelby smelled money and so did she.

Everywhere they cast their eyes, the Divas, who had champagne tastes and caviar dreams on a beer budget, were surrounded by wealth. Posh shops, ritzy restaurants, and obviously well-dressed, well-heeled residents and tourists alike. Proof that Mr. Frommer hadn't been off the mark. Tony he wrote, and tony it was.

Deciding it was time to rub elbows with the Italian rich and famous, and time to pay homage to Bacchus, the ladies were shown to an outdoor table at *Caffé Principe*[38] in the middle of all the action.

Seated next to Dena and Shelby was an elegantly attired lady who had most likely been a contemporary of Queen Victoria. The queen and any other contemporaries having died long ago, the woman was alone that afternoon.

As women often do, Dena and Shelby took a quick inventory of the lady's Chanel suit, matching hat and gloves, and expertly

---

[38]Caffé Principe, Via Carducci 2, Ph 0584/89238

applied makeup. They watched as she sipped her cocktail and enjoyed idle chatter with the waiter.

"What wouldn't I give to be like her in fifty years?" Dena swore.

"More like thirty years, but I know what you mean," Shelby said.

As their eyes assessed the woman from head to toe, the faux Divas agreed the elderly woman looked fabulous. Like a million bucks. But it was not simply her outfit. No, this woman had a certain *je ne sais quoi*. An aura of confidence with herself and the world around her that was enviable. She was alone, no man at her side, not even a girlfriend, and seemed comfortable being so. She was doing as she pleased and looked content. And damned what anyone thought of it.

A true Diva.

One appeal of train travel in a foreign country is the chance meeting and interaction with locals. It is the perfect way to learn helpful tidbits about different customs and discover less touristy haunts with more authentic flavor. From a broader perspective, these chance encounters reinforce the inescapable fact that wherever they happen to be from, people have similar hopes and dreams, as well as concerns and fears.

Given this, Dena and Shelby were enchanted when on their way home from Forte dei Marmi, a young Italian woman seated opposite them spoke up when she heard the ladies speaking English. Where they were from, she asked.

"Oh, New York! I've always wanted to go there," the Italian responded enthusiastically.

Where were they staying, she queried. And, upon hearing Dena and Shelby were visiting Florence, Francesca di Firenze was off and running. "I live in Florence. I wasn't born there, but I have been there many years."

Her tale spared no detail, as she regaled her captive audience with the epic, *The Life and Times of Francesca the Florentine Nurse*. Part One was entitled *Francesca in Utero*.

Roughly an hour later, there was a brief intermission as she checked her cell phone for messages. By then, Dena and Shelby were privy to Francesca's date of birth, shoe size, the number of fillings in her head with the precise breakdown of how many were porcelain and how many were mercury, the number and length of her romantic relationships and why they went sour, the names of her cats and dates of their scheduled inoculations, and the hospital at which she worked and no doubt tortured her patients with her incessant chatter.

On the other hand, should anyone ever have the misfortune of bumping into Francesca the Florentine Nurse, they should not expect to obtain any information from her about the Divas. During their encounter, the nutty nurse did not so much as enquire as to the ladies' names let alone anything more significant.

Soon Shelby could not stand one more second of the self-absorbed woman's mind numbing narcissism. Her only defense was to feign sleep. Shelby let her head nod once, then twice, before closing her eyes, abandoning Dena to Francesca as she picked up where she'd left off in her saga. For another thirty minutes, Dena listened as she droned on.

"And tonight for dinner..." the Italian finally paused for her first breath.

Smelling weakness, Dena seized the opportunity like a dog with a bone, determined to turn this meeting from hell to her advantage and glean any useful information out of Chatty Caterina that she could. Quickly, she asked the Italian woman for beach recommendations.

"You should go the island of Elba. It's beautiful."

Okay, finally, now we're getting somewhere, Dena complimented herself. But Francesca was a worthy opponent, managing to use an innocent island to her egotistical advantage.

"I love Elba. I used to go there every summer as a child. My parents had a summer house there. They bought it when I was five years old. We were so happy there...for a time. Then Mama caught Papa with a neighbor. It was awful."

Here we go again, Dena thought. Let me try one more time. "How's the nightlife there?"

This is what Francesca told Dena. Elba, the island to which Napoleon was exiled, is a must see with its pristine waters, great beaches, and, of particular interest to Dena, all-night discos.

"But don't go in July or August," she advised, warning of the hordes of European tourists descending on the tiny island.

To give the devil her due, the ladies' magpie companion also answered the burning question of where all the Italians were at night this past week.

"At the festival, of course," Francesca answered with an insufferable air of superiority. "Everybody knows about the festival!" One could almost hear the silent "you rubes!" at the end of her sentence.

"What festival?" Dena asked, ignoring the rudeness.

"The *Festa del'Unita* at the *Fortezza da Basso*. I go tonight. We can go together, if you like," she offered.

Dena smiled at the Italian woman's kind offer. Could be fun, she thought. "Well, thank you. We'd love to..."

Though she wasn't sleeping, Shelby was sure she was in the middle of a nightmare. If she didn't do something quick, she'd be tortured by *Francesca, the Wonder Years* later that evening. Forgetting any pretense of sleep, she opened her eyes and interrupted her friend.

"Oh, that's so nice of you. But we have so much to do to get ready to leave tomorrow. We really can't make plans."

Notwithstanding Shelby's protestations, later that evening, the ladies decided to investigate Francesca's claims. Obtaining directions to the Fortezza, they made their way to the outdoor festival.

As they approached the fort, Shelby once again was overcome with a feeling of familiarity. "I know this place," she declared.

"Let me guess. Another bleed through?" Dena laughed.

"Giancarlo brought me here for a crafts fair," Shelby continued without acknowledging the remark.

"Tell me, did you ever bother to find out the name of anyplace he took you? Or did you just hang on his arm and let him drag you willynilly from one end of Tuscany to another with a silly grin on your face?"

For a brief moment, Shelby was transported back six years. The simpleminded grin her friend spoke of lit up her face even now. She nodded and didn't even try to contradict Dena. "It would be the latter," she admitted.

The Fortezza da Basso was built as part of a trio of fortresses in the 16th century to give protection to the ruling Medici family from their enemies within the city. Today, the imposing brick complex is used as a conference hall and exhibit grounds for expos, trade shows, fashion fairs, and concerts.

That evening, the sprawling grounds teemed with people, overwhelmingly Italian...young and old, gay and straight, families with children, and single people. Music resonated from every corner with at least five bands playing simultaneously. Booths with vendors selling their wares were everywhere. Other booths tempted the palate with a wide selection of foods.

When Dena and Shelby came upon one selling a variety of sandwiches, Shelby quickly scanned the meats with hopefulness. "Ohmigod, they have *porchetta!*" she practically squealed with delight. "You simply have to try this."

Porchetta is the meat from a pig roasted whole over wood. The pig is heavily salted and stuffed with garlic, rosemary and other herbs. Generous slices of the meat are served on a thin unsalted roll.

Each lady ordered one of the Italian sandwiches along with a beer. They found a seat at one of the long picnic tables. Eagerly taking her first bite, Shelby was immediately disappointed. It was not nearly as tasty as those she had eaten six years ago. "A bit tough and somewhat dry."

"I'll say," Dena concurred. "If I want muscles in my jaw, this will do it!"

Unfortunately, the ladies couldn't recommend the porchetta sandwiches they sampled that night. However, Shelby still insists that anytime a tourist has the opportunity to try a porchetta sandwich, they seize it. A well-made one is a not to be missed treat for the taste buds.

Last swigs of their beers swallowed, the women decided to wander the grounds a while longer listening to music, "window shopping" at the booths, and enjoying the sights and sounds of Italians having fun.

"It figures we find out where all the Italians in Florence are our last night here," Dena groaned.

"This is something a travel guide should note. Once again, thank you Messrs. Frommer and Fodor," Shelby agreed.[39]

Yes, everyone was at the festival, including two of the ladies' admirers.

"Oh, no...don't tell me you actually ran into Giancarlo and Nicola at the festival?" India asked incredulously.

"No, here's a little hint," Dena said. "The male duo we encountered were friends."

"Oh," said India. The Englishwoman furrowed her brow in thought. "Let me see, who could it be? Oh, I know...Giancarlo and Fatso?"

Dena shuddered at the memory of Fausto. "Lord, no!"

"How about Nicola and Due?" came India's next attempt.

This time, it was Shelby's turn to recoil at the vision of Due in her mind's eye.

---

[39]Should our readers decide to visit beautiful Florence from mid-July until early August, be aware that the *Festa del'Unita* is an annual affair. If you're looking for the Florentines, this is where they'll be.

"No, poor Due never set eyes on his strong, hard woman again," she laughed. "Next!"

India frowned. "Who could it be?" she whispered more to herself than anyone else. "Oh, maybe that hot policeman and his shoemaker friend?"

While Dena got a silly grin on her face at the thought of Marco, Shelby didn't have such gleeful memories of Geppetto, the young cobbler.

"I'm right, aren't I?" India challenged.

As soon as their eyes fell on them, Shelby grabbed Dena.

"Ohmigod! Jeffelli and Muttelli. Quick let's get out of here!"

But Dena was still on a mission. If it killed her, she was going to prove Devil Doctor wrong. This was their chance to find out if Frankenstella was lying. She tugged on Shelby's sleeve, preventing her friend's bid for escape.

"Let's find out if they're from Florence!"

Shelby pulled herself free of Dena's grasp. "Who gives a damn? They could be crowned princes of the damned city for all I care," she growled.

Still, Dena was determined. She turned, ready to approach the two men. Shelby had to act fast. She reminded Dena this was their last night in Florence, and there was a beautiful woman they still needed to bid adieu.

"Let's go say our last goodbye," she suggested.

Making a quick getaway, the duo headed for the Duomo to say a final arrivederci to their beloved cathedral. They each said a silent prayer for a speedy return to the city they adored.

Chapter 19

They awoke to their last full day in Italy and the monumental task of repacking all that they had brought with them, plus everything they had purchased during the trip. A few days earlier, Shelby had begun to panic. She was no physicist, but it didn't take Albert Einstein to know that two plus two still make four, a square peg won't fit into a round hole, a rose is a rose is a rose, and a suitcase by any other name will still be the same size suitcase tomorrow. She would never fit all her belongings, old and new, in her luggage.

"There's only one thing left to do," she decided. She needed to rid herself of a few items.

"Well, that doesn't make any sense?" India was confused. "How much space do a bracelet and a wine cork take up?"

Dena and Shelby looked at each other with sheepish embarrassment.

"Well, we have a little confession. Maybe we did buy one or two more things than we mentioned," Shelby confessed.

The nasty truth started oozing forth, lava from an erupting volcano.

"Not much, just some small leather goods. You know, change purses and whatnot. And that Fendi bag," Dena admitted.

"Oh and then, Dena bought a few new outfits. Not too bulky; hardly worth mentioning," Shelby added.

Dena shot her friend an exasperated frown. She fought fire with fire. "And don't forget those three beautiful pairs of shoes you couldn't resist, Shelby."

Shelby fumed. "They were summer shoes, not very heavy," she justified.

"Oh yes, we almost forgot the artwork from San Gimignano. Beautiful renderings of sunflower fields and the antique wood doors of Italy. Who could blame us really?" Dena said, ignoring her friend's look.

By the time the ladies finished, their companion was shaking her head in amazement. Well, they say Americans are conspicuous consumers. These two prove the point.

It was not hard to imagine what the skinflint Brit was thinking.

"Oh, we're not that bad," Shelby answered back, a trifle offended.

"No? You ladies should consider yourselves a two-woman economic boost to the local economy. No wonder you had to get rid of some stuff."

Certain things were non-negotiable. The cinghiale sausage was going home with Shelby if she had to wrap it in a baby bunting and paint on eyes, nose, and mouth. Maybe when she got it home, she could claim little Porky as a dependent.

On the other hand, she had sworn revenge on a few pairs of shoes that had turned her feet into hamburger. They'd never see the States again.

Dena watched in utter amazement as her friend discarded valuables like a desperate crew jettisoning cargo from a sinking ship. Unlike Shelby, she was not worried. She had spent a considerable amount of time and money making purchases both here and at home, and she was not about to part with any of her nearest and dearest.

Nevertheless, halfway through her efforts, Dena's suitcase was groaning, her beach bag bulging, her hatbox sagging under the weight, and her shopping bags overflowing. And, on her bed, still lay a small mound of miscellaneous items without a home.

"I'll be back soon," she called over her shoulder to Shelby. "I need to go out and buy a duffel bag for the rest of my things."

Shelby was torn. Let her friend make this one last purchase or break down and reveal the almost scary extent of her delusion. What the hell. Did it really matter anymore? She routed through her suitcase until she found what she was looking for.

"If you want, you can use this," she offered. In her hand, she held up a rather large weekender bag made of ultra lightweight parachute material.

"Where'd you get that from?" Dena asked.

"I brought it with me in case I needed it," Shelby answered quietly.

"Needed it for what?" was Dena's next question.

Shelby turned away, unable to meet her friend's eyes as she explained.

Those beach bags the ladies thought would double as overnight bags for their romantic trysts? Well, Shelby had thought her trysts might be of the more extended variety. You know, a week at Giancarlo's villa in Grosseto or a side trip to romantic Portofino. The beach bag would have been woefully inadequate for that, wouldn't it?

"So, I brought this just in case," she finished her wretched admission and waited for the laughing to begin.

But Dena had a choice now, too. Kick her friend while she was down...quite a tempting reversal of roles for just once in their lives. Or, button up.

Let's face it, she needed that bag or she would be smuggling her pictures home in her underwear. So, Dena kept her own counsel regarding Shelby's lunacy.

Suitcases, beach bags, hat boxes, shopping bags, and bags formerly known as tryst bags packed, the ladies crammed into the tiny elevator down to the lobby. Within minutes, they learned that there was a wrinkle in their plans to take a bus to Pisa. No buses run to Pisa. Back to dreaded Plan A and getting their foot lockers onto the train before it took off without them.

A pained look swept across Dena's face as she remembered the ordeal of hoisting their luggage on the train at the onset of their trip. Her injured foot still tingled at the very memory.

"How much do you think a cab to Pisa would cost?" she inquired of the desk clerk.

When she heard the figure, Shelby's hand went to her heart. She felt a small palpitation. Was she having a heart attack? "Too much," she decreed with hauteur.

Mere minutes later, their cab to the train station arrived. As the lady cabdriver assisted the Divas in loading their cargo into the car, she asked their destination.

"Just around the corner to the train station," the ladies replied with straight faces.

They sank into the soft leather seats of the Mercedes. The air conditioning felt like a cool autumn breeze on the ladies' skin. Could they really leave all this luxury for the promise of a hot, sweaty train car and the unthinkable task of hauling their luggage onto and off of that train? Shelby got a hernia just thinking about it.

"How much to Pisa?" she asked, ready to negotiate.

Roughly 100 dollars, her brain quickly calculated.

"Keep driving!"

Words alone could not express the anxiety that lifted from the Divas' shoulders with the mere utterance of those words. The forty-five minute drive to Pisa was comfortable and informative. The ladies never found out the cabdriver's name, but will always think of her as their little angel. To this day, they call her Angela.

Angela dropped them off in front of the much anticipated *Grand Hotel Duomo*.[40] The name bespoke luxury and elegance. Shelby had found it through their travel agent, Mr. Web, and eagerly reserved a room for their last evening in Italy. Key in hand, the ladies showed themselves to the room.

If they were expecting the royal treatment for their last hurrah, they were sorely disappointed. So much for ever being recognized as the Divas they believed themselves to be. Their last night in Italy and they had been allotted a room smaller than the shower stall at the Hotel Aldini.

"Well, maybe there is a great view of the Leaning Tower," Dena offered hopefully. Drawing back the curtains to let in the warm Italian sun, she let out a scream.

Shelby rushed over to the window to check out what had Dena in more of a dither than usual. No, there was no view of the famed twelfth-century tower. There was no lovely flower-bedecked courtyard below them. Perhaps, a romantic view of a narrow cobblestone street? Nope.

Greeting the ladies was a flat tar roof slightly below their window, an extension of the hotel. And then, Shelby saw it. They had a neighbor. Sprawled out in the middle of the roof was a dead crow. He was providing a feast for a few of his best friends: flies, ants, and maggots.

Horrified, the women closed the drapes, offered a little prayer for the bird, and contemplated requesting a change of accommodations. However, the mere thought of moving their belongings one inch farther was more than either lady could stomach. And with that, they re-christened their new lodgings.

"Grand Hotel Duomo, my eye! More like the Grand Hotel Dumpo." The ladies chuckled heartily at their little joke.

There is one oft-overlooked benefit of staying in an unappealing hotel. Guests would rather be out and about than in a Hotel Dumpo, so they actually get more sightseeing done. In the ladies' case, substitute wine tasting for sightseeing. Time for Chianti.

So traumatized were they by the crow carcass, Dena and Shelby couldn't make it more than a few steps from the hotel. They ended up at the outdoor café of the nearby *Pizzeria Trattoria Toscana*.[41] Notwithstanding its proximity to Dumpo, the ladies actually found the pizzeria to be a culinary treat.

---

[40]Grand Hotel Duomo, via Non Andate Mai,1, which roughly translates to One Don't Ever Go Street.
[41]Pizzeria Trattoria Toscana, Via S. Maria.163, Pisa, Ph 050-561876

Shelby decided to start with the arugula salad with shaved parmesan cheese and the requisite extra virgin olive oil and sprinkled with salt. As an entrée, Dena chose a typical Tuscan soup of mussels, clams, octopus and bread in a tomato-based broth, while Shelby ordered a delicious dish of mussels in garlic and olive oil.

Both women enjoyed their meals immensely. But, unbeknownst to Dena, she would pay for her meal twice…once, with legal tender, and later on, with the agony of acid indigestion. And actually, Shelby was forced to pay for it again, too. By listening to Dena's moaning and groaning.

Intense heat, a downed liter of Chianti, and sated stomachs conspired to rob the women of any energy or desire to spend their last day exploring Pisa. Reluctantly, they retreated to the confines of their room with a revolting view for a little nap.

Hours later, they awoke to darkness and the knowledge that it was now or never. They only had a few hours left in Italy. They needed to make the most of them.

Deciding to heed the recommendation of their lunch waiter for a place to hear music, Dena and Shelby headed across the Arno River in search of yet another medieval fort, *Fortezza Nuova*. Had they known before they started out that their walk would rival a trek across Siberia, they might have hailed a cab. Still, the walk did yield some interesting finds.

Along the way, the wandering women came upon the Royal Victoria Hotel.[42] Shelby pointed a polished finger in its direction.

"Oh, that is the only Pisa hotel recommended in my book. I believe Teddy Roosevelt stayed there," she exclaimed. "Let's check it out."

It is not really as important to tell what the Hotel Victoria is like as much as to relate what it is not like. And what this hotel is not like is the Grand Hotel Dumpo, where the Divas had quite literally pigeonholed themselves.

Once inside, Shelby couldn't resist a small request of the hotel clerk. She wanted to see what the guest rooms looked like.

"No, no rooms free," he answered condescendingly and quickly shooed the women back out into the inky night.

Notwithstanding this rather unceremonious treatment, the ladies made note of a few things. The historic and stately building in which the Hotel Victoria resides dates back to the

---

[42]Royal Hotel Victoria, Lungarno Pacinotti 12, Pisa, Ph 050/940111

tenth century and served as an inn and headquarters to the winemakers' guild. Later, it became the University of Pisa. The eventual hotel has been operating under the ownership of the same family since 1839. The lobby of the Hotel Victoria is quite lovely with wide arched doorways, exquisite marble floors, and antique furniture.

How to describe Shelby's feelings as she stood outside on the sidewalk, knowing she had ignored Mr. Frommer and would be spending the night so near and yet so far? Well, let's just say that if she had had balls, she would have kicked herself in them. And Dena would have been happy to assist.

Forlornly, the ladies continued on their search for *Fortezza Nuova*. The rambling fort consists of several parts, and finding the music wasn't easy. They first happened upon *Giardino Scotto*. In the summer, the garden grounds host concerts and run current films in the open air. That night's offering was an Italian film, but many American films dubbed in Italian are also featured. Seeing no sense in paying money for a film they wouldn't understand, the women moved along.

On they continued, following the strains of reggae music. They came upon a sunken, outdoor dirt pit masquerading as a club located in the fort. As the Divas peered down the staircase into a brick-enclosed arena, they had the sensation of entering the Colosseum.

"All that's missing are the seats, the spectators, and the lions," Dena said with a little shiver.

It didn't look like anyplace for the Divas. But right now neither woman was too particular. They had just walked for what seemed like forever, and beggars couldn't be choosers. If it had wine and a seat, it was their kind of place. And with that, they headed down the stone staircase, crossed the dirt floor, leaving a cloud of dust in their wake.

"*Due vini rossi, per favore.*"

The ladies were not quite sure who this place was for, but before they finished their first glass of wine, they were quite certain it was not for them. They were old enough to have given birth to everyone there and maybe their parents.

The two were overdressed, having left their halter tops, cut-off jeans and sneakers at home. And, as far as finishing whatever was floating in their plastic cups, they both preferred their wine not come from a milk carton. In short, the ladies were fish out of water. Not uncomfortable enough to waste the wine they'd ordered, mind you, but out of place, nonetheless.

Once their cups were drained, so was their patience and ability to stand anymore of the music or the lack of suitable men. Bidding a fare thee well to no one in particular, they high-tailed it out of there.

On the walk back to their hotel, the ladies once again passed by the Giardino Scotto. Only this time, the cashier collecting the ticket fee for the movie had closed up shop. With no gate barring their admittance, Dena and Shelby were curious.

"It wouldn't be right to just walk in," Dena said.

"It wouldn't?" Shelby echoed unsurely.

"You didn't?" the very proper Englishwoman asked. She was aghast.

"We spent an hour last night working our last DIQ Test Question. What do you think of it?"

Once again, Dena shoved the purple book under India's nose.

What did the Divas do when confronted with an un-manned ticket counter and no gate to keep them out of the movie?
- A) Left the admittance fee under the door of the ticket booth and proceeded to the movie,
- B) Decided to continue on their way without checking out the movie,
- C) Scaled the walls of the fort and watched the movie from their makeshift aerie, or
- D) Went back to the dirt pit, got themselves another hit of wine as a snack, and slipped past the ticket counter to enjoy the show.

India was deep in thought. Okay, now let me recall what I've learned about these two in the last few hours. So far, they've been thieves (remember the confiscated wine at Sostanza), would-be smugglers (remember Shelby's plans for Baby Porky), and pagans (thank you, Lord Bacchus). Do I really think they have any compunction about evading the cost of a movie ticket? Eliminate choices A and B.

India continued her deliberations. Throughout this tedious tale, it has been patently obvious that the Divas are interested in climbing atop only one thing. Yes, it may be hard, standing tall and upright like a fort, but...

"This is the final boarding call for Flight..."

"Oooh, oooh, that's us!" said Dena. She sprang up and start-ed gathering her belongings.

"Final boarding call! How could we have possibly missed the first announcement?" India complained, as she furiously raked her things together and started running for the gate.

"Guess we were just caught up in The Divas' Diary,*"* said Shelby.

"You mean The Delusional Divas' Diary,*"* Dena corrected her friend.

Then she called out to the Englishwoman's back. "Make sure to look for it in a book store near you!"

"I certainly will, ladies. Good luck to you!" India chirped as she hustled through the gate, laughing quietly to herself.

The only thing she would make sure to do was to call up Annabel as soon as she touched down in London. That was one thing she silently thanked the ladies for.

But, a book? Hah, the Englishwoman chuckled. Now that really is the ultimate delusion.

Epilogue

*T*he authors are sure that their readers have a few lingering questions. Did anyone else but the Delusional Duo ever acknowledge who they really were? Was Shelby successful in smuggling Baby Porky into the country? Did they ever discover the answer to the burning question: Do Florentine men date only Florentine women? And finally, why did the Delusional Divas put pen to paper and write this book?

Divas, the Delusional Duo
(sung to the tune of Rudolph, the Red-nosed Reindeer)

Divas, the Delusional Duo
Had a very simple plan
And if it were suck-sex-full
They would both hogtie their man.
All of the men they wanted
Used to hide and run away.
They never joined our Divas
In their sexual foreplay.

Then one steamy July morn
The doctor came to say,
"Divas, with your American names
Florentine men won't play your games!"
Then how the Divas scorned her
Disbelieving what she said.
Still they have no ide-aa
Who the Florentine men bed.

Divas, the Delusional Duo
Had a very simple plan.
And it's not hard to see that
They would never get their man.
However, things weren't all bad,
Baby Porky got home fine.
The sniff dogs never found him,
And he tasted good with wine.

Then one steamy August eve
The stewardess came to say
"Divas, with your smiles so bright,
you'll be in First Class tonight."
Then how the ladies realized

That they'd learned a thing or two.
Using a little delusion
Changed their lives and will yours, too.

They hope you enjoyed their little tune and its inspiring message. Most authors would be quite content to end on such an uplifting note. But the Divas aren't most authors...in fact, some would posit that anyone who could write such drivel blasphemes the entire profession. Nevertheless, the ladies found it quite impossible to leave their readers without one last parting shot, i.e., the final DIQ Test question. So, here it is.

The answers to all the DIQ Test questions followed a distinct pattern. All of the answers were:
A) A for Astute,
B) B for Brainiac,
C) C for Clever, or
D) D for Delusional Divas.

If you chose, Answer A, you're not astute...you're an...well, let's just say, take the "tute" off astute, add an "s," and there you have it.

If you chose Answer B, you're no braniac, you're brainless. Our suggestion. Grab a small dog, hop on a bike, pedal as fast as you can, and demand an audience with the wizard.

If you chose Answer C, it's not for clever. It stands for cretan. Do the world a favor. Please practice safe sex. No, we're not concerned about STDs. The world will simply be a better place without any of your progeny.

And for those of you discerning enough to choose Answer D, you're correct. Well, except for that little question regarding Massimo the Merchant of Florence, of course. Nevertheless, you're ready for the ultimate Diva Do/n't.

Diva Do/n't

When you find the right delusion for you, do use it and watch your dreams come true.

And once you've gone out there...found a delusion of your own...and seen the wonderful things that can happen, should you feel moved to reward the Divas for their assistance and inspiration, they leave you with this final Diva Do/n't.

Diva Do/n't

Don't forget the Divas' offshore account. Do, do, do make a deposit in any amount.

Thank you in advance!!

DEBRA KNAPP RINALDI and STEPHANIE JONES are the real-life inspiration for the *Delusional Divas* Dena and Shelby. Raised in Poughkeepsie, New York, the ladies met on their first day of high school, and their friendship has endured and grown stronger throughout college, careers, marriages, children, divorces, writing a book, and whatever else good or not so good life has seen fit to throw their way.

As a wife and mother of three in upstate New York, Debra earned a degree in business management and has held positions as tax preparer, bookkeeper, and lecturer in accounting. Stephanie immediately skedaddled out of sleepy upstate New York for college and law school and had a varied career as a legislative attorney and law librarian before returning to school for a Masters in teaching English after her marriage failed, in order to fulfill her long-held dream of traveling the world.

Looking on as her friend took off on her journeys, an eventually not-so-happily-married Debra soon caught the traveling bug, and then, she and her BFF headed off together for parts unknown. When they are not traveling, Debra still lives in the beautiful mountains of upstate New York, and Stephanie divides her time between New York and Hamburg, Germany.

The *DELUSIONAL DIVAS* are available for select readings and public appearances. To inquire about a possible appearance, please feel free to visit us at www.DelusionalDivas.com or call (202) 580-8660.

www.ingramcontent.com/pod-product-compliance
Lightning Source LLC
Chambersburg PA
CBHW051721040426
42447CB00008B/922